The Life of Sharks

The Life of Sharks

Paul Budker

Director, Laboratoire de Biologie des Cétacés
Ecole Pratique des Hautes Etudes, Paris

Revised by Paul Budker and Peter J.Whitehead
English version by Peter J.Whitehead

Columbia University Press
New York

Published 1971 in Great Britain by
Weidenfeld and Nicolson, London
Printed in the United States of America
Library of Congress Catalog Card Number: 71-148462
ISBN: 0-231-03551-9 *Clothbound*
ISBN: 0-231-08314-9 *Paperback*

Sixth cloth and fifth paperback printing.

Contents

Plates

Acknowledgements

The author and the publishers would like to thank the following for providing photographs for this volume:

The Australian Museum, Sydney, plate 1 (upper picture); The United Nations Food and Agriculture Organisation, Rome, plate 1 (lower picture); Photo Researchers, plate 2 (upper picture), plate 5 (lower picture); Les Requins Associés, plate 2 (lower picture) and plate 8; Fox Photos, London, plate 3 (upper picture) and plate 5 (upper picture); Topix, London, plate 3 (lower picture); The American Museum of Natural History, plate 4; Paul Popper, plate 6 (upper picture); Oceanographic Research Institute, South Africa, plate 6 (lower picture); Australian News and Information Bureau.

Figures

1 Hexanchiform sharks
  a Six-gilled or Cow Shark *Hexanchus griseus*
  b Narrow-headed seven-gilled Shark *Heptranchias perlo*
  c Broad-headed seven-gilled Shark *Notorhynchus maculatum*
  d Frilled Shark *Chlamydoselachus anguineus*

2 One Heterodontiform and three Galeiform sharks
  a Port Jackson Shark *Heterodontus phillippi*
  b Sand Shark *Odontaspis taurus*
  c Goblin Shark *Mitsukurina owstoni*
  d Great White Shark *Carcharodon carcharias*

3 Galeiform sharks
  a Mackerel Shark *Isurus oxyrinchus*
  b Porbeagle *Lamna nasus*
  c Basking Shark *Cetorhinus maximus*
  d Thresher Shark *Alopias vulpinus*

4 Galeiform sharks
  a Nurse Shark *Ginglymostoma cirratum*
  b Zebra Shark *Stegostoma fasciatum*
  c Whale Shark *Rhincodon typus*
  d Larger Spotted Dogfish *Scyliorhinus caniculus*

5 Galeiform sharks
  a False Cat Shark *Pseudotriakis microdon*
  b Smooth Hound *Mustelus canis*
  c Tiger Shark *Galeocerdo cuvieri*
  d Small Black-tipped Shark *Carcharhinus limbatus*

6 Two Galeiform and two Squaliform sharks
  a Lemon Shark *Negaprion brevirostris*
  b Common Hammerhead Shark *Sphyrna zygaena*
  c Spur Dog or Piked Dogfish *Squalus acanthias*
  d Humantin *Oxynotus centrina*

Author's Preface

The original French version was published in Paris in 1946. For me, this was a kind of farewell gesture to the first part of my scientific career, which had hitherto been devoted to tropical fisheries in general and sharks in particular. Even at that time, however, I had already relinquished sharks and turned my attention to cetaceans (whales and whaling problems) and this was to be my main preoccupation for the next thirty years. In those thirty years, however, research on sharks has taken such giant strides that when the London publishers decided to bring out an English edition of my shark book it was clear that I had a monumental task in front of me catching up with the literature of the intervening years. Since the end of the war the literature has grown at a prodigious rate and every day brings some new contribution to our knowledge of these enigmatic creatures. Even so, there still remains much to be discovered.

It is perhaps because sharks have been exploited commercially from time to time that research workers have been led to study them more closely. This, and the very important part played by skin-divers in stimulating interest, have reinforced the popular demand for more knowledge, both for its own sake and to help cope with and prevent shark attack.

Thus a complete revision of the book became necessary. Making use of a technique much in vogue nowadays, I decided to graft new organs on to the old body, a task that I probably would not have been able to complete properly on my own. Here, however, chance stepped in, in the person of Peter Whitehead, who offered to adapt the text for the English version. I refrain, and from the very best of motives let it be said, from referring to Mr Whitehead as a 'translator'.

There is a famous saying from the First World War: liaison between the French and English armies was established through three types of interpreter – those who knew French but no English, those who knew English but no French, and those who knew neither! Peter Whitehead, however, represents the fourth and rare category – those who know both languages (although as far as England is concerned, I have been particularly lucky in finding such people, for I should mention here Dr N.B. 'Freddie' Marshall who, in like fashion, made a masterly translation of my book on whales and whaling). The quality of these 'translations' stems also from the fact that both Mr Whitehead and Dr Marshall combine their linguistic skill with considerable scientific ability, and this makes all the difference.

To return to the sharks. It is a great pleasure to acknowledge the important role played by Mr Whitehead in the presentation of this *Life of Sharks* and of his handling of the grafting technique mentioned above. As an ichthyologist, he was able to draw my attention to certain relevant literature which I had overlooked during my years on marine mammals. And with a truly English sense of 'cricket' and a rare understanding of the brotherhood of scientists, he has insisted on my authorship of a revision that has in many ways been a fruitful collaboration between us. So much so that my impression of the English text is that it is better than the original!

Having said this, and just tribute having been paid to Mr Whitehead, I must now record my debt to all those others who have helped this ageing ichthyologist to return to the subject that first captured his interest. I should like to thank: Henry B. Bigelow, Elgin Ciampi, Ralf S. Collier, the late Dr V.M. Coppleson, the late David H. Davies, Jeanette d'Aubray, Dr W.I. Follett, Dr J.A.F. Garrick, Professor Perry W. Gilbert, the late Dr E.W. Gudger, Bruce W. Halstead, Edmund S. Hobson, Robert F. Hutton, Leonie Joubert, Carleton Ray, William C. Schroeder, Elvira Siccardi, Stewart Springer, Victor C. Springer, Dr Donald W. Strasburg, Wilfred Templeman, Albert L. Tester, and Mr Gilbert P. Whitley.

To these I must add, last but not least, my diving friends, notably Captain Cousteau and Jean Foucher-Créteau. They have never hesitated in our friendly talks to give me the benefit of their experience as 'weightless' men and readily produced photographs to enliven the text of this little book.

Paris, September 1970   Paul Budker

Translator's Preface

The wolf, dark bogy of the medieval forests, has an aquatic counterpart –
the shark. Fortunately, the forests and the wolf now live a harmless life in
legend. Not so the shark, for today the waters of the world have become the
playgrounds of millions. There is a new class of people who enter this
'forest', and for pleasure: the skin-divers, the sport-fishermen, the yachts-
men and the humble bathers. For them, sharks are still a potential source of
danger; for them, 'shark' is an emotive, shocking word, as once was 'wolf'.
But for them, the myths are not enough – they want the facts, for only
knowledge will finally eradicate the danger and the fear.

To most people, a fish is a creature with a backbone, fins and tail that
spends its life in water. In fact, there are four distinct classes of such
animals inhabiting the oceans: *mammals*, such as whales and dolphins, that
breathe air and suckle their young like any mouse or elephant; *bony fishes*,
such as cods, herrings and salmon, that have proper jaws, usually breathe by
means of gills, and have a skeleton partly or wholly of bone; *cyclostomes*, such
as lampreys and hagfishes, which are jawless and have a skeleton of cartilage;
and finally, the *elasmobranchs*, such as sharks and rays, which possess jaws,
have a skeleton of cartilage, and show many other peculiarities which set
them apart from the true fishes. In recent years, and particularly since the
Second World War, scientific investigation into sharks, no less than popular
interest, has intensified.

To a large extent, this increase in the attention paid to sharks has found its
impetus in the search for an effective shark repellent. During the last war,
acute problems arose for safeguarding – and perhaps more important,
reassuring – airmen and sailors who faced the possibility of being cast adrift
for hours or even days in shark-infested waters. Nowadays, the protection of
bathing beaches and the safety of ever-increasing numbers of skin-divers,
have assumed equal importance. That shark attacks are in fact infinitesimal
compared with the annual toll of our over-crowded roads – or even of deaths
by lightning – is irrelevant: a single shark fatality can ruin a lucrative
seaside resort, perhaps for weeks. But, just as space research has its 'fall-out',
in the form of technological discoveries of more general application, so the

study of the aggressive behaviour of sharks in their relations with man, has ramifications which extend into every branch of biology, physiology, biochemistry, palaeontology, and so on. The result is a huge increase in the amount of scientific literature on sharks, bringing with it the need for a periodic confrontation of popularly held ideas with a review of recent scientific advances.

The three nations which have a special interest in the shark problem are the United States, Australia and South Africa. An English version of Paul Budker's *La Vie des Requins* should be most welcome to English-speaking readers, the more so because it has been revised to include results which have emerged since the publication of the first French edition. The subject of man-eaters, which holds for the public much the same fascination as do the more lurid reports in the Sunday newspapers, has been enlarged, and now carries all the authority of the data amassed by the Shark Research Panel, an international body established in 1958 to collect and collate material on this subject. Man-eaters do not, however, dominate the book, and rightly so, for sharks as a group now command a scientific and popular interest which reaches far beyond the occasional, but often fatal encounter with Man, tragic and horrifying though such accidents may be.

There are an estimated 250–350 species of sharks. Of these, only 27 or so have been implicated in attacks on man, and, in some cases at least, such attacks have been provoked. The number of species of bony fishes has been variously estimated at between 25,000 and 30,000, and it is not difficult to find amongst these two dozen or so species which, by reason of their toxicity or aggressive and defensive use of teeth or spines, are also injurious or fatal to man. The percentage is smaller, the means less spectacular, but the results are the same. Yet it is sharks that are almost universally condemned. Their very name conjures images of greed and wanton maliciousness, cunning and ruthless rapacity: and above all – teeth.

> Who see the *Shark's* capacious Jaws disclose
> A thousand Swords erect in flaming Rows
> Dispise the Tuskéd Boar.
>
> (Oppian, *Halieuticks*)

In one sense, sharks have not redeemed themselves. They are not of outstanding benefit to mankind, contributing to world fisheries to the extent of only about 1 per cent of total catches; their by-products (hides, liver oils, fins, etc) have mainly supported only luxury markets. But in another sense, and one that is often overlooked, sharks have certainly made their contribution, for it has been justly said that 'Only anatomists and embryologists realize how much the study of elasmobranchs has contributed to our understanding of the present structure and past history of the human body.' It is not merely sterile tradition that presents to the medical student and the aspiring zoologist the classic dissection of the dogfish. Embedded in this dissection, whether for cranial nerves or for more general anatomy, is a carefully preserved record of one of the major lines in vertebrate evolution.

It remains only for me to record my enjoyment in translating Dr Budker's informative book and to acknowledge my mother's valuable assistance in critically reading the manuscript, using almost the last of her failing sight with an interest and enthusiasm that speak eloquently of Dr Budker's ability to capture his reader.

Introduction

Sharks have an extremely bad reputation, so bad in fact that in everyday language the word 'shark' is ranged high up amongst the long succession of unflattering terms borrowed from zoology. It is curious, however, that nearly every time language has recourse to the animal kingdom to augment its collection of abusive terms, it picks on useful animals, at least amongst the vertebrates; insects are an exception. This does not apply only to the farmyard animals. Some of the most useful marine creatures have helped to swell the ranks of derogatory similes. There seems to be no semantic reason why fishes, for example, should be so unfairly treated, particularly in French. While in English we have phrases like, 'an ancient and fish-like smell', 'a fishy business' as well as various colloquial meanings for the verbs 'to fish', 'to angle' and 'to flounder', the French have evolved a series of colourful and often quite unprintable double-meanings around some of their commonest table fishes.

On the other hand, when it is a matter of praise or flattery, the same everyday language picks on the most useless, often quite noxious, of animals, and usually those with much overrated reputations. Examples are less numerous here, possibly because men are more eager to insult than to praise. But strength, prudence, loyalty and majesty all have their zoological prototypes on which, by a curious reflexive process, we unconsciously bestow those qualities that we so much admire in men. Thus the eagle, when all is said and done, is only a kind of scavenger of limited intelligence in spite of its royal adoption and its appearance on the crests of noblemen, banking houses and countries. Who could now question its noble, poetic, even fabulous reputation?

A more typical example is the lion. When Donna Sol coos softly '*Vous êtes mon lion superbe et généreux*', Hernani understandably swells with pride. It is flattering to be compared with *Panthera leo*, to whom is attributed the virtues of majesty (granted, but a virtue common to most of the cat family), generosity, bravery and nobility of spirit. There is a very long tradition here, both in poetry and legend. When Dante wanted to depict the fire and imposing demeanour of the troubador Sordel, he compared him to a lion:

Ella non ci deceva alcuna cosa:
Ma lasciava ne gir, solo guardando
A guisa di leon, quando si posa.
(*Purgatorio*, Canto VI)[1]

This is the lion, the heraldic beast, the presumptive figure, worked in silk, in paint or in metal on numerous armorial bearings. It seems almost ridiculous to talk of sharks in this context, but they do appear in a few British coats-of-arms. Significantly perhaps, they are shown in at least three cases in the act of swallowing human prey; in one instance this records the loss of a leg by the first baronet, Sir Brook Watson, in the harbour at Savannah (Moule, 1842). The incident is celebrated by a painting by Copley at Christ's Hospital.

The real lion, for those that have studied the species, does not live up to its reputation. Its devotion to Androcles has no more of a basis in truth than does its supposed bravery and generosity. The noble lion feeds, in fact, on gazelles and antelopes, graceful creatures which it exterminates regardless of the sentiments bestowed upon it by man. A lion's meal is a revolting, bloody orgy.

Sharks too feed on living prey, and it is hardly reasonable to be squeamish about them in particular since the animal world is full of carnivores, from spiders to whales. Sharks seize their quarry with a snap of their jaws, neatly and accurately. When a shark, with superb grace, glides through the blue-green water, it is a spectacle of such enthralling natural harmony as to win the admiration of the least artistic observer. To reproach sharks is to be anthropomorphic. Certainly, I am not coming to their defence by trying to deny their carnivorous habits, and the chapter on man-eaters is presented as objectively as possible. But if many tragic accidents can be attributed to them, one can be sure that these have not resulted from any motive of malice or intentional wickedness. No more than in any other carnivorous animal is there an element of 'spitefulness' in sharks – and probably much less than in human beings. We need only study our own species to realize that, all in all, sharks deserve their reputation rather less than the men with whom they are compared.

At the outset, there is a most intriguing etymological problem to consider, for it is a remarkable fact that amongst the Western European languages there seems to be no relationship between the various words used for shark. In English, these fishes are termed *shark*, in German *Haifisch*, in Spanish

[1] (The soul of Sordel) told us nothing
But let us continue on our way,
Looking only like a lion at rest.

tiburon and in French *requin*. Coppleson (1959) has said that, at the time of the exploratory voyages into tropical waters, sharks 'were so little known in those days that there was not even an English word for them. They were known by their Spanish name, *tiburon*', which was not replaced by the word shark until much later, 'about 1569 when the sailors of Sir John Hawkins' expedition brought home a specimen and exhibited it in London'. McCormick (1963) suggested that the word shark may have been derived from the German word *Schurke*, the word for a villain, or again that it recalls the Anglo-Saxon word *sceran*, meaning to shear or cut.

The French word *requin* is also puzzling. Since the time of Antoine Furetière (1619–88)[1] there has been a somewhat naïve explanation, still quoted occasionally, that the name was given because, once someone has been attacked by a shark, there is nothing left but to sing a requiem! Indeed, the grey sharks or Carcharhinidae are often referred to in English books as the requiem sharks. Obviously this explanation is a little too good to be true, and serious philologists do not accept it. Darmesteter and Hatzfeld, in their *Dictionnaire général* of 1932, felt that the second part of the word *requin* was related to the Normano-Piccardian form of *chien*, a dog (the word had long been written as *requien*). Albert Dauzat (1938) was more positive; he felt that this explanation was improbable and that the word resulted from a modification of some obscure, exotic word (evidently he dismissed Furetière's fanciful idea). Again, it was thought in the last century that *requin* was a corruption or French adaptation of *haakierring*, a word which signifies in Scandinavian dialect 'a dog that catches or seizes'. This word could have been brought to France by the Normans. This explanation is ingenious and merits further study, for even nowadays the French fishermen of the Channel coast from Brittany to Normandy give the name *haut* or *hâ* to the Tope (*Galeorhinus galeus*), a species which could well pass for a shark.

For the moment, however, the derivation of the various words for shark remain baffling and offer an interesting field for further study.

Fifty years ago, the American naturalists Murphy and Nichols (1916) wrote concerning sharks: 'A comprehensive study of the life history of any fish of this interesting group has yet to be made.' This is no less true today, but it is certainly not my intention in this little book to do more than rather rapidly review the problem. The literature concerning sharks has been prodigiously enriched during the last twenty years, thanks to the interest aroused by

[1] French scholar, Abbé of Chalivoy, who was expelled from the Académie for pillaging its Dictionary for one of his own, published in 1690.

oceanographical research and, it should be added, by the popularity of skin-diving. The mass of works published on sharks each year might indeed lead one to suppose that we now have sufficient data to undertake such a comprehensive study. But a monograph on even a single species would still require much more information.

General works on the anatomy of sharks are quite numerous. Books on zoology and comparative anatomy contain extensive descriptions, as for example in one of the most up-to-date, the *Traité de Zoologie* edited by P.Grassé (1958). J.F.Daniel's book *The Elasmobranchs* (1934) is still a classic, and there are numerous short papers testifying to the interest that biologists are bringing to bear on this group of vertebrates. A photographic atlas of shark anatomy by Gans and Parsons (1964) is one of several modern works for the student. For the general reader, one of the best of recent books is *Shadows in the Sea* by McCormick, Allen and Young (1963). *The Natural History of Sharks* by Lineaweaver and Backus (1970) is also most readable and contains much useful information on shark biology.

But if we now have a fairly good knowledge of the anatomy of sharks, we still know very little of their biology. In this respect, it is notable that our knowledge bears an exactly inverse relation to the size of the species concerned; of the largest species we know the least. Besides many well-known facts and careful observations and experiments, there are still far too many uncertainties. This is not because sharks have only recently come to our notice. On the contrary, these monsters have down the ages excited men's imagination on account of their size, appearance and their real or imagined ferocity. But the history of sharks, like the history of peoples, is a complex story where legend and truth are closely interwoven, sometimes making it almost impossible to separate the one from the other: some well-established facts – but as many unknowns. I will try to deal with both, without pretending to speak a final word on either, yet I hope even this may make a small contribution to our general outlook and knowledge of sharks.

4

TABLE 1

Classification of the Chondrichthyes

CLASS: CHONDRICHTHYES	Elasmobranchs or Cartilaginous fishes	(=ELASMOBRANCHII; plus Chimaeras = Regan's SELACHII)
1 Subclass **SELACHII**	All recent and fossil sharks and rays	
A *Superorder Protoselachii*	Protoselachians or fossil sharklike forms	(= Regan's subclasses Pleuropterygii +Acanthodii + Ichthyotomi)
i Order Cladoselachiformes	(e.g. *Cladoselache* of Upper Devonian)	
ii Order Pleuracanthiformes	(e.g. *Xenacanthus* of Carboniferous & Permian)	
iii Order Hybodontiformes	(e.g. *Hybodus* of the Jurassic)	
B *Superorder Euselachii*	Selachians, i.e. all modern sharks and rays	(= Berg's SELACHII; = Plagiostomes of early authors)
i Order Pleurotremata	*SHARKS* (i.e. sharks, dogfishes, hounds, topes, etc)	(= Selachii of Bigelow & Schroeder; = Division Pleurotremata of Berg)
ii Order Hypotremata	*RAYS* (i.e. skates, rays, torpedoes, etc)	(= Batoidei of Bigelow & Schroeder; = Division Hypotremata of Berg)
2 Subclass **BRADYODONTI**	*CHIMAERAS* Ratfishes	(= HOLOCEPHALI of Regan)

TABLE 2

The Suborders and Families of Sharks

ORDER PLEUROTREMATA

	(*Common name*)	(*Principal genera*)
Suborder **Hexanchiformes**		
1 Family HEXANCHIDAE	Cow Sharks, Combtoothed, Six- or Seven-gilled Sharks	*Hexanchus, Heptranchias, Notorhynchus*
2 Family CHLAMYDOSELACHIDAE	Frilled Sharks	*Chlamydoselachus*
Suborder **Heterodontiformes**		
3 Family HETERODONTIDAE	Port Jackson Sharks, Horn Sharks or Bull-headed Sharks	*Heterodontus*
Suborder **Galeiformes**		
4 Family ODONTASPIDIDAE (formerly Carchariidae)	Sand Sharks	*Odontaspis* (= *Carcharias* of authors)
5 Family SCAPANORHYNCHIDAE	Goblin Sharks	*Mitsukurina* (fossil genus *Scapanorhynchus*)

5

6 Family ISURIDAE	Mackerel Sharks	*Carcharodon, Isurus,* *Lamna*
7 Family CETORHINIDAE	Basking Sharks	*Cetorhinus*
8 Family ALOPIIDAE	Thresher Sharks	*Alopias*
9 Family ORECTOLOBIDAE	Carpet Sharks	*Orectolobus,* *Ginglymostoma,* *Stegostoma*
10 Family RHINCODONTIDAE	Whale Sharks	*Rhincodon*
11 Family SCYLIORHINIDAE	Dogfishes, Cat Sharks, Swell Sharks	*Scyliorhinus, Galeus,* *Apristurus,* *Cephaloscylium*
12 Family PSEUDOTRIAKIDAE	False Cat Sharks	*Pseudotriakis*
13 Family TRIAKIDAE (formerly Galeorhinidae)	Smooth Hounds or Smooth Dogfishes	*Triakis, Mustelus,* *Triaenodon*
14 Family CARCHARHINIDAE	Grey Sharks, Requiem Sharks	*Carcharhinus,* *Negaprion, Prionace,* *Galeocerdo, Scoliodon,* *Galeorhinus,* *Hemipristis*
15 Family SPHYRNIDAE	Hammerhead Sharks	*Sphyrna*
Suborder **Squaliformes**		
16 Family SQUALIDAE	Spiny Dogfishes	*Squalus, Etmopterus,* *Centroscymnus,* *Oxynotus, Centrophorus*
17 Family DALATIIDAE	Sleeper Sharks, Spineless Dogfishes	*Somniosus, Isistius,* *Euprotomicrus,* *Squaliolus, Dalatius*
18 Family ECHINORHINIDAE	Bramble Sharks	*Echinorhinus*
19 Family PRISTIOPHORIDAE	Saw Sharks	*Pristiophorus,* *Pliotrema*
20 Family SQUATINIDAE	Monkfishes, Angel Sharks	*Squatina*

Chapter 1

Classification

For the ancients, and even for authors as late as Pierre Belon (1551, 1555) in the 16th century, the word 'fish' referred to almost any animal living in fresh or salt water, thus including whales, frogs, crustaceans and molluscs, as well as fish in the true sense. Remnants of this outlook are still apparent in our term 'shellfish' for many marine animals far removed from the true fishes. Amongst the molluscs we have the Hosefish (*Solen ensis*), the Spontfish (*Solen marginatus*), the Butterfish (*Tapes decussatus*) and the Cuttlefish (*Sepia officianalis*); in the Coelenterates we have the jellyfishes; in the Echinoderms we have the starfishes; in the crustaceans we have the crayfishes; and finally, amongst the cetaceans we have the whalefish and the blackfish. These animals have nothing in common with true fishes except perhaps life in an aquatic environment. Whales are certainly fishlike (except that their tails lie horizontally and not vertically), and so too are the lancelets, at the other extreme of the size scale. Yet neither of these are fishes.

The problem of what is a fish, is far more complex than is commonly imagined, even when one abandons everyday language and enters the realm of science. Indeed, the overall classification of the vertebrates is still hotly disputed among zoologists, and this is no place to review the whole problem. Nevertheless a broad outline of this classification will make a useful preface for what is to follow. The scheme given here, which is based on that devised by Save-Söderberg (1934), is one of several modern classifications but one which is now accepted by a great many specialists.

In the first place, the vertebrates can be divided into two major groups.

1 AGNATHA. No true jaws, gills contained in a series of separate pouches. Lampreys, hagfishes and many fossil forms.

2 GNATHOSTOMATA. Jaws present. This group includes the true fishes, as well as the amphibians, reptiles, birds and mammals.

It is with the second of these two groups that we are here concerned since neither the lampreys nor the hagfishes are considered to be true fishes. This second group can be divided up in the following way.

I ELASMOBRANCHII

   1 Acanthodi (fossil sharklike fishes: *Climatius*)

2 Placodermi (armoured fossil sharklike fishes: *Coccosteus, Bothriolepis*)

3 Holocephali (the chimaeras) ⎫ These two groups are combined
4 Selachii (sharks and rays ⎬ in Table I under the heading
⎭ CHONDRICHTHYES

II CHOANATA

(A) 1 Dipnoi (fossil and modern lungfishes)
2 Urodela (newts, salamanders)
(B) 1 Crossopterygii (lobe-finned fishes: fossil and modern coelacanths)
2 Eutetrapoda (frogs etc, *Batrachomorpha*; reptiles, *Reptiliomorpha*; birds, *Aves*; mammals, *Mammalia*)

III ACTINOPTERYGII

This group includes all those fishes not placed in previous divisions, that is to say, all the modern bony fishes and a few primitive forms.

There is, as I have said, no general agreement on this scheme, but as far as the fishes are concerned the position is perhaps best stated by Bertin and Arambourg (1958):

It goes without saying that the present classification does not pretend to be definitive. The group Teleostei [i.e. the bony fishes] in particular, is so polymorphic and polyphyletic that it will perhaps never be possible to achieve a natural classification. Diverse characters have evolved independently one from another. Descent and convergence have become entwined in an inextricable manner. . . . In short, one can only act, in the matter of classification, in a group so involved and confused as the teleosts, with the most extreme circumspection.

The chondrichthyes, or fishes with a skeleton of cartilage, the group which contains the fossil and modern sharks and rays, stands in contrast to the teleosts or bony-skeletoned fishes by presenting a remarkable homogeneity and at the same time a complete independence from the teleosts. Almost the only thing that the sharks and rays have in common with the bony fishes is their aquatic life. In most other respects, in their physiology and anatomy, the two groups are totally different. The skeleton of sharks and rays, their method of reproduction, their external covering (placoid scales), their system of salt regulation and so on, separate them so completely from the bony fishes that authors have suggested that it would be more convenient to refer to them as 'fishlike vertebrates' rather than as fishes. This has, of course, already been done with the lampreys and hagfishes. The eminent palaeontologist Erik Jarvik (1960) stated recently:

The accepted classification has become more and more difficult to maintain; some of the older classes, such as the Cyclostomes and Amphibians, are each diphyletic; a man and a frog, which belong to different classes, are much closer one to the other, than are a herring and a shark, for example, which are included in the same class (Pisces).

For the present, however, it does not seem wrong to continue to refer to sharks as 'fishes' in the accepted sense.

There is no one species of shark, as there is one species of lion or one species of warthog. There are some 250–350 species of sharks, all clearly related to each other but differing sufficiently one from the next for the specialist, and often the layman, to distinguish them. The name shark is rather loosely applied to the larger species and may include such different animals as the Mackerel Shark (*Isurus*), the Man-eater (*Carcharodon*) and the Hammerhead (*Sphyrna*). The term 'dogfish' is often used for the smaller species. There is no zoological basis for this division; all belong to the order Pleurotremata, the dogfishes being merely small species of shark. Amongst the Grey Sharks (*Carcharhinus*) there are species which, even as adults, are no larger than a dogfish, and the Tope (*Galeorhinus galeus*), one of the three species loosely termed 'dogfish' off British coasts, could well be mistaken for a young 'shark'. By the same token, the domestic cat could fairly be called a dwarf tiger, for the cat is much more closely related to the tiger than is a Mackerel Shark to one of the dogfishes. The same difficulties arise with the turtles and tortoises, or the frogs and toads, neither popular term quite matching the zoological classification. For the purpose of clarity, therefore, I shall use the term 'shark' to include all the species placed in the order Pleurotremata, from the largest to the smallest.

The sharks and rays, here termed the subclass Selachii (see Table 1), are a close-knit group, and the uncertainties surrounding the separation of the sharks and the dogfishes are repeated in the difficulty encountered in trying to separate the sharks from the rays. The extreme forms are quite distinct, but between the two are species which combine the characters of both groups. The rays can be considered as greatly flattened sharks[1] but the degree of flattening varies, and such intermediates as the monkfish, the guitar fishes and the sawfishes are difficult to place. However, one can class as sharks all those fishes with the gill-slits on the side of the head, while those with the gill-slits underneath the head can be termed rays. The

---

[1] Burying, according to von Wahlert (1965) 'was the major factor that stimulated and directed the course of evolution leading to the skates and rays from the ancestral fusiform sharks'. The shift of the gill openings to the underside (see key) not only enabled 'jet-propelled' take-off, but allowed the forward expansion of the pectoral fins. The spiracle, a vestige of a former gill-slit, was thus the only opening suitable for taking in water without the danger of clogging by sand and mud. In the skates and rays the spiracle is on top of the head, immediately behind the eye.

9

monkfish is then placed in the former group and the guitar fishes and sawfishes in the latter.

The sharks and the rays can be separated by the following key.

(1) Gill-slits at least partly lateral; edges of pectoral fins not attached to the sides of the head in front of the gill-slits; upper margin of orbit free from eyeball (eyelid free); body usually not flattened. PLEUROTREMATA – Sharks, topes, dogfishes.

(2) Gill-slits confined to the under surface of the head; edges of pectoral fins attached to sides of head anterior to gill-slits; upper margin of orbit not free from eyeball (no free eyelid); body usually flattened. HYPOTREMATA – Skates and rays.

As might be expected, the classification of the Pleurotremata, or sharks, is no less controversial than the higher classifications already mentioned. New studies on one particular group of sharks, or a special study of one particular feature in all groups of sharks, inevitably lead to new schemes of grouping the various orders, suborders and families. One very irksome result of this, as far as the non-specialist is concerned, is that those vernacular group-names that have been derived originally from a Latin or Greek group-name then lose their original meaning. This is nowhere more confusing, even for the specialist, than in the case of the term 'selachian', a word which will be constantly used in this book. C. Tate Regan, whose classification of fishes is still widely used, employed the term Selachii for *all* cartilaginous fishes, that is to say, also fossil sharks and rays, as well as the chimaeras (the ratfishes). Under Regan's classification, all these are selachians. The great Russian ichthyologist L. S. Berg, on the other hand, recognized a subclass Selachii which included only the present-day sharks and rays. Finally, the Americans Henry Bigelow and William Schroeder, whose work on the sharks and rays of the Western North Atlantic stands as the most authoritative account to date, restricted the name Selachii to cover only the modern sharks (i.e. the Pleurotremata), as opposed to the Batoidei or modern rays (here termed Hypotremata).

The choice made here is to use the term selachian in Berg's sense: all modern sharks (dogfishes, topes, hounds, etc) *plus* all modern rays (skates, torpedoes, etc). This is not a wholesale endorsement of Berg's system, nor a rejection of the other two, for each system has its strong and weak points. It is more a recognition that, for the scope of the present book, the most convenient collective term for the sharks and rays is the one used by Berg.

We are now left without an all-inclusive term for the entire group of cartilaginous fishes. Having used selachian in Berg's restricted sense, we cannot use it again as Regan did for the whole group. In many books the word Elasmobranch is used, stemming from Ranzani's term Elasmobranchii (= strap gills). There is, however, an older name, Chondrichthyes (= cartilage fishes) deriving from Carl Linnaeus (1707–78), the founder of our modern system of nomenclature. It is nowadays agreed among zoologists that the prior name shall always be given precedence unless, and very rarely, there is some special reason for preserving another name which has been used so often in the literature that its replacement would cause more confusion than order. Critics have pointed out that the two hundred years of modern classification and nomenclature are a drop in the ocean compared with the immense period ahead during which we hopefully anticipate naming animals and plants; that a slight inconvenience in names in 1967 will be long forgotten in 5067. Hence the Law of Priority is taken as the basic rule, and to return to the cartilaginous fishes, the earlier name Chondrichthyes must replace Elasmobranchii for this group. For the vernacular, on the other hand, there is no such rule of priority. The term elasmobranchs is so deeply rooted in textbooks that it would be misleading to try to replace it with the more clumsy chondrichthians. In the sense defined here, however, the two are entirely synonymous. To clarify the matter, the terms used here and the equivalents used by other authors are set out in Table 1. The scheme adopted is essentially that set out by P. H. Greenwood in his revised version of Norman's *History of Fishes*.

Having defined terms and presented a framework into which the sharks can be fitted, it now remains to review the various families and the principal genera contained. The actual number of species of sharks is variously placed at between 250 and 350, the figure being augmented every year through the discovery of new species. Yet it is also being depleted, as further work shows that what were once considered two species are in fact merely variants of the same species. The species are grouped into about 60 different genera, and once again the number varies as our knowledge increases. The genera are here grouped into twenty families, some with only a single genus and some with many. Finally, these twenty families are placed in four suborders, an indication of the probable relationships of the families one to the other – and thus as open to controversy as any of the other man-made divisions within the group.

ORDER PLEUROTREMATA
(Sharks)
A *Suborder Hexanchiformes*
  1 **Family Hexanchidae** – Cow Sharks, Comb-toothed, Six- or Seven-gilled Sharks.

Immediately recognized by having six or seven pairs of gill-slits (five in all other sharks except the Saw Shark genus *Pliotrema*); a single dorsal fin; teeth in lower jaw comb-like, with a series of descending cusps (Figure 18a); primitive slender-bodied fishes. Three genera, with perhaps only a single species in each:

Hexanchus griseus (Bonn.), the Six-gilled or Cow Shark; world-wide, up to 15 feet in length (the record of a specimen 26 feet 5 inches from Polperro, Cornwall, is an error according to Lineaweaver & Backus, 1970) (Figure 1a).

Heptranchias perlo (Bonn.), the Narrow-headed Seven-gilled Shark; Australian waters, the Mediterranean and Eastern Atlantic and also off Cuba, reaches 7 feet (Figure 1b).

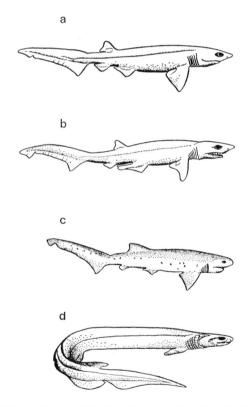

Fig. 1 Hexanchiform sharks. (a) Six-gilled or Cow Shark *Hexanchus griseus*. (b) Narrow-headed seven-gilled Shark *Heptranchias perlo*. (c) Broad-headed seven-gilled Shark *Notorhynchus maculatum*. (d) Frilled Shark *Chlamydoselachus anguineus*.

Notorhynchus maculatum Ayres, the Broad-headed Seven-gilled Shark; Australia, Indo-Pacific, California, reaches 10 feet (Figure 1c).

2 **Family Chlamydoselachidae** – Frilled Sharks (Figure 1d). Body very elongated, cylindrical, snake-like. A single dorsal fin, near the tail, the lower lobe of which is barely apparent. Six gill openings, the partitions of which project to form a kind of frilled collar; first gill-slit extends right across throat. A single species, *Chlamydoselachus anguineus* Garman, first caught off Japan in 1884 but now known from California and from Portugal to Norway. A rather rare deep-water species, reaching $6\frac{1}{2}$ feet in length.

B *Suborder Heterodontiformes*

   3 **Family Heterodontidae** – Port Jackson Sharks, Horn Sharks (Figure 2a).

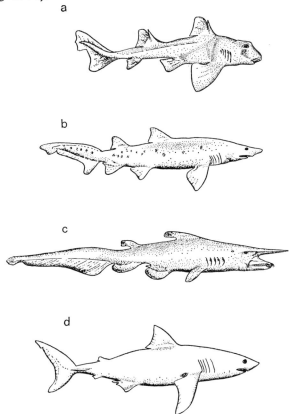

Fig. 2   One Heterodontiform and three Galeiform sharks. (a) Port Jackson Shark *Heterodontus phillippi*. (b) Sand Shark *Odontaspis taurus*. (c) Goblin Shark *Mitsukurina owstoni*. (d) Great White Shark *Carcharodon carcharias*.

13

Five gill-slits. Two dorsal fins, each preceded by a spine. Space between eyes with two longitudinal crests, hence another name, Bullhead Sharks. A single genus, *Heterodontus* (= different teeth), with two different types of teeth in each jaw, a primitive character linking them with the hybodonts of the Carboniferous period (Figure 19). Feed on molluscs and sea urchins, which are crushed by the molar-like teeth; Australia, eastern Pacific, East Africa, East Indies, but not in the Atlantic or Mediterranean. About ten species of small sedentary forms, reaching a maximum of 4–5 feet.

C *Suborder Galeiformes*

This group contains the 'typical' sharks. Two dorsal fins, without a spine in front. A single anal fin. Tail often asymmetrical, upper lobe larger, the axis of the tail more or less straight and the upper lobe notched. Five gill-slits. Teeth similar in both jaws.

4 **Family Odontaspididae** (formerly Carchariidae) – Sand Sharks (Figure 2b)

A single genus *Odontaspis* (formerly *Carcharias*), characterized by its large, awl-shaped teeth, with or without lateral cusps according to species (Figure 18d). The Grey Nurse Shark (*O. arenarius*) and the Sand Shark (*O. taurus*) are both reputed to attack swimmers. Reach 10 feet in length, possibly 15 feet in South Africa.

5 **Family Scapanorhynchidae** – Goblin Sharks (Figure 2c).

Known only from the fossil genus *Scapanorhynchus* until the discovery of a modern form, *Mitsukurina owstoni*, from deep water off Japan in 1898. Later recorded off India and Portugal, reaching a length of about 14 feet. Also known as the Elfin Shark.

6 **Family Isuridae** – Mackerel Sharks, Mako Sharks, Great White Shark.

Tail almost symmetrical (homocercal). Body streamlined for fast swimming. Three genera.

a Carcharodon carcharias, the Great White Shark, White Pointer or Man-eater (Figure 2d). Teeth triangular, with coarsely serrated edges, no lateral cusps (Figure 17a). Snout conical. Said to reach 30–40 feet in length but the largest recorded specimen was 21 feet and weighed 7,302 lbs (from Cuba). The most dreaded of all man-eating sharks.

b Isurus paucus and *I. oxyrinchus*, the Mako or Mackerel Sharks of the Indo-Pacific and Atlantic respectively, the former referred to as the Blue Pointer in Australian waters (Figure 3a). Teeth slender, awl-shaped, without lateral cusps (Figure 18b). Both are recognized as fine game fishes reaching weights of over 1,000 lbs (Plate 5).

a

b

c

d

Fig. 3   Galeiform sharks. (a) Mackerel Shark *Isurus oxyrinchus*. (b) Porbeagle *Lamna nasus*. (c) Basking Shark *Cetorhinus maximus*. (d) Thresher Shark *Alopias vulpinus*.

c *Lamna nasus* and *L. ditropis*, the Porbeagles or Blue Sharks (Figure 3b). Teeth as in *Isurus* but with lateral cusps (Figure 18c). The first occurs in the Mediterranean and Atlantic, the second off the Pacific shores of America. Game fish records of over 400 lbs are known.

7 **Family Cetorhinidae** – Basking Sharks (Figure 3c).
A single species, the Basking or Bone Shark (*Cetorhinus maximus*), next in size to the Whale Shark. Specimens of 20–30 feet are not rare, and they may grow to 40 feet.

8 **Family Alopiidae** – Thresher Sharks (Figure 3d).
Immediately recognizable by their enormous tail, which may account

a

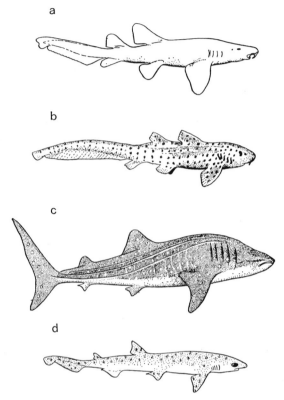

b

c

d

Fig. 4 Galeiform sharks. (a) Nurse Shark *Ginglymostoma cirratum*. (b) Zebra Shark *Stegostoma fasciatum*. (c) Whale Shark *Rhincodon typus*. (d) Larger Spotted Dogfish *Scyliorhinus caniculus*.

for almost half the total length of the fish. World-wide, *Alopias vulpinus* in the Atlantic and related species in the Indian Ocean and Pacific. The largest specimen caught on line was 922 lbs.

9 **Family Orectolobidae** – Carpet Sharks, Nurse Sharks, Wobbegongs, Zebra Sharks.

Some of the most colourful of all sharks, mostly harmless unless provoked. Examples: *Ginglymostoma cirratum*, the Nurse Shark of the Atlantic (Figure 4a); *Orectolobus* species, the Wobbegongs of Australia; *Stegostoma fasciatum*, a Zebra Shark (Figure 4b).

10 **Family Rhincodontidae** – Whale Sharks (Plate 1 and Figure 4c). A single species, *Rhincodon typus* (often misspelt *Rhinodon* or *Rhineodon*), the huge Whale Shark, said to attain a length of 60 feet. Like the Basking Shark, it feeds mainly on plankton.

16

11 **Family Scyliorhinidae** – Dogfishes, Cat Sharks, Swell Sharks.
Small sharks of 4–5 feet in length found in coastal waters mainly.
Examples: *Scyliorhinus caniculus* and *S. stellaris*, the Larger and the
Lesser Spotted Dogfishes of European coasts (Figure 4d);
Cephaloscyllium species, the Swell Sharks that can inflate the belly
with air or water.

12 **Family Pseudotriakidae** – False Cat Sharks (Figure 5a).
Two rare species of *Pseudotriakis* are known, one Atlantic and one
Pacific. Snout pointed, first dorsal fin long and low.

13 **Family Triakidae** (formerly Galeorhinidae) – Smooth Hounds,
Smooth Dogfishes.
Small fishes with pavement-like teeth. Many species, of which the
Atlantic *Mustelus canis* or Smooth Hound is the best known (Figure 5b).

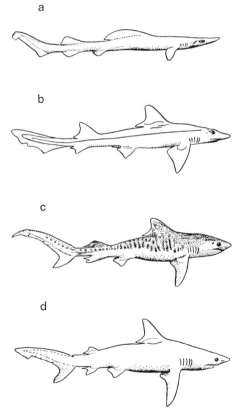

a

b

c

d

Fig. 5   Galeiform sharks. (a) False Cat Shark *Pseudotriakis microdon*. (b) Smooth
Hound *Mustelus canis*. (c) Tiger Shark *Galeocerdo cuvieri*. (d) Small Black-tipped
Shark *Carcharhinus limbatus*.

14 **Family Carcharhinidae** – Grey or Requiem Sharks (Plates 2 and 6). A rather heterogeneous family with a large number of species. Some are small (4½ feet) and are benthic or coastal; others live in freshwaters, such as *Carcharhinus gangeticus* (Figure 39); a third important group comprises the large species of 'typical' shark of tropical waters (up to 12–18 feet). In this latter group are the Tiger Shark (*Galeocerdo cuvieri*) (Figure 5c), the White-tipped Reef Shark (*Carcharhinus longimanus*), the Small Black-tipped Shark (*C. limbatus*) (Figure 5d), the Cub or Bull Shark (*Carcharhinus leucas*), and the Great Blue Shark (*Prionace glauca*), the latter a cosmopolitan species found in tropical and temperate seas. Also members of this family are the Lemon Shark (*Negaprion brevirostris* – Figure 6a) and the Soupfin Shark (*Galeorhinus zyopterus*).

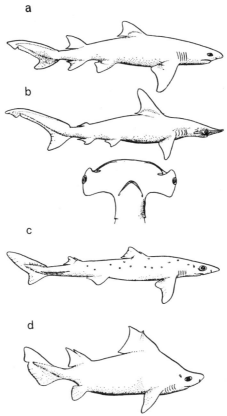

Fig. 6   Two Galeiform and two Squaliform sharks. (a) Lemon Shark *Negaprion brevirostris*. (b) Common Hammerhead Shark *Sphyrna zygaena*. (c) Spur Dog or Piked Dogfish *Squalus acanthias*. (d) Humantin *Oxynotus centrina*.

15 **Family Sphyrnidae** – Hammerhead Sharks (Plates 2 and 3). Similar to the Carcharhinidae but with the anterior part of the head greatly flattened and enlarged laterally, the eyes lying along the outer border. Examples: *Sphyrna zygaena*, the Common Hammerhead Shark, almost world-wide in its distribution (Figure 6b); *Sphyrna mokarran*, the Great Hammerhead, reaching a length of 15 feet; *Sphyrna tiburo*, the Bonnet or Shovel-nosed Shark, a New World species reaching 5 feet. A total of nine species, grouped into three subgenera.

D *Suborder Squaliformes*
Two dorsal fins but no anal fin. Five gill-slits, rarely six.
16 **Family Squalidae** – Spiny Dogfishes.

a

b

c

d

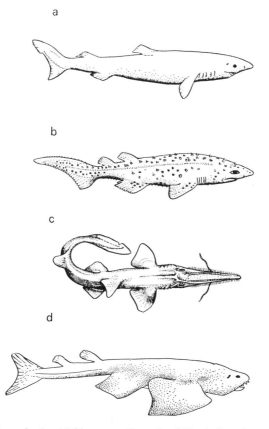

Fig. 7   Squaliform sharks. (a) Sleeper or Greenland Shark *Somniosus microcephalus*. (b) Bramble Shark *Echinorhinus brucus*. (c) Saw Shark *Pristiophorus nudipinnis*. (d) Monkfish or Angel Shark *Squatina squatina*.

19

Each dorsal fin preceded by a long or short spine, hence the common name. Of the many small species, the best known is the Spur Dog or Piked Dogfish, *Squalus acanthias*. Other members include the species of *Oxynotus* with high-standing dorsal fins (Figure 6d), *Etmopterus*, *Centrophorus* and *Centroscymnus*, a member of the latter (*C. coelolepis*) holding the depth record for sharks, having been caught at 8,922 feet in the Eastern Atlantic.

17 **Family Dalatiidae** – Spineless Dogfishes, Sleeper Sharks.

A rather mixed collection, including the large Sleeper or Greenland Shark, *Somniosus microcephalus*, which reaches 21 feet and is the only shark known to inhabit polar seas throughout the year (Figure 7a); the smallest of all sharks *Squaliolus laticaudus*, mature at only 6–8 inches; and three luminous sharks, *Isistius brasiliensis* and *I. plutodus*, and the very small *Euprotomicrus bispinatus* (maximum size 10½ inches).

18 **Family Echinorhinidae** – Bramble Sharks (Figure 7b).

A single genus with probably a single world-wide species, the Bramble Shark *Echinorhinus brucus*, easily recognized by its size (to about 9 feet) and its prickly hide.

19 **Family Pristiophoridae** – Saw Sharks (Figure 7c).

Small sharks, less than 3 feet in length, with either 5 gill-slits (*Pristiophorus*) or 6 gill-slits (*Pliotrema*). Remarkable for their long tooth-edged snouts, thus resembling the true Sawfishes (*Pristis*) but with gill-slits at the side of the head, not underneath.

20 **Family Squatinidae** – Monkfishes, Angel Sharks (Figure 7d).

Bottom-living species with a flattened body but gill-slits on side of head. About ten species placed in the genus *Squatina*. Largest up to about 8 feet.

Classifications are constantly changing, for each new study on a group of animals or plants will either confirm or contradict some facet of the existing classification, leaving the layman, and often the specialist too, bewildered and even a little irritated. A classification attempts two things. In the first place, it tries to give a picture of the evolutionary relationships between the various species included, advancing to broader and broader groupings much as one would follow the branches of a tree down to the trunk. Secondly, it aims to present a convenient framework so that groups at various levels can be compared and contrasted. Thus the 'tree' is to some extent pruned in order to prevent a hopelessly tangled briar. These two aims often clash, as in the case of the bony fishes mentioned earlier. A framework is, however, essential, and the present arrangement of the suborders and families will at least enable the reader to explore the world of sharks without the feeling of being in an endless jungle of species.

Finally, a brief word on the history of sharks. The modern sharks represent a very primitive group of vertebrates and, apart from the Grey Sharks (Carcharhinidae), all the other families contain genera that occur as fossils in rocks dating back to the Cretaceous period (70–140 million years ago), or even the Jurassic (140–170 million years ago). This is not to say that considerable specialization has not occurred, but merely that sharks have been by-passed by the rest of vertebrate evolution, lingering on as a relic of what was once the dominant vertebrate group in the oceans.

The earliest evidence that we have of sharks are the isolated spines, teeth and scales found in Upper Silurian and Lower Devonian beds. Even these show considerable diversity, suggesting a well-established group that was already launched on its 300 million year career. The strata of the Devonian period (320–265 million years ago) yield protoselachians such as *Cladoselache,* one of the most primitive sharks yet discovered. In *Xenacanthus,* from Late Devonian to Triassic beds (250–200 million years ago), 'claspers' are present, an indication of internal fertilization which is characteristic of all selachians of modern times. These early sharks share many primitive features (form of brain case, jaws, fin skeleton, teeth, etc) and as a group are said to represent the 'cladodont' level of organization (Schaeffer, 1967). The hybodonts (or 'hybodontid' level), which appear in the Carboniferous (270 million years ago), are much nearer to the modern sharks in general appearance. Some have sharp teeth in the front of the jaws, but flat crushing teeth at the back, an arrangement which links them with the present-day Port Jackson Sharks (Heterodontidae – see Figure 19). The Carboniferous was the heyday of the sharks, their zenith before competition from the bony fishes forced them into their present position.

The modern sharks, the remnants of this once dominant group, still show considerable diversity, a mark of biological success. They range in size from the tiny Midwater Shark (*Squaliolus laticaudus*), which is reported mature at only 6–8 inches, to the huge Whale Shark (*Rhincodon typus*), whose citation as 'length 45 feet' is usually qualified by the words 'but larger individuals can be expected'. The Whale Shark is, in fact, non-aggressive to man, but 6-inch fossil teeth closely resembling those of the man-eating Great White Shark (*Carcharodon carcharias*) suggest the existence of bygone leviathans of as much as 80 feet in length. Beneath the diversity of sizes, shapes and habits, however, the sharks, and even the broader group selachians, show a structural homogeneity which is at once characteristic of the group and a testimony to the success of this pattern down through the ages.

Chapter 2

General Form

When one studies a drawing or photograph of a shark – or indeed the live animal – one cannot help but admire the sheer elegance of its lines (see Plate 2 for example). We of the 20th century are undoubtedly far more aware of the beauty of such lines than were men in earlier times. Our eyes are accustomed to hydrodynamic and aerodynamic curves; the modern ship, car or aeroplane are infinitely more pleasing aesthetically than their counterparts of forty years ago and this simplicity of line nowadays finds expression in architecture and interior design, from furniture and fabric patterns to china and tableware. Such simplicity was perhaps not appreciated before, or at least in periods such as the Victorian era when detail and ornamentation sought to embellish objects almost to the exclusion of their actual form. This may explain why sharks, although much written about in the past, are rarely extolled for their purity of line and graceful contours. Of all fishes, sharks are the most striking in this respect. However, all this seems self-evident nowadays, even to the least observant, and engineers have not been slow to draw comparisons between the lines of aeroplanes and those of sharks.

Some of the figures illustrating the preceding chapter show clearly that, whichever family is taken, sharks exhibit such a characteristically hydrodynamic form that analogies quickly spring to mind – torpedo-shaped, like the body of an aeroplane, like a submarine. Moreover, one generally compares sharks with modern high-speed vehicles whose construction involves sophisticated mathematical formulae for determining the shape offering least resistance. It is, on the whole, with aeroplanes that the comparison is most usually made, for their lines clearly suggest the general appearance of sharks. The resemblance is even more striking in those in which the wings are set low on the body, like the pectoral fins in sharks (Figure 8). Regarding the first dorsal fin, especially in the family Isuridae, its profile is almost exactly reproduced in the tailplane of certain aeroplanes. During the last war, a German handbook describing some of the British aeroplanes (Wellington, Sterling, Sunderland) clearly specified: tailplane in the shape of a shark's fin (*Haifischflosse*).

But that is not all. A cast made of the pectoral fin of a shark by Mr Royer

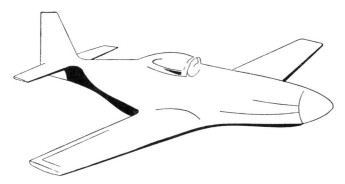

Fig. 8   Mustang P 51, to show the close resemblance between aerodynamic streamlining and the hydrodynamic streamlining found in sharks and certain fishes.

in 1913 revealed quite unexpected but close similarities with the profiles found in the wings of certain aeroplanes. Figure 9 shows the general outline of this fin, with the corresponding cross-sections in grey. The latter, numbered 1–15, are quite characteristic of those used in aeroplane wings, and it is even possible to state which particular aircraft they most resemble.[1] We shall have occasion, further on, to discuss the role played by these wing-like pectoral fins in the locomotion of sharks.

The fundamental difference between sharks and man-made aeroplanes and submarines is, of course, that the latter are rigid, allowing practically no deformation of shape, and are propelled by an engine. Sharks, on the other hand, are supple, swimming chiefly by sculling movements of the caudal fin but with the rest of the body participating in the propulsive effort to a greater or lesser degree, according to species; thus, members of the Scyliorhinidae undulate the body much more than do the Isuridae; Donald Nelson (1969) particularly noticed the stiff-bodied motion of a 12-foot Great White Shark (*Carcharodon carcharias*) as it approached him. An interesting study of the geometrical and physical characteristics of fishes and their relationship to swimming was made by Magnan (1929) following an earlier and more theoretical paper that he published with Sainte-Laguë the previous year. Such studies have hitherto been rather rare. They require a biologist with a first-rate understanding of both hydrodynamics and the biology of the fishes studied and a capacity to synthesize the data from these two disciplines. That the problem of swimming is not so simple as it first appears can be judged by the fact that even quite recently the *New Scientist* contained a paper arguing the theoretical impossibility of an animal body to swim at all! Some important contributions to an understanding of how fishes

[1] E.g. the article signed 'M.V.' in the periodical *Les Ailes* for 29 October 1936.

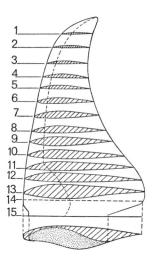

Fig. 9   Pectoral fin of a shark with fifteen cross-sections, the latter showing a striking resemblance to those of the wing of an aeroplane.

swim have been made by Kramer (1960), Aleev (1963), Alexander (1965) and Magnuson (1970), the latter making a particularly detailed study of the Wavyback Skipjack (*Euthynnus affinis*). Such studies are extremely valuable, both in themselves and in the light that they throw on other aspects of ichthyology. For example, Magnuson concluded that many of the specializations of his skipjack and probably other tuna-like fishes (family Scombridae) were not for the attainment of high speeds, as one might think, but were for the maintenance of continuous swimming movement through the water with the least expenditure of energy.

Magnan and Sainte-Laguë also found surprising results. They compared the speeds and power required in a Blue Shark (*Prionace glauca*) with those of a submarine. The ship chosen was the type O'Byrne, 170 feet in length, of 500 h.p. and capable of a speed of 8 knots under water. The shark measured 6 feet 6 inches, weighed 70·65 lbs and its speed was 21·3 knots. When the necessary calculations had been made, it was found that the shark required a driving power of about 6 times as little per pound weight as did the model of the submarine (which had been scaled down to the same size as the shark). Clearly, the shark was the more efficient of the two.

Sharks swim with all their fins erect. This is an anatomical necessity since it is quite impossible for the fins to be folded back against the body. This is quite the reverse of the condition in most bony fishes where the fins can not only fold back but often have a groove at their base into which the fin fits snugly during bursts of speed. In bony fishes, the spines and finrays of the fin supply rigidity when the fin is erected, but the thin membrane in between allows the fin to be folded neatly when the rays are depressed. The cross-sections of a shark fin in Figure 9 show that folding of the fin could only result in a disorganized crumpling which would pose more problems of turbulence than it solved. The fins of sharks are, however, beautifully streamlined and the permanent erection of the pectoral fins fulfils a most important function since they provide lift for the front part of the body. Magnuson (1970) found a similar situation in the tuna-like or scombroid fishes which either lack a swimbladder (like sharks) or else have a very reduced one that is incapable of supplying sufficient buoyancy. In these fishes the pectoral fins are spread out at slow or cruising speeds but progressively retracted until at high speeds they are folded back into a groove and the fish is travelling more like a high speed missile than an aeroplane, the body itself producing sufficient lift. Sharks cannot travel like this but the leading edges of the fins are often strongly swept back, especially in fast species like the Mako (*Isurus oxyrinchus*). Rather few precise measurements have been made on the speeds of sharks but for a Mako to leap clear out of the water it must require a starting velocity in water of at least 22 miles per hour (Lineaweaver & Backus, 1970). In one series of experiments on a Blue Shark (*Prionace glauca*) measuring 2 feet in length and weighing 1·3 lbs, the fish was able to hold its own against a current of 26 feet per second (24·5 miles an hour) and in short bursts of speed it attained 43 miles per hour.

On the whole, the sharks belong to the class of 'sprinters', as Slijper (1963) has pointed out. That is to say, marine animals which live a rather lazy existence but which are capable, should the necessity arise, of very sudden bursts of speed. Slijper characterized the sharks in this way, and contrasted them to the 'stayers', of which he considered the cetaceans (whales, dolphins, etc) examples.

Klausewitz (1962) has made a special study of swimming in cartilaginous fishes (Selachians), and in particular in the sharks themselves. As a result, he has divided the sharks into three groups, following their general form:

Group 1. Pelagic sharks with streamlined bodies; snout pointed (conical); caudal fin homocercal[1] or nearly so. Type: Mackerel Sharks (Figure 3a,b).

Group 2. Slender-bodied sharks, but much less streamlined than the preceding; caudal fin strictly heterocercal;[1] head flattened dorso-ventrally, the lower part in the form of flat plane; Klausewitz proposed, as type of this

---

[1] Strictly speaking, the terms homocercal and heterocercal denote shapes of the caudal fin (tail) as they result from the shape of the underlying skeleton. As used here: *Homocercal tail* – upper and lower lobes more or less equal; *Heterocercal tail* – upper lobe larger than lower, the Thresher Shark an extreme example.

group, *Carcharhinus menisorrah* and *C. melanopterus* (Black-tip Reef Shark). Generally speaking, one can include here representatives of the family Carcharhinidae, and some others (Figure 5d).

Group 3. Anterior part of head massive, heavy; tail slender, its axis noticeably horizontal, the lobes little developed, e.g. the Zebra Shark (*Stegostoma fasciatum*) (Figure 4b).

These three groups can also be distinguished by the angle formed between the axis of the body and the axis of the upper lobe of the caudal fin: *Group 1*, 50°; *Group 2*, 30°; *Group 3*, 0°.

There is a direct relationship between the way of life of species within these three groups and their body form. Thus, members of the Mackerel Shark group lead a pelagic existence, hunting fast-swimming or shoaling fishes such as mackerel, flying-fishes and herrings. The two *Carcharhinus* cited by Klausewitz are coastal species, frequenting coral reefs, living mainly in fairly shallow waters and feeding on small littoral animals such as flatfishes, crustaceans and so on. As for the Zebra Shark (*Stegostoma fasciatum*), it well exemplifies those forms which live wholly at the bottom, feeding on bottom-living animals.

In general, Klausewitz's scheme is an attractive one, but it does overlook some exceptions. For example, the Basking Shark (Figure 3c) and the Whale Shark (Figure 4c) are slow and sluggish creatures but possess strictly symmetrical (homocercal) caudal fins. Moreover, the Whale Shark has a head which is flattened dorso-ventrally, quite comparable to the condition found in members of Group 2. On the other hand, there are well-known pelagic sharks which have a heterocercal tail, the upper lobe being larger than the lower in for example the White-tipped Shark (*Carcharhinus longimanus*), which should be placed in Klausewitz's Group 1.

Confining ourselves to the pelagic and coastal sharks (Groups 1 and 2) it should be possible to classify them into two approximate categories: those in which the caudal fin is definitely symmetrical (i.e. *Carcharodon, Lamna, Isurus, Cetorhinus* and *Rhincodon*), and those in which the caudal is noticeably heterocercal (i.e. *Carcharhinus*). This distinction is quite an obvious one. One can add to this the fact that, with the exception of the Whale Shark, the remainder of the first group have conico-cylindrical bodies, while those in the second group show in varying degrees a reversal of the plane of flattening (i.e. horizontally flattened in front, changing to vertical flattening, that is to say, lateral compression, behind). This latter type of body form will be dealt with later (p. 31).

The very name of the Mackerel Shark (Group 1) suggests a close analogy with the scombroid fishes (the fast-swimming tunas, mackerels, etc). Many authors (Hesse and Kramer particularly) have made comparisons between different kinds of fishes which show a tendency towards the same type of body form. Hesse (1910) established that the caudal fin was the major propulsive organ, and that the most efficient shape for it was that of a crescent (i.e. homocercal) combined with the greatest possible rigidity. However, forward movement is not solely due to the caudal acting like a propeller pushing a rigid hull. To the oarlike action of the caudal fin is added the gentle undulation of the body running back from the head along the length of the body of the fish. The pivot or fulcrum of this undulation lies at a point behind the head, in the nuchal region. The lateral oscillation augments the main propulsive effort supplied by the tail. In passing, it can be noted that the same side to side movement is found in small craft propelled by means of a single oar over the stern; but in this case, the actual side to side movements of the boat add nothing to the forward movement of the craft, and indeed, an expert sculler can almost eliminate this and pursue a straight course. One should not press the comparison too far, for one cannot equate the rigid hull of a dinghy with the movable body of a Tuna or Mackerel Shark. These fishes, as the authors just cited have observed, are able to swim by oscillating motions of the body, even if such movement is only slight. It is to this group that Breder (1926) has given the term 'carangiform movements' (after the carangid fishes, the jacks, horse mackerels, etc).

In their morphology and way of life, the sharks in Group 3 are in complete contrast to the pelagic species in Group 1. The Zebra Shark (*Stegostoma*), for example, always swims slowly, close to the bottom. In doing so, the anterior part of the body oscillates very strongly from left to right, the point of oscillation being set back much further along the body than in the Mackerel Sharks, in fact somewhere under the first dorsal fin. The posterior part of the body also oscillates in an exaggerated manner, and it would appear that this oscillatory movement plays a highly important role in the swimming of sharks in Group 3, the action of the tail being correspondingly reduced. According to Breder, this can be termed the 'anguilliform movement' (more or less approximating to that found in eels). In fact, this author considers that pelagic sharks, such as the Great White Shark (*Carcharodon*) tend towards the carangiform movement, but without reproducing it exactly. In the same way, the sharks in Klausewitz's Group 3 would approach the anguilliform movement. However, the two definitions tend to break down in the sharks, and Breder considered that typical sharks 'display swimming movements intermediate between the anguilliform and the carangiform'. He then gave some criteria characterizing the two types of

27

movement, based on the extent of the undulations passed along the body: '*Anguilliform*: more than one half a sine wave is formed by the body, typically several entire waves. *Carangiform*: Not more than one-half a sine wave is formed by the body and frequently it is anatomically impossible to form even that much.'

Breder believed that in the carangiform movement the axis of oscillation, the pivot or fulcrum, is at the base of the skull 'at the beginning of a stroke, but migrates backward with it'; on the other hand, Klausewitz located this point very much behind the head and below the first dorsal fin in species of *Stegostoma* (sharks of Group 3), with a marked tendency towards the anguilliform movement. Be that as it may, between these two extremes there are, in Group 2, some typical sharks with a decidedly asymmetrical heterocercal tail, of which the numerous members of the family of Grey Sharks (Carcharhinidae) are good examples.

Hesse (1910) examined the movements and effects of an asymmetrical tail and found that the oarlike movements of the upper and most developed part tended with each sweep to drive the front part of the animal downwards. Counteracting this, as mentioned earlier, is the lift provided by the pectoral fins and the lower surfaces of the body. These two forces cancel each other out and the final result is a horizontal passage through the water. In horizontal swimming with no turns, the hind edges of the pectoral fins are inclined downwards so that the fin shows a slight angle of attack to the water. Contrary to the belief of some authors, the fins are not *absolutely* rigid and it seems that the hind edges can be further depressed to produce more lift; presumably this is done at slow speeds when there is more of a tendency for the body to sink. Magnuson (1970) showed in his skipjacks (in which the pectorals are retractable) that the pectoral fins rotate as they are folded back so that the angle of attack becomes greater although the area of the fin is reduced. Sharks cannot do this but there seems to be constant control over the hind edges of the pectorals not only to adjust the lift but to alter swimming angle and to assist in making turns (see Plate 2).

By studying successive frames in ciné films taken by Hans Hass, on the *Xarifa* Expedition, Klausewitz was able to make an analysis of the swimming of *Carcharhinus acutidens*. Without entering into the details of this work, one can summarize by saying that the head oscillates rather feebly (about 10°) from left to right; the pivot is situated immediately behind the head, and the curve begins to increase at the second dorsal fin reaching its greatest amplitude in the region of the caudal, where the caudal fin begins to oscillate 50° or more. Thus it has been possible to follow a single wave from its origin to the tip of the caudal; on the film, this occupied 61 frames

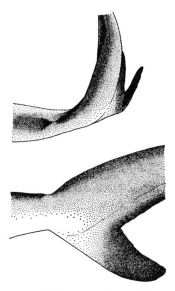

Fig. 10   Caudal fossette or small pit at the base of the tail, seen here in a species of Grey Shark (*Carcharhinus*). Base of tail seen from above (top) and from the side (lower).

at a projection speed of 24 frames/second, i.e. it took $2\frac{1}{2}$ seconds to complete. The shark was at the time swimming at what could be called a normal cruising speed. Recent theoretical work by Wu (1961) has shown that swimming is most efficient when the wave amplitude increases as it progresses down the body towards the tail. This confirms earlier views, and is fully discussed by Alexander (1967) in an excellent little book on body form in fishes.

At the same time, Klausewitz noticed a pronounced to-and-fro movement in the anal fin, and he thought that, together with the two dorsal fins, these three vertical fins acted as stabilizers. One can note, in passing, that certain sharks have only a single dorsal fin, and that in others there is no anal fin. With regard to the ventral or pelvic fins, they showed an undulatory movement which perhaps helps to maintain stability (Harris, 1936, 1938).

Fishes that lack a swimbladder are heavier than the water surrounding them and thus tend to sink. Average figures for the specific gravity of such fishes are between 1·06 and 1·09, that is to say, more than either freshwater (1·00) or sea water (1·026). The result is that these fishes must constantly swim in order to avoid sinking to the bottom. Most of the bony fishes have a swimbladder which provides buoyancy, enabling the fish to 'hover' in the water. In certain sharks the problem seems to have been solved by using the

29

liver as a buoyancy organ. Since the liver may comprise 20 per cent of the weight of the shark and contains oils with a very low specific gravity (0·86), one can understand how species like the Basking Shark and the Whale Shark can appear to lie motionless at the surface. Most sharks, however, do not seem to achieve this neutral buoyancy and must keep swimming. This has had a profound effect on their body form as well as on their behaviour and swimming technique. The high degree of streamlining discussed earlier has clearly been an evolutionary necessity, for the history of all animal species has involved balancing the amount of energy used in maintaining life against the amount actually gained through feeding. With the evolution of the swimbladder in the bony fishes, tremendous diversity in body form became possible since swimming was not essential to buoyancy. The sea horses and boxfishes are extreme examples of the kind of experiments that have proved successful.

It was stated earlier that sharks belong to the class of sprinters or animals that are normally slow moving but can make sudden spurts when necessary. This is reflected in the type of muscle that they have. There are two types of muscle used in swimming. The first is red muscle, which functions aerobically, that is to say it obtains its energy by actively oxidizing fats (which is twice as efficient weight for weight than using carbohydrates or protein). The individual muscle fibres in the red muscle are rather slender, well supplied with blood and contain myoglobin as an oxygen transporter, which gives them their reddish colour. The second type of muscle is the white muscle, which functions anaerobically by converting glycogen to lactate.

A certain amount of work has been done on the swimming muscles of dogfishes (*Scyliorhinus*) by Bone (1966), who showed that the red muscle, which forms a thin layer lateral to the much greater bulk of white muscle, is chiefly used in cruising. The white muscle is used as an additional source of energy for spurts of speed but cannot be used for long. As might be expected, oceanic fishes and those which must swim to avoid sinking (e.g. most sharks except those that live on the bottom) have relatively large amounts of red muscle. Conversely, the 'lurkers' like the pike, which hover and make short fast rushes at their prey, have rather few red muscle fibres.

Also connected with the swimming of sharks is the surprising discovery that in two of the fastest species, the Porbeagle (*Lamna nasus*) and the Mako (*Isurus oxyrinchus*), the body temperature is above that of the surrounding sea. It is well known that certain tunas and bonitos (family Scombridae), which are also extremely fast and powerful fishes, have body temperatures as much as 10° C higher than that of the surrounding medium, but this was not suspected in sharks until the work of two American physiologists working at the Woods Hole Oceanographic Institution, Francis Carey and John Teal. Commenting on this discovery, Lineaweaver and Backus (1970) point out that with each 10° C rise in temperature muscle contraction will triple (although the actual force exerted remains the same). Since the Bluefin Tuna has been found to achieve over forty miles an hour in short bursts, the advantages of 'warm' muscles are clear. According to Carey and Teal, the Porbeagle and the Mako (and probably the two other members of the Isuridae, the Great White Shark and *Isurus paucus*) have a counter-current heat-exchanger system similar to that found in the tunas; the close apposition of arteries and veins in the muscles enables heat to pass from the warmer to the cooler vessels rather than be lost at the gills.

A few words can be said here regarding the idea of the reversal of the planes of flattening mentioned earlier in connection with the body form in some sharks. Frédérick Houssay (1912) amongst others examined this hydrodynamic phenomenon in its application to fishes. It is well known that a jet of liquid, leaving a rectangular or elliptical orifice under pressure, assumes the shape shown in Figure 11. This is the reversal of planes, each segment forming an angle of 90° to its neighbour. Following this principle, Houssay took a rubber bag and filled it with a mixture of oil, vaseline and white lead, of a specific gravity of 1·0. Then, having sealed it hermetically, he pulled it through the water and obtained in this way, with a maleable solid, the reversal of planes shown in Figure 11. Having already noted that

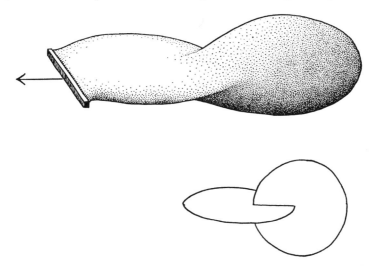

Fig. 11   The phenomenon of 'reversed planes'. Drawing of a rubber bag showing the characteristic shape assumed after being drawn through water from right to left (redrawn after Houssay).

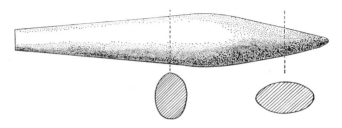

Fig. 12   Diagrammatic representation of body form in certain sharks, showing the
tendency towards reversal of planes, the front of the body being flattened
horizontally and the rear part vertically.

in certain fishes, the anterior part of the body is flattened horizontally
(dorso-ventrally) while the posterior part is flattened vertically (laterally),
he deduced that this shape was not only the most advantageous for fast
swimming, but that one should find it, more or less accentuated, in all fishes
without exception (Figure 12).

Certainly, some of the sharks show very clearly this flattening of the head
and lateral compression of the posterior part of the body, the latter cul-
minating in the upper lobe of the caudal fin. At first sight, the Carcharhinidae
are typical examples. Moreover, there are forms in which this feature is
particularly well shown, even exaggerated: the rhinobatids, rhynchobatids,
sawfishes and monkfishes. All these fishes – intermediates between the
sharks and the rays – have the head and the anterior part of the body considerably flattened, above all with a greatly flattened snout or rostrum
(Rhinobatidae) resembling a flat, triangular plate; while the dorsal fins,
placed well back, complete the vertical aspect of the second 'plane'. But
all these animals are slow swimmers. They lead a benthic life, feeding on
molluscs and crustaceans for which a concerted rush or lively pursuit is not
necessary. In this respect, they approach the rays, to which they bear considerable anatomical resemblance. It does not seem, therefore, that in
pushing the principle of the reversed planes to its ultimate conclusion, one
necessarily obtains a body form adapted to speed. Some authors have con-
tested the whole idea, in particular Amans (1906), who believed that in the
vast majority of cases the principle was not evident, particularly in good
swimmers.

The Mackerel Sharks, pelagic fishes which are known to be fast, powerful
swimmers, are a case in point. In them, the phenomenon of the reversed
planes is least apparent. It is concealed to the extent of being invisible; only
the methods of a Magnan or Houssay could reveal it. At first sight, the body
of these fishes is much more akin in shape to a malleable substance which

has been spun at high speed, i.e. conico-cylindrical. Moreover, with the presence of lateral 'keels', the caudal peduncle shows a decided tendency towards a dorso-ventral flattening, as if a supplementary, horizontal plane had been interposed between the posterior part of the body and the caudal fin (Figure 13). The presence or absence of these keels is an important character in generic diagnoses. The question arises what is the function of these keels, since they are found also in the scombroid (mackerel-like) fishes? Houssay was of the opinion that the presence of caudal keels was associated with fast-swimming animals, and he suggested the following series in connection with homocercal tails: *Squalus*, *Cetorhinus*, *Lamna*. The Spur Dog (*Squalus acanthias*) is a small fish lacking keels, but the others possess them. But if *Lamna* can be considered a fast-swimming fish, the

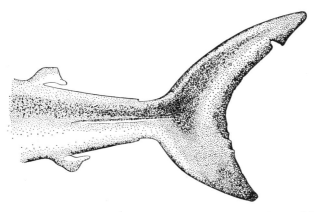

Fig. 13   Tail of shark showing the lateral keel on the side of the caudal peduncle.

same cannot be said for the Basking Shark (*Cetorhinus*), which is renowned for its placid lounging; or again, the huge Whale Shark, which possesses caudal keels but which certainly could not be classed as a fast swimmer.

On the other hand, Houssay claimed that the presence of these keels had as a corollary the development of the lower lobe of the caudal fin, so that *all* sharks with them also have a homocercal caudal. But this is not wholly true. If the Mackerel Sharks do in fact answer to this description, one finds, in the family Carcharinidae, the Tiger Shark (*Galeocerdo*) which has a caudal as heterocercal as is possible, together with long keels on the caudal peduncle (it is necessary to state that the latter have, for some reason, sometimes escaped the notice of authors). The relationship between cause and effect in these two characters is therefore still debatable.

For Houssay, the fish has been modelled by the water itself, and its form

33

must be that which offers least resistance. In fact, until this result is attained, he believed that the water collided with, pressed and modelled the obstacle until it had been effaced or at least as far as the 'plasticity' of the fish would allow. It seemed to Houssay that this process was unlimited in its application to the attainment of the maximum speed. This is to simplify what is in fact an extremely complex question, and one which poses problems of the highest order. We have seen that the hydrodynamics of sharks can be successfully verified by mathematical proofs. But one must also recognize that the liquid medium can, on occasions, be a very whimsical sculptor,

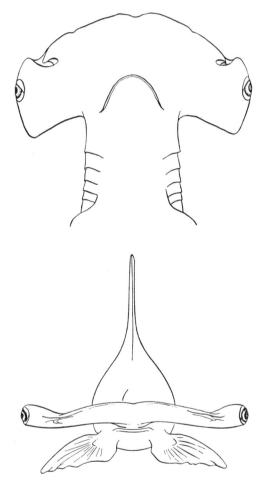

Fig. 14 The head of a Hammerhead Shark (*Sphyrna* sp.) seen from below and head on.

acting apparently blindly and without regard to proportions and balance. Two good examples of this are the Hammerhead Shark and the Thresher Shark.

The quite extraordinary shape of the Hammerhead Shark (more correctly, Hammerhead *Sharks* since there are in fact nine species), has always awed men and provided them with one of the classic types of sea monster. Truly, the lateral expansions of the head, with the eyes at the tips of these protuberances, give these fishes the appearance of something out of a nightmare (Figure 14 and Plates 2 and 3).

The 16th-century naturalist Guillaume Rondelet (1554) stated that the Hammerhead was also called the Jew fish because of the similarity between its head and the style of head gear worn by Jews in Provence. He also said: '*Il est horrible à voir . . . sa rencontre porte malheur aux navigateurs.*' The Hammerhead is referred to by Oppian as:

> The monstrous Balance-Fish, of hideous Shape
> Rounds jetting Lands, and doubles ev'ry Cape.

The head in this fish is strongly flattened dorso-ventrally, much more so than is generally the case in the family Carcharhinidae, to which it is closely related. A Hammerhead is, essentially, a carcharhinid in which the head has been expanded laterally while at the same time flattened into a rather thin platelike structure; this may be distinctly rectangular, as in *Sphyrna zygaena*, or shovel-shaped, as in *S. tiburo*.

Can one really attribute this shape to the sculptural action of the water? And what adaptive or functional value can such an unusual head shape have? It is found also in certain larval forms of bony fishes (teleosts), for example in *Idiacanthus fasciola*, the larva of which was described (mistakenly) as a quite different species, *Stylophthalmus paradoxus*. In this fish, however, the cartilagenous expansions of the larva are resorbed in the adult, and the eye assumes its normal position within the orbit.[1]

Murphy and Nichols (1916) stated categorically that one function of this specialized head is to act as a hydroplane, so that the animal can make rapid ascents or descents merely by raising or lowering its head. They considered these fishes to be the most agile, fast and excitable of all sharks and amongst the most lively of fishes. These authors believed the head to be *highly specialized*. It happens that the outline of the head is very suggestive of some of the early aeroplanes, and in particular the machine flown by the Wright

---

[1] In passing, it can be noted that there are some examples amongst the Diptera of forms in which the eyes are placed at the tips of greatly developed lateral expansions: *Sphyracephala, Laglaisia, Diopsis, Asyntona.*

brothers, in which the elevators controlling inclination were situated in the *front* – a practice which was soon abandoned. According to Murphy and Nichols, the head of the Hammerhead should not be supposed to function solely as a means of regulating depth. Fishes in general, and sharks in particular, can undulate the body laterally, but this is much more difficult and less effective in the vertical plane. These authors state explicitly that the Hammerhead uses its head to help it turn or swerve. In effect, the head complements and reinforces the pectoral 'hydroplanes'. When one views a Hammerhead from the front, one can clearly see that the head forms a plane which repeats that made up of the pectoral fins (Figure 14). All this serves to accentuate the 'reversed plane' body form which, though found in other sharks, is nowhere so pronounced as in the hammerheads.

Having stated this, it must be said that the hammerheads have not yet been established as faster or more agile swimmers than are the members of the family Carcharhinidae, to which they are closely related. Only a series of precise measurements, such as those carried out on the Blue Shark by A. Magnan, will allow us to make exact comparisons of their relative speeds. Possibly unduly impressed by the grotesque appearance of the Hammerhead, observers have in the past tended to attribute to it the appropriate qualities of speed and ferocity suggested by its appearance. We shall discuss this further in a later chapter.

All in all, the Hammerhead is only a *Carcharhinus* equipped with two protruberances on the sides of the head. It is enough to compare Figure 5d (*Carcharhinus limbatus*) with Figure 6b (*Sphyrna zygaena*) to see the truth in this (see also Plate 2). If we cut off the lateral expansions of the Hammerhead, we would arrive at some sort of *Carcharhinus*. These protruberances could, indeed, be a hindrance and a serious handicap. For example, in a tussle with a Tiger Shark or a White Shark, the adversary could easily inflict great damage with its jaws on these vulnerable parts. One can plausibly imagine that such an occurrence could happen frequently. This would indeed seem to be paying too dearly for a specialization whose utility is not clearly apparent. It has been suggested (Nelson, 1969) that the wide separation of the nostrils in Hammerhead Sharks provides these fishes with a kind of 'stereoscopic' sense of smell. The suggestion is ingenious but lacks experimental proof.

There is another remarkable example of 'modelling' in sharks which is also difficult to attribute to the effect of water acting against a malleable body in a manner calculated to produce the most ideal hydrodynamic form. This is the Thresher Shark, *Alopias vulpinus* (there are, in fact, three other closely related species of *Alopias*). This species shows a caudal fin which is as heterocercal as one could wish for: a perfect case of *hypertely*, i.e., excessive development of a character, the result being of problematical utility. In addition, the Thresher gives the impression, at first sight, of being unbalanced, almost ungainly, despite the undoubted elegance of its enormous but finely curved caudal fin; beside other sharks, the Thresher seems to be malformed (Figure 3d). It is difficult to imagine that the Thresher is designed for speed, and in fact it is not known as a particularly fast swimmer.

The general opinion nowadays is that the Thresher uses its huge tail to concentrate into a compact mass the fish on which it feeds. This 'threshing' behaviour is extremely effective. The Thresher swims round shoals of herrings, sardines or mackerel in ever decreasing circles, leaping into the air and then falling back into the water while thrashing vigorously with its tail. It follows these tactics until its victims, intimidated by this fantastic display, huddle together in a tight mass. Then, jaws open, the Thresher drives straight into the middle of this concentration of food and gorges itself. It would seem that on occasions, two or three *Alopias* combine in a communal hunt, and it is even recorded (Coles, 1915) that one particularly dextrous Thresher, with a flick of its tail, tossed the fishes into its mouth!

Such details are no doubt picturesque. But can one here again speak of *specialization*? If it were deprived of its cumbersome appendage, the Thresher would hardly die of starvation. There seems to be no doubt that it could do just as well as related species without somersaults and other antics and without behaving like a sheep dog. Moreover, it is curious that the Thresher should find it necessary to act like this in order to concentrate fishes like herrings and sardines which in any case are renowned for their gregarious habits and surely need no stimulus to form shoals of tightly packed individuals. It is not impossible, conversely, that these gymnastics are actually forced on the Thresher because of the extravagant caudal with which it is equipped; for what else can it do with such an appendage but thrash it from side to side? And if the unerring sculptural action of the water (in Houssay's sense) truly acted to the best advantage of the Thresher, then surely it would restore its caudal fin to dimensions more in keeping with its type of locomotion, since sharks, like other hunters, depend primarily on speed for their subsistence. There is, in fact, another shark that performs the same kind of antics as the Thresher but which has a quite normal tail. This is the Spinning Shark (*Carcharhinus maculipinnis*). According to Springer (1963), these sharks make spinning leaps which sometimes start below a school of very small fishes, through which the sharks pass with their mouths open.

Amongst the sharks, therefore, one finds two most interesting cases of

37

hypertely, on which contemporary biologists have been regretfully unable to throw light. It appears that the Hammerhead and the Thresher derive no obvious benefit from their deformities and the latter would even seem to be more of a liability than an asset to their owners (Cuenot, 1932; Rabaud, 1942). But this does not diminish the fact that, on the whole, sharks are remarkable 'swimming machines'.

With regard to the caudal keels, an interesting comparison can be made with the tuna-like fishes in which the caudal is lunate (i.e. strictly homocercal) and in which keels are variously developed. Aleev (1963) had suggested that although homocercal, the caudal in the common mackerel (*Scomber scombrus*) was actually tilted from the vertical during its sweeps from side to side and thus had an angle of attack which produced lift. Magnuson (1970) found the angle to be an insignificant 1° only in the Wavyback Skipjack, which would hardly produce any lift, and he suggested that the caudal keels are actually responsible for lift in the tail region. At first sight these narrow keels, like those in the sharks mentioned above, would appear to be capable of very little lift. Magnuson pointed out, however, that they travel through the water faster than the swimming speed of the fish and furthermore that the flow of water is not along their length but *diagonally* across them. In this way, they have a strong angle of attack even though they are set horizontally on the body. Magnuson concluded that the correlation between caudal keels and tail shape in sharks reflected the need for a source of lift behind the centre of gravity which could be supplied either by a heterocercal tail or by caudal keels. This does not overcome the difficulty of the Tiger Shark, with its caudal keels and caricature of a heterocercal tail, but it provides a more reasonable explanation than that given by Houssay, for whom the fish has been modelled by the water, each obstacle to the flow of water being buffeted and effaced until the species has achieved its maximum streamlining.

One must admit, however, that whether 'modelled by water' or answering to obscure hydrodynamic requirements, the shape of sharks can on occasion defy reasonable expectations of balance and proportion, producing an almost whimsical result. Two good examples are the Hammerhead and the Thresher.

Coloration

Form and colour are the two characters of marine life which first strike an observer, colour perhaps predominating. It must be said, however, that as regards colour sharks display no very exceptional qualities. The group as a whole in no way matches the beautiful and striking colours so much admired in the bony fishes.

In general, sharks show the well-known counter-shading found in most fishes, the back being dark and the belly lighter. This counter-shading has been much discussed and this is not the place to enter into explanations and arguments for or against its supposed survival value and its bearing on mimicry.

Among the vernacular names for sharks there are many which, quite justifiably, refer to the dominant colour of the fish (blue, brown, grey, white, etc) or to a particular colour pattern (black-tipped, marbled, leopard, tiger, zebra, etc). It is, of course, the colour of the dorsal surfaces which is referred to, the ventral surfaces usually being white or at least lighter than the back. (There are a few small sharks which are entirely black, but these are deep-water species.) The Blue Shark (*Prionace glauca*), for example, is aptly named, being a beautiful and quite characteristic blue in colour. The Great White Shark (*Carcharodon carcharias*), on the other hand, is not strictly white, as its name would suggest, but more a light grey-brown, with the belly a dirty white. A colour very common in the Carcharhinidae is a greyish-blue slate or brown, more or less dark. The full-term foetus in certain carcharhinids exhibits a very delicate colour reminiscent of Copenhagen porcelain.

There is nothing very splendid in the garb of sharks (except perhaps the blue of the Blue Shark), and for the most part they are rather drab. Some ornamentation is found in the fins, the tip often being black as if dipped in Indian ink, but in other cases the fin is without pigmentation and distinctly white. Regarding the stripes and various markings which adorn some sharks, these are above all juvenile colours which tend to disappear with age. This is exactly what occurs in the Tiger Shark (*Galeocerdo*), which is truly striped in the juvenile but in large individuals becomes a uniform greyish colour with only a faint reminder of the stripes from which it derives its name. Again, young Nurse Sharks (*Ginglymostoma*) have on their dorsal surfaces numerous black ocellated spots which disappear in the adults. On the other hand, the Whale Shark (*Rhincodon typus*) keeps its colour pattern throughout life, the quite distinctive colour pattern of the 30–40 feet adult being present at all sizes down to the only embryo ever found, a $14\frac{1}{2}$-inch specimen still in its egg case (well figured by Lineaweaver & Backus, 1970). The most colourful of the sharks are those members of the Orectolobidae (the Carpet Sharks or Wobbegongs of Australia), and the Zebra Shark (*Stegostoma fasciatum*). These are coastal species which can blend in with the colour of the substrata on which they are found.

This brings us back to the question of mimicry and adaptive coloration. For obvious reasons, colour and colour changes have been studied mostly in bony fishes, but some work has been done on selachians, showing that certain species have the ability to become lighter or darker according to the nature of the bottom. The mechanism of colour change is now fairly well understood: it is due to concentration or dispersion of the pigments within the pigment cells (chromatophores), so that more or less pigment is exposed to view. The principle can be illustrated by the following analogy. Imagine an aerial observer hovering over Trafalgar Square on a rainy day. The mass of open umbrellas would present a predominantly black ground, with perhaps here or there the brighter colours of a woman's umbrella. Then the rain stops. The umbrellas are folded away and from high above, Trafalgar Square would have a quite different appearance – a mixture of the varying colours of people's coats against the grey of the streets and pavements.

In the case of the chromatophores, the question is obviously much more complicated. What for example stimulates the pigment in the cells to aggregate or disperse? The process may take a few seconds, or again it may take hours or even days. Vilter (1941) has suggested the following sequence of events: LIGHT → RETINA → SYMPATHETIC NERVOUS SYSTEM → CHROMATOPHORE. Early investigators had found, however, that not all responses of the chromatophores were initiated by the nervous system. The discovery of hormonal communication explained many of these exceptions. Parker and Porter (1934), working on the Smooth Hound (*Mustelus canis*), attributed the functioning of the melanophores to 'pituitary secretions carried from the pituitary gland to the melanophores by the blood and lymph'. Similarly Waring (1938), working on dogfishes, attributed the expansion of the melanophores to the 'activity of a blood-circulated hormone derived from the neuro-intermediate lobe (of the pituitary)'. Besides neural and hormonal control of the chromatophores, there is a third possibility, the neurohormonal theory. This supposes that the neurons supplying the chromatophores produce chemical substances which activate the chromatophores, there being a *neurohumor* causing contraction and another causing dispersion.

As yet, experiments have been carried out on small selachians such as dogfishes (and the monkfish, Budker, 1937), but not on large sharks. In the latter, however, the colour remains relatively stable.

Chapter 3

Anatomy

It would no doubt have been more correct to have headed this chapter 'A *little* anatomy' (or perhaps, more truthfully, a *very* little), since there is no question of presenting an exhaustive study here. I merely wish to give a general picture of such anatomical facts as are necessary to the understanding of certain aspects of the lives of sharks.

As already noted, the selachians comprise an extremely homogeneous group, all members having in common the following features: cartilaginous skeleton, calcified to a greater or lesser extent; a thick skin bearing toothlike placoid scales; an intestine with a spiral valve, of rather variable form; 5 to 7 branchial openings (gill-slits), without a gill cover or operculum; carnivorous habits.

These features are common to both the sharks and the rays. Since we are here concerned only with the sharks, the following further features can be added to the list above: an elongate, fusiform body; jaws furnished with sharp-edged or pointed teeth,[1] in several series, some being replacement series; gill openings lateral and usually in front of the pectoral fins, but sometimes the 4th and 5th slit above the latter.

Such is a general definition of the sharks. In the synopsis given in Chapter I are the various morphological characters one can use to distinguish one family from another using the more obvious outward features. We shall now proceed to a swift review of the more important anatomical characters.

Skeleton
The skeleton of sharks is entirely cartilaginous, bearing no trace of bony material. Nevertheless, certain parts of the skeleton (the vertebral column in particular) show to a greater or lesser extent signs of calcification, i.e. the impregnation of the intercellular material with a complex mixture of calcium phosphates and carbonates to form apatite. For this reason, the cartilage may be relatively soft in some cases and quite easily cut with a knife,

---

[1] The only sharks having teeth in a 'pavement' are those belonging to the genera *Mustelus, Hexanchus* and *Heterodontus*, and these can be placed without hesitation in the category 'sharks'.

while in others it can be hard and have much the appearance of bone. It must be stressed that there is never found in sharks anything which approaches true bone. Even when, in some specialized species, the calcification has proceeded to a point where certain skeletal elements strongly resemble compact bony tissue, this is an illusion and without exception the cartilage is impregnated with calcium without any trace of canaliculi (the system of Haversian canals) which permeate the intercellular substance of bone. Recently however Zangerl (1966) has reported the presence of bone cells (osteocytes) in the denticles of the very ancient but specialized fossil shark *Ornithoprion hertwigi*. This is of great interest because it lends support to the suggestion that the cartilaginous fishes are ultimately derived from ancestors that later lost the ability to form bone and, for one reason or another, strengthened their skeleton by calcification of cartilage. The need for such strengthening would have been most necessary in the vertebral column of the larger species since the powerful swimming muscles of the trunk require to act against a stout but flexible rod.

In the vertebral column calcification occurs in more than one way. In the last century, the German worker Hasse (1879) recognized three types of calcification in the vertebrae: *cyclospondylous* (a ring of calcification), *tectospondylous* (two such rings), and *asterospondylous* (star-shaped zones of calcification). By sectioning the vertebral column of a shark or one of the dogfishes, one can clearly see the type of ring encircling the notochord; the rings appear yellowish white and opaque against the bluish and hyaline cartilage. The constancy of the form of these calcified zones in the centrum encouraged Hasse to use this character as the basis for a general classification of the sharks. Subsequently, exceptions have been found and the system can only be accepted with reservations. Nevertheless, some later authors revived the scheme in part, but with modifications in the interpretation of the terms asterospondylous and tectospondylous (e.g. E. Grace White, 1936; Applegate, 1967). More recently, two of the foremost workers on sharks at the present time, Springer & Garrick (1964) and Garrick (1967) have tried using vertebral number as a character in the classification of the sharks, with some success.

A further character which can be noted in connection with the vertebral column, is the tendency towards a doubling of the segments in the caudal region. The name *diplospondyly* has been given to this phenomenon. Daniel observed that this condition 'is to be interpreted as meaning that there is need for greater freedom of movement in the area preceding the caudal fin'. Springer and Garrick (1964) have shown that diplospondyly occurs mostly after the level of the pelvic fin has been reached.

When one cuts up a shark, one might be tempted to think that the animal has no ribs, and indeed there is nothing like the cage of ribs found in the bony fishes. Nonetheless, ribs are in fact present, in the form of lateral catilaginous expansions (apophyses) very reduced, but present at the bases of the vertebrae in the trunk region (absent in the caudal vertebrae). These are true but vestigial ribs, playing no role as supports.

Unlike the bony fishes, the shark's skull is not made up of many small pieces sutured tightly together, one to the next. On the contrary, it is a single compact cartilaginous block, enclosing, in addition to the brain, the olfactory and auditory capsules; there are a number of foramens for the passage of nerves and vessels, and the skull is more or less prolonged anteriorly, in some species forming a rostrum (e.g. Saw Sharks). These features render the skull of selachians particularly suitable for the demonstration of the relationships of the cranial nerves, and the dissection of the dogfish is a classic exercise for all zoology students.

In sharks, the jaws are rather loosely attached to the cranium. It is this which allows them to be removed so easily; a sharp but dextrous cut with a knife, and the trophy is yours. In the more primitive Hexanchidae (Cow Sharks) the jaw suspension is termed *amphistylic*: the upper jaw is connected to the cranium in two places, the hyomandibular (the next cartilaginous 'hoop' behind the jaws, the remaining hoops being those of the gill arches) playing little part in supporting the hind end of the jaw. In other sharks the suspension is termed *hyostylic*: a single muscular ligament secures the upper jaw to the cranium, and the hind end of the jaw is supported by a segment of the hyomandibular 'hoop'. In the Heterodontidae (Port Jackson Sharks) the suspension is intermediate between amphistylic and hyostylic, the upper jaw fitting into a deep groove in the cranium, but at the same time being support by the hyomandibular. In the Chimaeras (and lungfishes) the upper jaw is completely fused to the cranium (*autostylic*).

The gill arches are supported by cartilaginous but non-calcified rods like hoops. In most sharks there are five arches but *Hexanchus* and one Saw Shark (*Pliotrema*) have six, while seven occur in *Heptranchias*, *Notorhynchus* and *Chlamydoselachus*. The fins also are supported by cartilaginous rods, the most complex being those associated with the pelvic fins in males. In all male selachians the inner edge of the pelvic fins is modified to form an elongate mixopterygium or clasper, an erectile organ used to transfer sperm to the female during copulation. The cartilaginous skeleton of the clasper is sometimes extremely complex; that shown in Figure 27 for the Whale Shark has been drawn somewhat simplified. The claspers are erectile and during copulation are bent forward and are swollen. They may be armed with one or more hooks (modified denticles) or covered with denticles, presumably both to rupture the female hymen and to secure a firmer hold. In the live-bearing toothcarps (Poeciliidae) the copulatory organ or mixopterygium (highly modified anterior anal rays) has an equally complex structure and one that is characteristic for each species, thus tending to prevent hybridization between different species. Possibly the same principle holds in sharks. At the base of each clasper is an opening, the apopyle, into which the seminal fluid passes after being discharged from the vent. A muscular pump forces the fluid down the groove of the clasper and into the female. Credit for the first description of the function of the claspers or intromittent organs must be given to Louis Agassiz (1807–73). As might be expected, Aristotle had remarked on their presence in male selachians but had assumed that they were used to clasp the female, hence our use of the term clasper.

For a long time, the calcified cartilaginous skeleton was considered to be an undoubted archaic character. The selachians have, in fact, an ancient lineage, going back over 300 millions years to Devonian times, and the term 'living fossils' has been popularly applied to them. But in other respects, the sharks possess organs which are highly evolved, perhaps more so than in bony fishes; for example, their nervous system and their urino-genital organs. Thus the cartilaginous skeleton can be considered, not as an ancestral character which has been retained in the modern forms, but rather as a degeneration or regression from bony tissue in the ancestral selachians. Piveteau (1934) was of the opinion that there is a definite series of regression of bony tissue from the most ancient to the most recent forms, as implied by the discovery of bone cells in *Ornithoprion* (see above).

The problem of the origin of the vertebrates is by no means simple, and views have radically altered in the last few years. The old picture of an evolutionary progression from the jawless Agnatha (now represented by the lampreys and hagfishes) to the cartilaginous sharklike fishes, up to the bony fishes and thence through the amphibians and reptiles to the birds and mammals, has been seriously questioned. E. Jarvik (1960 and 1964) has reviewed this problem and shown that in important respects it is 'inconsistent with known, well established facts'. He concluded that the Agnatha 'do not include the ancestors of the gnathostomes' (i.e. jawed fishes), and indeed that the petromyzontids (lampreys) and the myxinoids (hagfishes) had themselves become quite separate by the end of the Cambrian period, 500 million years ago. He also concluded that the many qualities common to all vertebrates must have arisen prior to this; when the other vertebrate groups appear in the fossil record, much later in the Ordovician or more commonly in the late Silurian and early Devonian, they are already divided into a number of clearly defined main groups. As Jarvik put it: 'If we imagine that we cut off the trunk of a tree and then plant its branches well apart into the ground, we will get a picture of the evolution of the vertebrates which agrees fairly well with the available facts.' These branches, which represent the major groups, 'are all equivalent, and none of them may be derived from any of the others' which 'removes the very foundation of the accepted family tree'.

Denticles or placoid scales
One of the most characteristic features of sharks is their outer covering; handle a shark and you are immediately aware of the rough, sandpaper-like

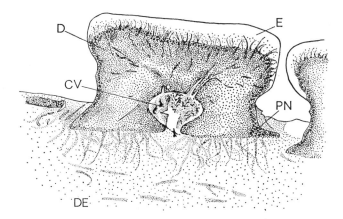

Fig. 15 Placoid scale from Nurse Shark *Ginglymostoma cirratum*, diagrammatic
D dentine. DE dermis. E enamel. CV pulp cavity. PN basal plate.

scales. The scales themselves are most distinctive and are of a type only found in selachians; they are termed *placoid* scales.

A placoid scale has the same structure as a tooth (Figures 15, 20). It is composed of a mass of dentine, at the centre of which is a pulp cavity, the whole being covered by a layer of enamel of variable thickness.[1] A basal plate secures the scale firmly in the skin. The similarity between the scales and the teeth in sharks is so exact that the scales are usually termed denticles or even dermal teeth to distinguish them from the jaw teeth.

There is a wide variety of shapes and sizes of denticles (see Figure 16). They may, for example, be closely juxtaposed in seried ranks, or they may

[1] The fine structure and properties of this enamel differ from those of mammalian enamel; the term *vitrodentine* has been used for it.

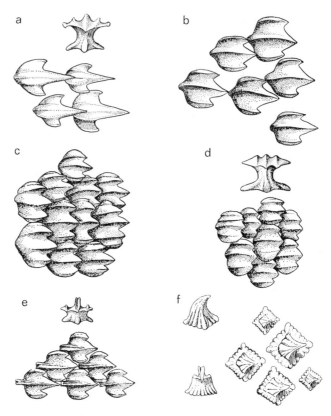

Fig. 16 Various types of placoid scale (denticle) found in sharks. (a) Spotted Dogfish (*Scyliorhinus* sp.). (b) Cow Shark *Hexanchus griseus*. (c) Dusky Shark *Carcharinus obscurus*. (d) Mackerel Shark *Isurus oxyrinchus*. (e) Piked Dogfish *Squalus acanthias*. (f) Greenland Shark *Somniosus microcephalus*.

be spread more sparsely, as in the Bramble Shark and the Greenland Shark. In some species the denticles are rounded, smooth and without points, while in others the crown of the denticle is pointed posteriorly and accounts for the roughness of the fish when it is stroked against the grain. Many sharks can be identified by their denticles, although difficulties arise when the shape and pattern of the denticles varies in different parts of the body.

The denticle is the original unit from which certain more specialized structures have arisen. The most obvious are the teeth. In the embryo there is almost no difference between the denticles round the mouth and those lining the jaws, but as development proceeds the jaw teeth take on their characteristic shape. In the rays (Hypotremata) the spines that often occur on the dorsal surface are merely modified denticles. Comparison of the enlarged spines or bucklers of the Thornback Ray (*Raja clavata*) with the denticles of the Basking Shark (*Cetorhinus maximus*) shows their common origin. Similarly, the spine or sting at the base of the tail in Stingrays is a greatly modified denticle, as also are the teeth along the edges of the saw in sawfishes (e.g. *Pristis*). Another modification of the denticles is seen in the spine that precedes the dorsal fins in the Port Jackson Sharks (*Heterodontus*) and the Piked Dogfish (*Squalus acanthias*).

One very specialized modification of the denticles is found in the Basking Shark. Along the inside of each of the five gill arches lies a series of a thousand or more stiff, bristle-like rakers which become erect when the mouth opens and thus serve to strain off the planktonic animals on which these fishes feed. These gillrakers are in fact greatly attenuated denticles. When feeding, the shark merely cruises along with its mouth open and Lineaweaver & Backus (1970) have calculated that a Basking Shark of 23 feet cruising at 2 knots will strain some 4,000,000 lbs of seawater in an hour. They note that a specimen that they examined had at least 300 lbs of plankton in the stomach, together with about 700 lbs of mucus. They were puzzled by the presence of mucus but the Basking Shark possibly operates the same filtration system as is found in many smaller fishes (e.g. certain species of the cichlid fish *Tilapia*) in which food organisms are caught and concentrated in a mucus film before being swallowed, the mucus later being resorbed in the gut and thus not wasted.

A curious feature of the Basking Shark gillrakers is that they are shed in winter and apparently regrown the following spring. This problem has been studied by Harrison Mathews (1962) who concluded that the energy expended by these fishes in feeding was so great that during the winter when plankton densities were low in northern waters the sharks would expend more energy in feeding than they could possibly replace by the food available. Therefore, the fishes retire to the bottom, shed their worn gillrakers and vegetate quietly until plankton levels rise once more in the spring. As Lineaweaver & Backus (1970) remark, this does not entirely explain the loss of rakers since Basking Sharks are present off the coast of central California throughout the year and it would be illogical if they went the entire winter without gillrakers.

The Whale Shark (*Rhincodon typus*) has feeding habits rather similar to those of the Basking Shark in that it strains out enormous quantities of plankton from the water. In this case, however, the sieving device is not by means of denticles elongated to form gillrakers but by cartilaginous rods between the gill arches supporting a fine mesh of spongy tissue.

At first sight the denticles, like the scales of bony fishes, would appear to

47

be a means of protecting the body. It is noticeable, however, that fishes with scales are no less preyed upon than those without. Similarly, the rigid spines preceding the vertical fins in many fishes may have only secondary importance for defence, their primary function being to hold the fin rigid during turning movements. It is possible that the primary function of the denticles is also a hydrodynamic one. It would seem, however, that such a roughened surface would enormously increase the drag effect and thus seriously affect both speed and the power required to attain it. In animals that must, of necessity, constantly swim to avoid sinking, such a drag would appear to be a poor evolutionary heritage, particularly since the basal plate of the denticles (see Figure 16) is all that is necessary to fulfil the function of forming a protective layer over the skin: for this, the upper parts of the denticles, i.e. the spines, keels, ridges, etc, are surely superfluous.

One possible function of the denticles was hinted at by Purves (1963). In sharks, the pectoral fins provide the lift for the front half of the fish against the downward and forward thrust of the heterocercal tail. Purves discussed the possible 'upwash' and 'downwash' effects of the obliquely-aligned denticles towards the tail region in dogfishes, the denticles forward of this being horizontally aligned. He compared this with the pattern of dermal ridges in cetaceans (whales, dolphins), and suggested that in the latter case at least, the ridges are arranged in the direction of flow over the body. This has some bearing on calculations of theoretical speeds of fishes based on the energy available in the muscles. Osborne Reynolds, who became the first professor of engineering at Manchester a little over a hundred years ago, made a detailed study of the way liquids flow over a body. In addition to the pressure drag caused by the shape of the body, there is a second form of drag due to the viscosity of the water in the thin layer immediately surrounding the body. Reynolds was the first to show that this latter type of drag was of two kinds. The skin of water surrounding the body may cause minute eddies where the two liquids meet (turbulent flow), or it may slide smoothly and with very little friction (laminar flow). This helps to resolve what is known as Gray's Paradox. James Gray showed that the locomotory power available to dolphins is theoretically insufficient to overcome the drag of the body at the speeds which these animals have been observed to attain. Gray suggested that the flow of water over the animal's body must, therefore, be *laminar* and not *turbulent*. This is now generally accepted and Lang (1966) has said: 'A large body of evidence suggests that cetaceans and many types of fish possess unusually low drag because their boundary layers remain laminar at high speeds, and do not become predominantly turbulent, as in rigid bodies.'

48

One is tempted, in this light, to re-assess the function of the dermal denticles. Is it possible that they are of such a design that a layer of water is held against the body to form a stable boundary layer, over which the water flows with reduced drag?

Research, however, rarely stands still for long. The concept of laminar flow solved Gray's Paradox and suggested a way in which aquatic animals could overcome much of the drag on their bodies and thus swim at speeds which were theoretically impossible. There is another aspect, put forward by M.W.Rosen (1959) on the basis of hydrodynamic experiments with live fishes (one of the Danios of aquarists, *Brachydanio albolineatus*). Using milky water, and later dyes, Rosen showed that far from slipping through the water smoothly, the fishes set up a series of vortices or whirlpools on either side of the body, starting just behind the gills and lying thereafter in each concave undulatory curve of the body. Puzzling over this, Rosen came to the conclusion that the fishes used these vortices rather like roller pegs, obtaining a certain amount of thrust from each vortex as it evolved and thus recovering a portion of the energy that went into setting the vortex in motion in the first place. He suggested that the lateral line organs gave information on the state of these vortices.

What then is the function of the denticles? The suggestion that they promote laminar flow is still possible, for it would still be necessary to prevent excessive drag against the vortices. Clearly, this is an exciting field for further experiments and the next few years may see a solution to the problem of how sharks and other aquatic animals swim with such efficiency.

Teeth

From dermal denticles, the transition to jaw teeth is easily made: the latter can be considered perhaps as placoid scales which have become differentiated for the purpose of seizing and cutting up prey. Only rarely are they used for crushing, as in *Mustelus*; also in small *Heterodontus* (Port Jackson Shark), which uniquely possesses two types of teeth – incisors for cutting and 'molars' for crushing (Figure 19). Since teeth play a major role in the life of sharks, and also in their classification, a word should be said regarding their form.

The polymorphism of shark's teeth is quite striking. The two basic actions, cutting and seizing or grasping, are carried out by teeth of various shapes and kinds. The differences shown are in fact so constant and characteristic that they can be used as an excellent character for distinguishing species, genera, even families. It is, indeed, essential to have at least a jaw in order to make an accurate determination of the identity of a particular

49

species. Often a jaw is sufficient on its own, and it is even possible to recognize species by the marks left by their teeth. In the family Carcharhinidae, for example, the tooth marks of each genus are quite characteristic of the teeth that made them.

In general, one can distinguish two main forms of teeth in sharks, the sharp, triangular plate used for cutting (Figure 17a,b); and the long, pointed, awl-shaped tooth, round or semicircular in cross-section, acting like a spike but incapable of cutting (Figure 18,b–d).

(*a*) The platelike, triangular tooth is the most common. The Great White Shark (*Carcharodon carcharias*) is a good example (Figure 17a), and all members of the Carcharhinidae have this type of tooth. Although usually triangular or subtriangular, they may depart from this shape (e.g. the Tiger Shark, *Galeocerdo cuvieri*, Figure 17b), sometimes strongly tapering from a broad base, as in *Carcharhinus obscurus*. Even so, they can always be identified as belonging to the group of platelike teeth and distinguished from the awl-like teeth both by the form of their cusps and the form of their root (see below).

Apart from some very rare exceptions (*Heterodontus*, already mentioned

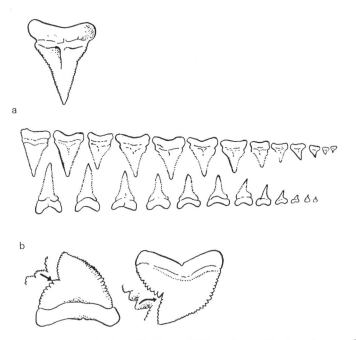

Fig. 17 Jaw teeth in sharks. (a) Great White Shark *Carcharodon carcharias*. (b) Tiger Shark *Galeocerdo cuvieri*.

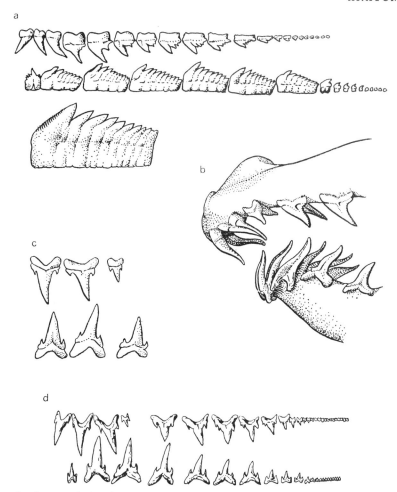

Fig. 18   Jaw teeth in sharks. (a) Cow Shark *Hexanchus griseus*. (b) Mackerel Shark *Isurus oxyrinchus*. (c) Porbeagle *Lamna nasus*. (d) Sand Shark *Odontaspis taurus*.

earlier; and *Paragaleus gruveli* from the West coast of Africa), the teeth in any one jaw are similar except only that those lying near the articulation of the jaw are neither as large nor as robust as those near the symphysis, the transition from large to small being very gradual. Frequently, however, the teeth of the upper jaw differ from those of the lower. There are numerous examples of this: in the Hexanchidae the lower teeth are in the form of a pavement, while those in the upper jaw are strongly cusped and accompanied by small lateral cusps (Figure 18a). Again, amongst the Carcharhinidae, one frequently finds that, as in the Dusky Shark (*Carcharhinus obscurus*), the upper teeth are triangular and sharp, while the teeth in the lower jaw are tapering and pointed. Jaws thus equipped can both seize and cut up their prey. Other species have only a single type of tooth in both jaws, as for example the Tiger Shark. There are a few examples of sexual dimorphism in the teeth, those of the male differing from those of the female. This is most pronounced in *Apristurus riveri*, a scyliorhinid shark from the Caribbean, in which the teeth of the mature male are twice the size of those of the female and also differ somewhat in shape (Springer, 1967). This may be an adaptation in the male to seizing a pectoral fin during copulation in order to secure a firm hold on the female.

The cutting teeth may have smooth edges or the latter may be furnished with fine serrations. One reads of shark's teeth being 'as sharp as razors', and Captain Young recounts how he once took from his pocket the tooth of a Tiger Shark and, to the astonishment of spectators, proceeded to shave his fore-arm with this natural razor. I can personally attest the truth of this, having demonstrated it myself on many occasions. One cannot, of course, equate the tooth of a Tiger Shark with one of Mr Gillette's products: the latter has a continuous edge, whereas the tooth, with its fine serrations, is much more akin to a bread knife and it cuts in much the same fashion. To say the least, these teeth are remarkably efficient cutting instruments, and it can happen that, in handling whole jaws in a careless manner, one can inflict on oneself gashes of almost surgical precision.

(*b*) The second type of tooth is rather different. It is restricted to the genera *Odontaspis*, *Lamna* and *Isurus*. In this case, the tooth has a double, forked root, and the cusp is massive, long and subcylindrical. At the base of the main cusp there is sometimes a small basal cusp (Figure 18d, Sand Shark, *Odontaspis taurus*), or two such basal cusps (*O. ferox*); in *Isurus oxyrinchus* there are none (Figure 18b). All these species possess teeth which are similar in both jaws. Such teeth have nothing in common with the cutting type, and function only to seize and hold on to prey without being able to cut it up before swallowing.

In general, the Ragged-toothed or Sand Sharks (*Odontaspis* species) live close to the bottom, feeding mainly on small fishes; on occasion they will take squids or crustaceans. Their long, tapering teeth thus appear to be designed for seizing their prey but not for crushing carapaces (Ray & Ciampi, 1956), a good example of an adaptation of tooth form to feeding habits. On the other hand, the Mako Sharks (*Isurus*), pelagic and powerful swimmers, are equipped with exactly this same type of tooth but hunt in open water the same fishes that are the food of the Carcharhinidae with their cutting teeth.

In sharks, unlike mammals, the teeth are not implanted in sockets but are simply attached at their bases to a collagen-rich sheath of connective tissue – the tooth bed – and the teeth are anchored by what may be termed a 'root', that is to say the equivalent of the basal plate of the denticles. In most cases, there is only a single series of teeth functional at any one time, the outer series. In some species, such as the Nurse Shark (*Ginglymostoma cirratum*), two or three series may be in use simultaneously. In the genus *Oxynotus* the arrangement of the teeth in the upper jaw is unique; the outer series has two or three teeth, the series behind it three to five, and so on to form a triangular patch of about six series. In the rays (Hypotremata) and in those sharks that also have a pavement of teeth in the lower jaw (e.g. the Smooth Hound *Mustelus* or the Port Jackson Sharks *Heterodontus*) there are several rows of functional teeth in operation, in this case forming a mosaic much like that of the denticles in those species with the latter densely packed (e.g. the Thresher Sharks *Alopias*). In most sharks, however, five or six reserve or replacement rows of teeth lie behind the functional ones, one on top of the other and covered by tissue. This is shown diagrammatically in Figure 21. The replacement teeth are thus ready, almost at a moment's notice, to take the place of functional teeth should the latter fall out for one reason or another. This does in fact happen quite frequently during the normal course of a shark's life, mostly as a result of purely mechanical damage.

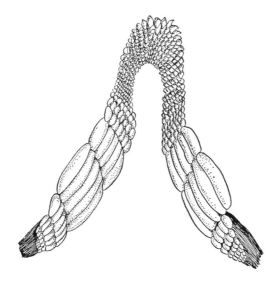

Fig. 19 Jaw teeth in the Port Jackson Sharks (*Heterodontus* spp.) showing the cutting teeth in the front of the jaw and the molar or grinding teeth behind.

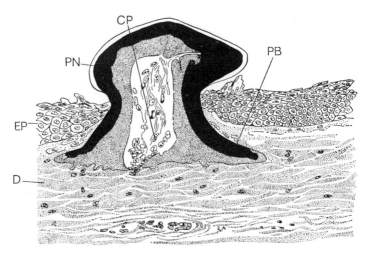

Fig. 20   Denticle from the mouth (buccal cavity) of a Nurse Shark *Ginglymostoma cirratum*. D dermis. EP epithelium. PB basal plate. CP pulp cavity. PN dentine.

Richard Owen, one of the great anatomists of the late 19th century, referred to the succession of teeth in a shark's jaw as a 'phalanx . . . ever marching slowly forwards in rotatory progress over the alveolar border of the jaw'. Although the actual mechanics of this process are not yet understood, the basic principle is now generally accepted. Experiments on the Lemon Shark (*Negaprion brevirostris*) have shown the replacement of lower jaw teeth in an average of 8·2 days and upper jaw teeth in 7·8 days, or respectively 10·0 and 9·2 days in starved sharks (Moss, 1967).

Here, we can return briefly to the analogy mentioned earlier between the jaw teeth in sharks and the placoid scales. The latter do not persist throughout life, but are easily shed (caducous) and subject to a process of destruction. The destructive cells (osteophagous monocaryocytes) first attack the basal plate, and then the dentine; the scale becomes white or milky-looking and finally is shed. Now, in certain jaw teeth one finds cavities in the root (the so-called lacunae of Howship) which are found in normal osteoporosis. There is a striking similarity between the microscopic picture of placoid scales which are on their way to destruction, and the macroscopic appearance of certain jaw teeth. In the latter one can recognize the same stages as in the scale, from the initial attack on the basal plate (= tooth root) to the more or less complete destruction of the dentine. Further, on 5 June 1934, on the coast of Senegal, I found in the flank of a net-caught shark the tooth of a Sand Shark deeply embedded in the skin. The tooth showed all the characteristics of an advanced stage of destruction: the root had all but gone and

Plate 1. The Whale Shark (*Rhincodon typus*), largest of all species of shark, stranded on an Australian beach (*upper picture*) and admired by a huge crowd from Mangalore after FAO master-fisherman G.S. Illugson had succeeded in conquering this 32 ft monster, estimated to weigh 5 tons (*lower picture*).

Plate 2. Graceful lines characterize many species of shark. Seen from the side, the grotesque Hammerhead Shark (*Sphyrna sp.*) (*upper picture*) closely resembles one of the Grey Sharks (*Carcharhinus sp.*) (*lower picture*). The latter is clearly dipping its right pectoral fin to aid in turning away from the cameraman.

Plate 3. Captain Emil Hanson displays the head of a Hammerhead Shark (*Sphyrna* sp.) to show the extraordinary lateral projections which still puzzle zoologists (*upper picture*). The normal shark head (*lower picture*) often has a conical and beautifully streamlined snout. Shown well are the spiracle, the half-closed nictitating membrane of the eye, the nostril and, speckled around the lower surface of the snout, the pores of the sensory canal system and ampullae of Lorenzini.

Plate 4. Reconstruction of the jaws (*upper picture*) of the giant fossil shark *Carcharodon megalodon* at the American Museum of Natural History, New York. An actual tooth (*lower picture*) is compared with the tooth of its modern relative, the Great White Shark (*Carcharodon carcharias*), a species which can reach over 30 feet.

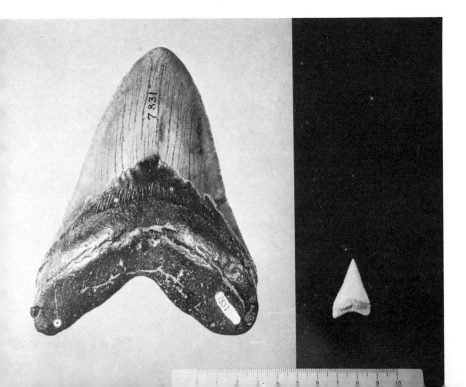

Fig. 21   Diagrammatic cross-section through the tooth-bearing region of the jaw, showing one functional tooth backed by five replacement teeth (after Ridewood).

the dentine showed the small cavities which can truly be considered analogous to the lacunae of Howship. These facts strongly suggest that in sharks the teeth are subjected to a process of destruction comparable to that found in the scales. Figures 22 and 23 show the various stages of this process in the tooth of a Sand Shark (the figures read from left to right). This concept has been known for twenty-five years without any full and rigorous research being directed towards it. Again, I have recorded indications which could be considered osteoclasty (breakdown) in jaw teeth belonging to the replacement series.

However, in a recent study, J. Cadenat (1962) has stated the view that this is not a case of resorption, but rather of building up, and that the series shown in Figures 22 and 23 should, as a result, be read from right to left and not from left to right. The spongy appearance of the root would therefore be due, not to the lacunae of Howship, but to the presence of ribs of material in process of being built up – the work of constructive odontoblasts and not of destructive odontoclasts. Cadenat's study, carried out with great care and on a large number of jaws, must be considered very carefully. Certainly the 'hollow' teeth appear very early on in the replacement series, and the build up of the teeth might well follow the plan suggested by this author. But this does not exclude the possibility of osteoclasy (breakdown) affecting certain of the jaw teeth. Cadenat rejects this: the functional teeth which he examined in a large number of jaws were all free of any trace of necrosis. According to him, their eventual loss could be attributed solely to the strains imposed on them while the prey was being seized. To this I would reply, that the example cited earlier, and also certain photographs showing sharks' teeth embedded in *muscular* wounds suggests that there may, nevertheless, be a prior loosening of the teeth. For example, there is the case of Iona Asai cited by Coppleson (1962): the man was bitten in the neck by a Tiger Shark and a tooth was left in the wound. Other examples are given in Gilbert's *Sharks and Survival* (1963).

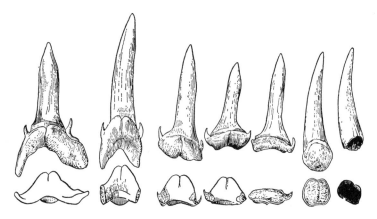

Fig. 22 Teeth of Sand Shark *Odontaspis taurus* in various stages during the process of tooth destruction (after Budker).

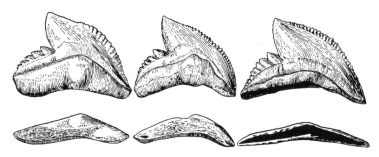

Fig. 23 Teeth of Tiger Shark *Galeocerdo cuvieri* in three stages in the process of destruction (after Budker).

Further views on this subject were kindly communicated to me by Dr W.I. Follett, Curator of Fishes at the California Academy of Sciences (and to whom I express my sincere gratitude). He stated:

The teeth of certain fossil species of *Carcharodon* are quite thick. It may well be that, in life, they were difficult to break. On the other hand, the teeth of the present-day *Carcharodon carcharias* are thin, hollow and quite fragile. In a mature upper tooth (40 mm in length, 31 mm in basal width, and 7·7 mm in greatest thickness) from a specimen of *Carcharodon carcharias* 511 cm in total length and 1·282 kg in weight (California Academy of Sciences 26245), the wall enclosing the hollow interior of the tooth is only 0·4 mm in thickness. Consequently, a tooth of this species is sometimes broken when the shark bites a mammal. I have examined a broken tooth of *Carcharodon carcharias* on three occasions, as follows:

1 An apical fragment taken from a sea-otter, *Enhydra lutris nereis*.
2 A fragment of a tooth taken from the leg of Alfredo Aubone (Coppleson, *Shark Attack*, 2nd edition, 1962, p. 218).
3 The fragment that you have mentioned, which was taken from the thigh of Jack Rochette (Collier, *California Fish & Game*, 50, (4), 264, fig. 2).
On the other hand, I have never examined a complete tooth of this species, which has been removed from the body of a mammal.

This shows that broken teeth can appear in the functional range of teeth and it tends to argue for an initial weakening of the tooth. The apical fragment of tooth, found in the back of the sea-otter just behind the shoulders, was reported by Robert T.Orr (1959), with a photograph of the tooth by Dr Follett which clearly showed the line of fracture some distance from the point of the tooth. For such a break to occur in soft muscle presupposes a particularly fragile tooth; even if the tooth had penetrated to the bone, it was specified that the sea-otter was 'sub-adult'.

Much more cytological and histological research is needed before this question can be resolved.

Liver
When one makes a cut down the belly of a shark, from the base of the pectoral fins to that of the pelvic fins, the first organ that one sees is the liver (Figure 24), the two lobes of which are sometimes so long that they occupy the entire length of the body cavity. They cover and to some extent wrap around the digestive tract, and it is necessary to lift them free to examine them properly. Where the two lobes join and on the inner face of one of them, is the gall bladder, dark green in colour and deeply embedded but still visible from the outside.

In sharks, the liver is a bulky organ, soft and oily to the touch, and varying from a clear buff colour to dark tawny. It is full of an oil which, as we shall see later, has many and varied uses; indeed, the oil from shark livers has been one of the most precious of all shark by-products.

The weight and volume of the liver in sharks is highly variable, depending on factors whose influence is still not fully understood. Sex, age, state of sexual maturity, feeding condition, all these probably play some part in determining the amount of oil present in the liver. Sharks are not fatty fishes. Their flesh is, in fact, noticeably dry since all their fatty reserves are concentrated in the liver. This explains the enormous size that these great oily 'sponges' can attain. The fat reserves in the liver may well serve to tide the animal over periods when food is unavailable. This would be particularly important in large oceanic species whose chances of encountering prey

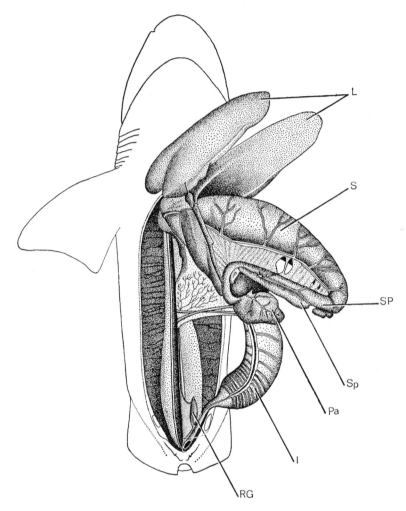

Fig. 24 Digestive tract in the Broad-headed seven-gilled Shark *Notorhynchus maculatum* (redrawn from Daniel). L lobes of the liver. S stomach. SP pyloric region of stomach. Sp spleen. Pa dorsal and ventral lobes of pancreas. I intestine. RG rectal gland.

were less than those of species frequenting coral reefs for example. Also, in some species there seems to be a feeding inhibition of mating males and pupping females, the liver reserves being used at this time.

It is not always easy to determine the exact weight of the liver in relation to the total weight of the shark. While fisheries often record liver weight, it is not usually feasible for them to weigh sharks of several hundred pounds.

This is most unfortunate, but the difficulty can to some extent be overcome by relating liver weight to total *length* of fish, and the figures in the following table are given in this way (they relate to a fishery in Senegal – Pêcheries de l'Ouest africain of Hann).

Species	total length (metres)	weight of liver (kg)
Galeocerdo cuvieri (male)	3·25	34
(female)	3·60	77
(female)	3·15	49
Galeocerdo arcticus (= *G. cuvieri*)	3.20	45
Sphyrna zygaena (female)	3.70	30
(female, gravid)	4.10	14
Sphyrna zygaena	4.20	65

This table shows clearly that considerable variations are found between individuals of the same species and nearly the same size. Tiger Sharks have a particularly bulky liver. All these measurements were made on fishes caught in June–July near Dakar. Appreciable seasonal variations have been recorded. For example, in Hammerheads (*Sphyrna*) of 4·0–4·5 metres total length, the liver was found to weigh 15–20 kg in July, while in individuals of the same length the liver attained 40–50 kg in October. As mentioned above, feeding inhibition will result in depletion of liver reserves. There is evidence (Springer, 1967) that in some species at least the males do not feed during the mating season; in one specimen of male Tiger Shark (*Galeocerdo cuvieri*) the liver was nearly oil-free and weighed only 10 per cent of the normal liver weight, suggesting a long period of starvation. This might account for the variations in liver weight cited above. There is here a wide field for research and one that has so far barely been touched upon.

In exceptional cases the liver may even reach 20–25 per cent of the weight of the shark. There are figures which occasionally exceed this, but these should not be considered usual. The average weight of the liver seems to be between 5 and 15 per cent of the gross weight of the animal, figures based on the rather few observations when the precise weight of the whole fish has been recorded.

With regard to the actual amount of oil present, this too is subject to great variation, both quantitatively and qualitatively. A figure of 90 per cent oil has been recorded, but this must be taken as an exceptional figure and unfortunately the species of shark involved was not determined accurately. On the whole, one can reckon on an average yield of about 50 per cent by

59

weight, with minor variations. For example, the liver of a Tiger Shark weighing 45 kg yielded 25 litres in one case, while in another some 28 litres were extracted. The constituents and uses of these oils will be discussed in another chapter (p. 193).

Digestive tract

When the lobes of the liver are lifted aside (Figure 24), the whole or almost the whole length of the digestive tract is exposed. In sharks, it is difficult to specify an actual oesophagus. Sometimes a kind of stricture or narrowing of the anterior part of the stomach is found, but more often there is a gradual transition from the pharyngeal region to the stomach proper. At the most, it can be said that the oesophagal region begins where the buccal denticles end.

The stomach in sharks has the general form of a 'U', the arms being unequal in length. The part immediately following the oesophagus (and intimately united with it) is voluminous and like an elongated sack. It is here that an autopsy reveals identifiable material, food or other objects, often little digested by the animal. This part of the stomach is sometimes referred to as the cardiac stomach.

The vast sacklike stomach becomes restricted and doubled back on itself at 180°, passing into a narrow pyloric region (pyloric stomach) which is sometimes as long as the cardiac stomach itself but is usually shorter so that the whole stomach region then forms a 'J'. This second arm is traversed throughout its length by the spleen, an elongate dark red organ, triangular in cross-section, the anterior part capping the angle formed between the stomach proper and the pyloric region. Finally, the pancreas is also found in this area. Its form is variable, but in general it is made up of two parts, a ventral lobe near the duodenum, and a dorsal lobe in the anterior region of the pyloric branch of the stomach.

The pyloris ends in a duodenum, always very short, which leads to the intestine. The latter is large and bulky in sharks and is furnished with a spiral valve, the exact form of which varies between species. In some it resembles a spiral staircase, in others a series of cones one inside the next like elongated trumpets (Figure 25); or again it may resemble longitudinal coils rolled back on themselves. The spiral valve is a primitive feature. Lineaweaver & Backus (1970) state that it is unique to sharks but this is not strictly true; a spiral valve, albeit of simpler construction, is found in the primitive sturgeons, bichirs, lungfishes and bowfins although it is virtually absent from the higher bony fishes (a vestigial form occurs in *Gymnarchus* and *Osmerus* but not in *Chirocentrus*, as was previously thought). The presence of a spiral valve in fossil sharks can be demonstrated by the characteristically

a

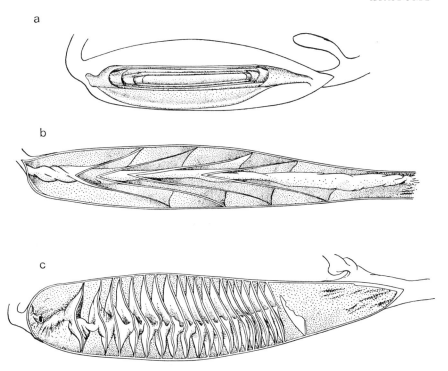

b

c

Fig. 25   Spiral valves in the intestine of sharks. (a) Common Hammerhead Shark
Sphyrna zygaena. (b) A Grey Shark (*Paragaleus pectoralis*). (c) Narrow-headed
seven-gilled Shark *Heptranchias perlo*.

twisted shape of coprolite (fossil faecal material). One important aspect of
the spiral valve seems to be the increase in the absorptive surface of the
intestine without a comparable increase in intestine length. In herbivorous
fishes, for example, the intestines may be many times the total length of the
fish to provide the necessary absorptive surface. Thus, sharks have found an
alternative solution.

The posterior end of the intestine leads into the rectum and the latter
terminates at the cloaca. Along the dorsal surface of the rectum is the rectal
or digitiform gland, an elongate, fingerlike organ whose function is still not
properly understood. Burger & Hess (1960) have suggested that the rectal
gland is responsible for getting rid of excess sodium chloride, but this is
another facet of shark physiology that needs more study.

Urino-genital organs
Removing the oesophagus, rectum and mesentaries, and drawing aside the

digestive tract and its associated organs, one finds close to the dorsal surface of the body cavity the urino-genital organs.

The genital organs are first encountered, particularly in a mature animal. The kidneys are more dorsal to them and appear as two long ribands of dark red lying on either side of the vertebral column and reaching the length of the body cavity. On the whole, they are slightly larger posteriorly than at their anterior tips, this being more or less pronounced depending on the species. The diagram (Figure 26) gives an idea of the general layout of the urino-genital system.

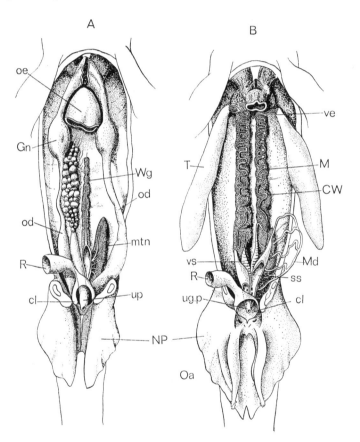

Fig. 26 The urino-genital system of a Dogfish (*Scyliorhinus* sp.) (after Bourne). A female. B male. oe oesophagus (stomach cut away). cl cloaca. R rectum. NP pelvic fins. od oviduct. Gn shell gland. Wg mesonephros with ureter. mtn metanephros. up urinary papilla in female. T testis. ve efferent canals. M mesonephros. CW Wolffian duct. vs seminal vesicle. ss spermatic sacs. ug.p urinogenital papilla in male. Oa claspers. Md canals of metanephros.

In an adult female, one first notices the ovaries, which have the appearance of a transparent sac through which the eggs can be seen. The latter, which vary in size, may have a diameter of 3–5 cm. The ovary is usually a double organ, but in some species the left ovary atrophies in the adult and only the right ovary completes its development. This is the case in certain dogfishes, and in the Hammerhead Shark, and is considered to be the norm in all large sharks by Lineaweaver & Backus (1970).

When an egg becomes detached from the ovary, it passes into the body cavity and then enters one of the oviducts through a flared trumpetlike opening (the oviducal aperture) which is shared by the two oviducts. The oviducts themselves are long, whiteish tubes. In the first third of their length there is a 'nidamentary' or shell gland which secretes the outer case (the 'shell' or capsule) for the embryo (the capsule may be permanent or temporary). Fertilization may take place in the anterior part of the oviduct, between the gland itself and the trumpet-shaped opening, a region which can be thought of as analogous to the Fallopian tubes in higher vertebrates; in other cases, fertilization may occur in the nidamentary gland itself, as we shall see later on. With regard to the posterior part of the oviducts, this region plays a part in viviparous sharks which can be likened to a uterus, and this name is given to it. It is here that the foetus develops. It should also be noted that, in female sharks, there is no connection between the ovaries and the kidneys, the latter discharging through the Wolffian ducts and the former through the oviducts, that is to say, the Müllerian ducts.

In the male, on the other hand, the Müllerian ducts are atrophied and the Wolffian ducts (i.e. the vas deferens) are used to discharge from both the testes and the kidneys (Figure 26, CW). The testes are paired organs, elongate, and may be bulky or not depending on the species or the state of maturity. In some cases they are regular in shape, as in Figure 26, or again they may be lobed or crenulated. Each Wolffian duct ends in a seminal vesicle, the latter being in connection with a urino-genital sinus and two spermatic ducts (Figure 26, VS and SS). The spermatozoa then pass along the mixopterygia or claspers (Figure 27) and are thus introduced into the cloaca of the female during copulation. The claspers can be erected experimentally, by adrenalin or by electrostimulation of the appropriate spinal nerves. It can be noted that the claspers of sawfishes and some other rays are too far apart for them to be drawn together and used simultaneously. This may be correlated with the fact that some rays (e.g. stingrays) have only one functional oviduct (Springer, 1967), while two functional oviducts appears to be the rule in all sharks. As noted below, however, only the right clasper appears to be used by the Horn Shark (*Heterodontus francisci*).

63

In selachians, the kidney is a mesonephros; at the same time, however, one can recognize the presence of a metanephros, lying in the posterior part of the coelomic cavity (Figure 26, mtn) and equipped with excretory canals which in the male unite in a ureter (Md) and rejoin the base of the Wolffian duct (vas deferens).

Water and salt balance
The problem of regulating the balance of water and salts has been solved in the marine sharks in a manner which has been referred to as 'regulation by evasion' as opposed to the method of 'regulation by correction' in the marine and freshwater bony fishes as well as the freshwater sharks. Marine bony fishes have a salt concentration in the blood and body fluids which is below that of the surrounding sea water and as a result they must drink copiously in order to avoid dehydration through osmotic loss. The reverse holds for freshwater bony fishes, whose body fluids are more concentrated than the surrounding medium and they must, therefore, excrete dilute and copious amounts of urine. In the marine sharks, on the other hand, the concentration of solutes in the blood and other body fluids is slightly higher than that of the sea. Expressed in terms of osmolarity (i.e. the osmotic gradient determining in which direction liquid will tend to flow), a figure of 930 mosmole per litre for sea water might be matched by 980 mosmole per litre for the body fluids of the shark, with the result that the shark is able to absorb liquid (mainly through the gills) without any expenditure of free energy. By contrast, the bony fish must not only expend energy by drinking but also by desalinating this liquid by extraction at the gills (univalent ions) and in the tubules of the kidneys (divalent ions).

Clearly, these are radically different answers to the problem of how to regulate the balance of salts and water. Cartilaginous fishes are, however, even more remarkable. Sharks, rays and chimaeras (but not lampreys and hagfishes) have the ability to retain the nitrogenous waste products urea and trimethylamine oxide (TMAO) and to use these to maintain the high concentration of solutes characteristic of their body fluids. Normal levels of urea in marine sharks range from 200 to about 350 mosmole per litre (100 to 200 in sharks moving into a freshwater environment, over 300 in chimaerids). Under normal circumstances, the gills are almost impermeable to urea, but loss of urea from the gills can be induced by artificially raising its concentration in the blood (Boylan, 1967).

Urea is synthesized almost entirely in the liver. About 95 per cent of the urea and up to 98 per cent of the TMAO filtered by the glomerulus of the kidney is then reabsorbed as it passes down the tubules of the kidney – quite the reverse from frogs, for example, which actively secrete urea *into* the tubule fluid from whence it is excreted as urine.

The only other fishes that have this ability to retain urea are the coelacanth (*Latimeria chalumnae*) and the lungfishes, the latter doing so during their periods of aestivation in a cocoon of mud on a dried-up lake bottom. Urea retention is also found in a few frogs (e.g. *Rana cancrivora*) which periodically migrate into salt water.

It has been suggested that the ability of the cartilaginous fishes to synthesize non-toxic compounds (i.e. urea and TMAO) from ammonia may be correlated with the very long gestation of their young (Forster, 1967). In fact, gestation periods are some of the longest in the vertebrate world, up to two years in some cases, and it is obviously necessary that the developing embryo should not be poisoned by its own waste products. Burger (1967) has shown that during the almost two-year pregnancy in the Spiny Dogfish (*Squalus acanthias*), the uteri are sealed off for a time but, with the breaking of the egg cases, sea water in volumes up to several hundred millilitres per female is periodically introduced and the uteri are flushed out. In bony fishes, the eggs are usually surrounded by water into which the waste products can quickly diffuse, while in the live-bearing species the eggs are held not in the uterus as in sharks but in the ovary, so that waste material can readily diffuse through into the maternal circulation and be eliminated. It is interesting, too, that urea retention is not found in the cyclostomes (lampreys and hagfishes). Possibly, this method of water and salt regulation arose after the jawed fishes (Gnathostomes) had split off from the jawless Agnatha. If this is so, then the presence of claspers (for internal fertilization and thus internal development of the embryo) can be correlated with a urea retention system and one could hazard that the two evolved in conjunction with each other.

Reproduction

The presence of claspers in sharks, as well as in skates and rays, means that fertilization is internal and therefore that an act of copulation must take place. For many years an apparent exception to this seemed to be provided by the Sleeper Shark (*Somniosus microcephalus*), many authors stating that this species was not only oviparous, but eggs were fertilized after deposition on the sea floor. Lütken (1880), although believing this shark to be oviparous, pointed out that functional claspers are present, so that fertilization could occur before the eggs are deposited. Bigelow & Schroeder (1948), in their comprehensive work on the sharks of the Western North Atlantic, made the following comment:

65

Fig. 27 Left clasper or myxopterygium in male Whale Shark *Rhincodon typus* to show the complex skeletal arrangement for transfer of sperm to the female. The erectile spurs ensure firm union during copulation.

Adult females have been found repeatedly containing great numbers of soft eggs without horny capsules, with as much as $1\frac{1}{2}$ barrels of them in large specimens, the eggs ranging in size up to that of goose eggs. This combined with the fact that none of the many examined have been found with embryos, supports the general belief that this shark unlike other squalids is oviparous. If so, it seems likely that the eggs are deposited on the bottom in mud, but eggs naturally laid have not been found as yet.

In 1957, however, Einar Koefoed gave a description of one out of ten embryos from the right uterus of a Sleeper Shark of 5 metres length. Possibly because Koefoed used an old and misleading name for the shark (*Acanthorhinus carcharias*), this record was overlooked by many later workers. Thus internal fertilization is the rule in all selachians. This method of fertilization obviously requires an act of copulation, and at the turn of the 18th century Lacepède (1798), with a characteristic display of lyricism, described this act in the following way (something of the original naïveté is unfortunately lost in translation).

And often, after the male has survived a dangerous and bloody battle against a rival, they [i.e. male and female] apply themselves one against the other in such a way as to bring their anuses into contact. Held in this position by the hooked appendages of the male [i.e. the claspers], by their mutual efforts, and by a kind of entwining of their many fins and the extremities of their tails, they float in this constrained position, but one which must to them be full of charm, until the life fluid of the male animates the eggs which have already reached a degree of development susceptible to receiving it. And such is the force of their active passion, which is aflame even in the midst of water, and whose heat penetrates even to the most abysmal depths of the sea, that the male and female which at other times would be so formidable to one another and would only seek to devour each other if they were pressed by violent hunger, are now softened and surrender to emotions quite different from those of destructiveness, mingling without fear their murderous weapons, bringing together their enormous jaws and terrible tails, and far from inflicting death, expose themselves to receive it rather than be separated, and not ceasing to defend with fury the object of their passionate enjoyment.

This passage is coloured by the flame of a lively imagination, and indeed such would have been needed by Lacepède since, without any doubt, he had never been witness to the things about which he writes with such apparent authority. In truth, even now one can hardly hold forth on the manner in which the large species of shark copulate: it is neither easy to observe nor often seen in nature. But in the course of the last few years, great advances have been made in the construction of large pens suitable for keeping even quite large species in captivity, and new opportunities for all kinds of observations have been opened up. Thus, Eugenie Clark (1963) records that on 1 May 1957, at midnight,

Dr and Mrs Duguld Brown, who were working in the laboratory, walked out on the dock and saw two Lemon Sharks in copula. The sharks were side by side, heads slightly apart but the posterior half of their bodies in such close contact and the swimming movements so perfectly synchronized that they gave the appearance of a single individual with two heads, as they swam in slow counter-clockwise circles around the pen. . . . This position is quite different from that postulated by Springer (1960) for large sharks. When the observers left the dock a half hour later, the sharks were still in copula.

Here, therefore, is one precise observation on a large species of shark. Otherwise, mainly the smaller species, which can be kept in small aquaria, have been studied. Bolau (1881), for example, had noted that when copulating, the male Spotted Dogfish (*Scyliorhinus*) wraps itself tightly round the female (Figure 28), the latter for its part remaining stretched out and immobile. Such a position is possible in the Scyliorhinids, which are supple and rather sinuous fishes, almost eellike. It would certainly not be possible for large sharks, such as the Mako Shark (*Isurus*). However, the observations recorded by Eugenie Clark offer a useful clue.

Copulation in Nurse Sharks (*Ginglymostoma cirratum*) has been fairly

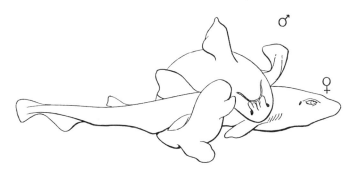

Fig. 28   Copulation in the Dogfish *Scyliorhinus caniculus* (after Bolau).

often observed. McCormick, Allen & Young (1963) cite Gudger's description of the act, in which the male grasps the hind edge of one of the female's pectoral fins and with this hold turns her on her back and inserts his claspers (it is not stated whether one or both claspers are used). During the breeding season, many females are seen with torn and scarred fins; as mentioned in the discussion on teeth (p. 52), the better developed teeth in the males of some species may be an adaptation connected with copulation.

Another case where actual copulation has been observed is that cited by Robert Dempster and Earl Herald (1961) of the Steinhart Aquarium for the Horn Shark *Heterodontus francisci*. Apparently, a worried visitor to the aquarium reported a 'terrific fight' between two Horn Sharks in one of the large display tanks. One fish was about to kill the other and 'something should be done to prevent this tragedy'. The 'lethal battle' turned out to be courtship and mating. The 27½-inch male had seized a slightly larger female by the left pectoral fin and was firmly holding on to her with his mouth. Shortly after, the male was able to manipulate his body so that his tail was over her back immediately in front of the second dorsal fin and, using the latter as an anchor and with her pectoral fin still firmly in his mouth, he was able to thrust his right clasper into her vent. The fishes copulated for about half an hour, the female remaining passive and the male making a gentle rhythmic motion with the hind part of its body. In subsequent matings of this species it was always the right clasper that was used.

Whatever the details of the act, the next step is for the spermatozoa, deposited in the female cloaca, to pass to the oviducts, fertilization occurring, as we have said, in the anterior part, that is to say, in the trumpet-shaped oviducal funnel. Metten (1939), however, has shown that the nidamentary or shell-forming gland in *Scyliorhinus* also acts as a seminal receptacle and that the egg is fertilized at the same time that the egg capsule is formed. The presence of spermatozoa in the shell gland in adults of these fishes is certain. Raghu Prasad (1945) has confirmed this observation during a study of placental sharks of the genera *Carcharhinus, Hemigaleus* and *Scoliodon*.

Leaving the nidamentary or shell gland, the fertilized egg passes to the lower part of the oviduct and then to the uterus. It can be noted, in this connection, that the uterus is separated from the oviduct by a valve.

From this point, one of three things may happen.

(1) During its passage through the shell gland, the egg may be enveloped in a horny shell; it then traverses the whole length of the uterus and is extruded to the exterior. The embryo thus completes its development without further contact with the mother. During its entire sojourn in the capsule, the embryo is nourished by a sac filled with yolk, which is progressively resorbed

up to the moment of hatching. At hatching, the shell is ruptured by mechanical means, that is by movements of the embryo, aided by a secretion from a hatching or 'frontal' gland situated on the anterior part of the head. Leaving the capsule, the young shark begins its free-swimming life, and is inclined to search for food straight away. This is, in rather general outline, the kind of pattern found in the Dogfishes (Scyliorhinidae) off British coasts whose egg capsules are rectangular with long spiralling tendrils at each corner; these are sometimes termed 'mermaid's purses', although the true mermaid's purses are the egg cases of certain rays with only a very short tendril at the corners. The shapes of shark egg cases are characteristic of the family or the genus, sometimes of the species. In the Port Jackson Sharks (Heterodontidae) the egg cases are conical with a curious spiral flange and the tendrils may be up to seven feet long (Figure 29). The largest of all egg cases is that of the Whale Shark (*Rhincodon typus*). Only one has ever been found and that was hauled up from 31 fathoms in the Gulf of Mexico in 1953. The case measured 12 inches in length, $5\frac{1}{2}$ inches in breadth and $3\frac{1}{2}$ in thickness. When opened with a knife, out came a $14\frac{1}{2}$-inch embryo which was such a perfect replica of the adult in both shape and colour pattern that there could be no doubt of its identity. Embryo and egg case are figured by Lineaweaver & Backus (1970). The Port Jackson Sharks (Heterodontidae) and the Whale Shark (Rhincodontidae) are oviparous, as also are most members of the Scyliorhinidae and Orectolobidae. It is

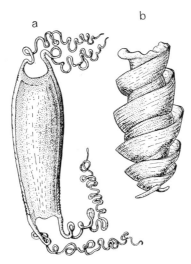

Fig. 29 Egg cases in sharks. (a) Spotted Dogfish (*Scyliorhinus* sp.). (b) Port Jackson Shark *Heterodontus phillippi*.

TABLE 3

Methods of Reproduction in Sharks and Rays

Order PLEUROTREMATA (sharks)

Suborder HEXANCHIFORMES

Family Hexanchidae	All ovoviviparous
Family Chlamydoselachidae	Ovoviparous

Suborder HETERODONTIFORMES

Family Heterodontidae	Oviparous

Suborder GALEIFORMES

Family Odontaspidae	Ovoviviparous
Family Scapanorhynchidae	Presumed ovoviviparous
Family Isuridae	Ovoviviparous
Family Cetorhinidae	Ovoviviparous (presumed)
Family Alopiidae	Ovoviviparous
Family Orectolobidae	(Transitional between oviparous and ovoviviparous)

Chiloscyllium *Hemiscyllium* *Parascyllium* *Nebrius* *Stegostoma*	Oviparous
Brachyaeturus *Orectolobus*	Ovoviviparous
Ginglymostoma	Intermediate, either oviparous or ovoviviparous
Family Rhincodontidae	Oviparous
Family Scyliorhinidae	Most or all oviparous, but *Galeus polli* ovoviviparous
Family Pseudotriakidae	?
Family Triakidae	Viviparous
Family Carcharhinidae	Ovoviviparous to viviparous
Family Sphyrnidae	Probably all viviparous or ovoviviparous

Suborder SQUALIFORMES

Family Squalidae	All ovoviviparous
Family Dalatiidae	Ovoviviparous
Family Echinorhinidae	Ovoviviparous
Family Pristiophoridae	Ovoviviparous
Family Squatinidae	Ovoviviparous

Order HYPOTREMATA (rays)

Family Rajiidae	Oviparous
All other families	Ovoviviparous or viviparous (e.g. the 'placental' connection by means of trohonemata in *Pteroplatea*)

interesting to note, however, that *Galeus melastoma* lay eggs, whereas the very similar and closely related *G. polli* gives birth to live young.

(2) In the second possibility, the fertilized egg follows the same route, but the shell gland merely coats it with a very thin, membranous and often delicate shell. Instead of being extruded straight away, the egg remains within the uterus. Soon, it is rid of its temporary shell and grows and develops within the uterus until the moment when, at full term, it is born. As in the preceding case, it also is provided with a yolk sac, a vestige of which still remains when it is born. Thus the foetus remains independent of its mother, although completing its development within the uterus. This is termed ovoviviparity, or perhaps more logically 'aplacental viviparity'. A typical example is found in the Nurse Shark, *Ginglymostoma cirratum*. Ranzi (1929) first showed the importance of the uptake of water and inorganic salts by the embryos of oviparous species such as the Spotted Dogfish (*Scyliorhinus caniculus*). In the ovoviviparous species the uterine secretions play a similar role, and in some species are rich in organic substances. The embryo is thus in part nourished by the mother, suggesting a transition stage to full viviparity.

(3) The third possibility is the stage which can be considered viviparity in the true sense, that is to say, 'placental viviparity'.

In this case the nidamentary gland is very reduced. The development of the embryo again takes place in the uterus, but the essential feature here is that, instead of subsisting almost solely on an independent yolk sac, the embryo is nourished by the mother herself.

Without entering too deeply into details, this third method needs rather fuller treatment than the other two. The embryo, arriving in the uterus, develops there and is equipped with an 'umbilical cord' which grows until it has become a tube of about 20 cm in length. At its tip is the yolk sac, which starts to branch and undergoes modifications which lead to the formation of a 'yolk placenta' (Figure 30b). According to Cole (1944), the Danish anatomist Steno (Niels Stensen, 1638–86) was the first after Aristotle to claim that the connection was a functional placenta whose blood vessels were responsible for transferring food materials from the parent to the yolk sac cavity and thence to the embryo. In the Smooth Hound, *Mustelus canis* (studied by Ranzi, 1932, 1934), the latter forms when the embryo is 10–16 cm in length. At the time that the yolk sac becomes applied to the lining of the uterus and starts to become a placenta, it still contains a certain amount of yolk; on the other hand, the distal portion in actual contact with the uterine lining begins to absorb the nutrient material provided by the mother, so that at this stage the placenta has a double role. Thereafter,

a

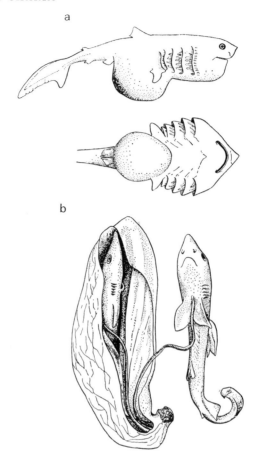

b

Fig. 30   (a) Embryo of the Porbeagle *Lamna nasus*. (b) Foetuses of Smooth Dogfish *Mustelus manazo*, showing connection to 'placenta' and general resemblance to the situation found in mammals.

following the final disappearance of the yolk, the placenta becomes structurally more complex, and five different placental types can be recognized according to the number of membranes interposed between the maternal and foetal blood (Needham, 1950). These five, beginning with the most permeable, are classified as: (1) Epithelio-chorial; (2) Syndesmo-chorial; (3) Endothelial-chorial; (4) Hemo-chorial; (5) Hemo-endothelial.

The connection between the placenta and the embryo is effected by the umbilical cord, which contains three vessels: the umbilical artery (or vitelline artery as Ranzi terms it), the umbilical vein (Ranzi's vitelline vein), and between them the vitelline canal (*ductus vitello-intestinalis*). In some cases the umbilical cord is completely smooth (as in *Carcharhinus* for example), or it may be variously ornamented with arborescent appendages, or *appendiculata* (as in *Scoliodon, Paragaleus, Sphyrna*), which give it a characteristic 'bushy' look. One would suppose that the presence or absence of these appendiculata would have some systematic value. So far, all species of *Carcharhinus* examined have been found to have a smooth cord, whereas members of the three genera named above all have appendiculata. But the number of specimens examined has been insufficient to establish a general rule (Budker, 1949, 1953).

The presence of these arborescent appendages leads on to the question of the method by which the foetus is nourished in these placental species. While the foetus is within the uterus, attached to its lining by means of the umbilical cord and placenta, two kinds of relationship between mother and foetus can be recognized.

(1) *Embryotrophic* or *histotrophic*. In this type of nutrition, substances produced by the uterine lining (which undergoes modification directly gestation begins) are absorbed by the embryo directly. The embryo is bathed, in fact, in a liquid containing the dissolved nutritive substances produced by the uterine epithelium. This liquid has been aptly named 'uterine milk'.

(2) *Hemotrophic*. In this type of nutrition, substances dissolved in the blood plasma of the female pass into the blood of the foetus at the point where the blood vessels of the two are in contact, i.e. at the placenta.

The structure of the smooth type of umbilical cord does not seem to be conducive to the absorption of the intra-uterine liquid (uterine milk). On the other hand, the structure of the appendiculata strongly suggests that they play a part in the histotrophic nutrition of the embryo.[1] However, the way in which the nutritive substances in the uterine milk are absorbed has yet to be elucidated satisfactorily. Certain cells of the embryonic epithelial tissue, the ectoderm and the lining of the yolk sac, etc, may contribute in this absorptive process. Later on, the intra-uterine liquid can be taken in by the mouth and by the spiracle when present.[2]

Finally, in certain ovoviviparous (i.e. aplacental) sharks, the embryo after resorption of the yolk begins actively to feed on unfertilized eggs passed down into the uterus. In the Porbeagle (*Lamna nasus*) especially, one finds

[1] TeWinkel (1963), studying early stages in the Smooth Hound *Mustelus canis*, found in the surface of the yolk stalk (smooth in this case) cells with brushlike borders, and suggested that they might have an absorptive function by a process of pinoclysis.

[2] In some genera of rays (e.g. Butterfly Rays, *Pteroplatea*) long villi develop from the wall of the uterus and these enter the spiracle of the embryo and extend down into the pharynx of the embryo. They have been referred to as '*trophonemata*' (Gudger, 1952).

an enormous 'yolk stomach' distended by the quantities of eggs ingested before birth and afterwards sustaining the young shark for some time before feeding commences (Figure 30a). This 'oophagy' also occurs in the Mako (*Isurus oxyrinchus*) and the Sand Shark (*Odontaspis taurus*), the whole process being very well described for the latter by Stewart Springer (1948). He showed that 15 to 20 very small eggs were discharged by the right ovary (the left not being functional) and were coated by the shell gland before passing to one or other of the oviducts for fertilization. Only one embryo would hatch, however, and it would then feed on the yolks of its surrounding eggs once its own was finished. A similar situation would obtain in the other oviduct and for about a year the two embryos would continue to feed on eggs passed down from the ovaries, finally being born at a length of some 30 inches.

During this rather rapid review of viviparity in sharks, the word placenta has been used. It must not, in spite of its morphological similarity, be too closely compared with the placenta in mammals. In fishes, of course, an allantois and amnion are not present. For this reason, many authors prefer the term 'pseudo-placenta'. However, the function is the same and the similarity is nonetheless striking: fully formed young are born which, during the whole of their intra-uterine development, have remained directly in contact with the uterus by means of an umbilical cord and a placenta.

This can give rise to rather amusing errors. For example, in a book called *Child of the Deep*, published about twenty years ago, a young American woman gives an interesting account of her memories of a childhood spent entirely on board a sailing ship of which her father was both owner and skipper. Describing the capture of a female shark, she declares categorically that sharks are not fishes! They are mammals! She had seen more of sharks than the experts in their laboratories! She had even found the young ones in their bellies, proving that they are true mammals! Irrefutable proof indeed, but no doubt it would have been useless to have explained to this young lady that there are numbers of *viviparous* sharks, and also many viviparous bony fishes. She had *seen* it, with her own eyes. I have already quoted this anecdote in another book (*Whales and Whaling*) as I find it interesting and at the same time typical of a certain state of mind which is fairly prevalent.

Amongst the species of the genus *Mustelus* (Smooth Hounds) are examples currently cited as being viviparous. As far as can be judged, viviparity seems to be equally the case in the large pelagic sharks. In the Carcharhinidae, at any rate, it appears to be a general rule, both in the genus *Carcharhinus* and in *Scoliodon*. Unfortunately, when they catch a gravid female, fishermen do not always recall whether the foetuses were attached by their umbilical cord to the lining of the uterus. There are also many sharks which are claimed to be placentally viviparous without there being any confirmatory evidence. This is true of the White Shark (*Carcharodon*), as well as many other species. But certainly, all the gravid females of *Carcharhinus* which I have dissected up to now (in tropical regions) have shown an attachment of the umbilical cord to the lining of the uterus.

The uterus on each side functions simultaneously, at least in the sharks. The quantity of foetuses which they can hold varies considerably, but in general the number is equal on the two sides with a total ranging from two (Sand Shark, *Odontaspis taurus*) or four (small *Carcharhinus*) to about fourteen (large Hammerhead) and 26–28 in the Nurse Shark (*Ginglymostoma*). Tortonese (1950) reported that eighty-two were found in a Tiger Shark of 14 feet 7 inches length caught off Cuba. When the number is unequal, evidently one uterus must contain more than the other, but even numbers are normally recorded. A rather curious problem involves the distribution of the sexes on each side. Some years ago, a fisherman off the coast of Africa told me that he had seen a Hammerhead Shark containing sixteen foetuses, eight males and eight females. The males were all found in the right uterus and the females in the left. According to him, this distribution of the sexes was apparently commonly found. Separation of the sexes in the two uteri is doubted by Aristotle: Males are generated on the left-hand side of the womb and females on the right-hand side, but also males and females on the same side together (*Historia Animalium*, **6** : 10). Elsewhere, Aristotle gives this in reverse: The male embryo is in the right uterus, and the female in the left (*De Generatione Animalium*, **4** : 1), but this seems to be merely the opinion of Anaxagorus, Empedocles, Democritus and 'some other naturalists' whom Aristotle wishes to refute. Even now, one hesitates to reject any of Aristotle's observations until definitely proved otherwise, and certainly in all the gravid females that I have dissected the sexes have always been mixed in each uterus. Sauvage (1888) also found this to be so in the Piked Dogfish (*Squalus acanthias*).

It may be that this separation of the sexes is peculiar to certain species of sharks and not others. Only through more precise observations on a large number of individuals can the question be settled satisfactorily. The problem is not without interest, for it raises the question of which is the heterogametic sex in sharks, the male or the female. In mammals, the genetic mechanism is such that the female is the homogametic sex (designated XX), and the male the heterogametic sex (XY). The opposite is true in birds, the female having the XY chromosome set and the male the XX. In fishes, however, both mechanisms are found, occasionally within the same species.

Considerable genetic interest attaches to this since the pattern can be followed in breeding experiments where an external character is linked to one of the sex chromosomes. There is also the consideration of the details of copulation, for which at the moment we have only a vague outline based solely on anatomical studies. There is here a vast field of research awaiting study, although obviously not an easy one to investigate.

For centuries, the viviparity of sharks has been well-known.[1] But Rondelet (1558), in his *Du Renard* (*Alopias vulpinus*) stated that: 'It takes its young ones, neither more nor less than does the Aguillat (i.e. the Spur Dog) and receives them inside itself, as Aristotle wrote and as is the truth.' Aristotle, in fact, reported this extraordinary phenomenon not only in the Thresher (*Alopias*), but also in the dogfishes in general and in the Electric Ray (*Torpedo*).[2] Again, certain fishermen have claimed that the female Thresher Shark swims in company with its young, doting on them in a most attentive fashion and taking them under the shelter of her pectoral fins in times of danger. According to Moreau, a female Thresher has taken a juvenile under each pectoral and has swum off rapidly, even leaping, but all the while guarding the young ones. This requires confirmation but it is rather different from the conclusions drawn by Aristotle and Rondelet that some sharks behave like veritable kangaroos. The latter myth was also repeated by Aelian (*ca* 140–220 AD) and appears in Oppian's *Halieuticks* of about the same period, where it is accredited to the Blue Shark:

> Thus the Blue Sharks, secure from chasing foes,
> Within their widen'd mouths their young enclose.

Sensory organs

Fishes are equipped with an assemblage of cutaneous sensory organs which cannot be equated with any of the sense organs of land animals, and thanks to which they can sense certain things which are outside our ken and which we even find difficult to appreciate fully. In this respect, sharks are especially well provided, and the role that these organs play in the life of sharks can be discussed briefly here. The function of these organs has long been guessed at or assumed, and it is only in recent years that it has been to some extent clarified.

Early observations on dogfishes had revealed that these animals appeared

---

[1] However, it was only in 1667 that Nicolas Steno at Florence dissected a female dogfish, recognizing the exact nature of the ovaries.

[2] Aristotle states, however, that 'the spiny dog-fish (i.e. *Squalus acanthias*) is an exception to the rule, being prevented by the spine of the young fish from so doing' (*Historia Animalium*, 6: 10).

capable of 'sensing with their skin' (Nagel, 1894). A little later Sheldon (1911) showed that the Smooth Hound (*Mustelus canis*) sought for and found its food by a chemical sense; according to this author, the chemical sense was entirely olfactory, the dogfish finding its food chiefly, if not entirely, by its smell, sharks having a true olfactory sense comparable to that found in terrestrial vertebrates.

Sharks, however, have three other types of sensory organs by means of which they register conditions and changes in the external medium. These are the sensory canals, the Ampullae of Lorenzini and the sensory pits.

(1) *Lateral line sensory canals.* The lateral line system on the flanks of fishes is common to almost all groups. In only a few families is it missing; in the Clupeoids (herringlike fishes) for example, the canal is limited to the anterior two or three scales. But in the vast majority of cases a lateral line canal is present, and in the bony fishes, can be seen quite easily. The scales of the lateral line have a pore at their centre and a small canal which is clearly visible, these scales forming a longitudinal series down the flank of the animal.

In sharks the situation is rather different. The placoid scales are in no way involved in the lateral line sensory system, the latter being made up of true canals, mucus filled tubes which are buried in the thickness of the skin and communicate with the exterior by means of numerous tubular openings or pores in the epidermis spaced at regular intervals. One of these canals, the lateral canal, follows exactly the same course as the lateral line canal in bony fishes. The other canals, situated in the head region (the cephalic canals) have many branches – supra-orbital, infra-orbital, mandibular and supra-temporal canals (Figure 31). These branches are found in bony fishes, at least as far as their general layout is concerned, but in bony fishes they differ somewhat in their morphology from the lateral line canal proper. In sharks,

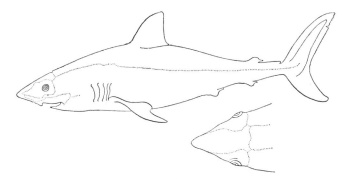

Fig. 31   Sensory canals in the Porbeagle *Lamna nasus* (after Garman).

77

on the other hand, the whole assemblage of sensory canals is quite homogeneous.

The canals in sharks are filled with mucus, and for this reason are sometimes referred to as 'mucus canals'. Sensory organs, the neuromasts, are arranged along the length of these tubes and external stimuli are transmitted to them by the mucus which itself is in contact with the water through the openings along the canal.

For a long time, the function of the canals was something of a mystery. In sharks, moreover, the openings of the canals are masked by the presence of the dermal denticles and the course of the canals is not always easy to see. However, it is now known that these canals play a part in perception of vibrations in the external medium, that is to say, they are sensitive to stimuli of a mechanical nature. Whereas in water the higher frequency vibrations (i.e. sound) are probably picked up by the hearing apparatus, low frequency vibrations, such as result from a struggling fish, are perhaps detected by the lateral line system (Backus, 1963; Dijkgraaf, 1963).

Hoffer (1908) found that with the Pike (*Esox lucius*) a strong current of water would result in the fishes turning to face in the direction of the current. This type of behaviour is known as *rheotaxis* (positive rheotaxis if the fish faces into the current, negative if it swims with the current). Dijkgraaf (1934), however, denied that the lateral line was the chief organ involved in this rheotactic behaviour. 'Distance perception' (*Ferntastsinn*) as a function of the lateral line system is apparently well established (Grassé, 1958).

The role of the lateral line system formed the subject of a recent symposium held at Yeshiva University in New York (Cahn, 1967). This was, in fact, the first conference to be devoted exclusively to this sensory system. Like many such conferences, the papers posed as many questions as they answered. One interesting paper was that by Sven Dijkgraaf (1967) on the biological significance of the lateral line organs. He had shown thirty years earlier (Dijkgraaf, 1934) that fishes have the ability to sense moving objects in the water. His recent experiments suggested that some fishes with particularly sensitive lateral line organs are able to sense *motionless* obstacles as they approach them. He admitted that the lateral line is used to register small differences in water velocity but claimed that these organs are not involved in rheotactic behaviour towards large water currents, of the kind that carry the whole fish away.

Very much remains to be done on this subject before the complete significance of the lateral line organs are properly understood.

(2) *Ampullae of Lorenzini*. Over much of the anterior part of the head in

sharks, especially the snout region, there are a large number of small, round porelike openings which, when pressed, ooze transparent mucus. These pores are the openings of sensory organs termed the ampullae of Lorenzini (Figure 32 and Plate 3, lower). They are elongate tubes which internally terminate in a kind of ampoule or sac containing mucus cells and sensory cells. Discovered by Marcello Malpighi in 1663, the ampullae were first described in detail by Stephano Lorenzini in 1678, after whom they are now named.

These organs have been subjected to a certain amount of research leading to rather contradictory conclusions. The ampullae themselves are composed

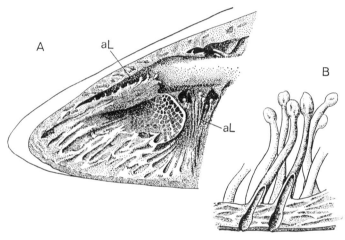

Fig. 32   The ampullae of Lorenzini. Cross-section of the snout of a shark (A) showing the ampullae (aL) and their fine structure (B).

of two types of cells, sensory cells (flask cells of some authors) and supporting (pyramid) cells. But for a long time, authors have disagreed over the identity and function of the one and the other. Recent research (Barets and Szabo, 1962), made with the aid of the electron microscope on the ampullae in the Electric Ray (*Torpedo marmorata*) has thrown some light on the nature of these two types of cell. However, it is the general function of the ampullae of Lorenzini which concerns us. But even here, there is still considerable uncertainty and controversy. Many research workers have tackled the problem and thought that they had found a solution. Parker (1912), and above all Dotterweich (1932), linked anatomical with behavioural studies and concluded that the ampullae of Lorenzini are used in the perception of variations in hydrostatic pressure, acting in fact as depth gauges. Injecting

79

distilled water into the ampullae, causing the gelatinous contents to swell and thus exert a pressure, Dotterweich showed that dogfishes (*Scyliorhinus*) then swam snout upwards as if trying to rise from the depths and so reduce water pressure. This view had been generally adopted when Sand (1938) took up the study of the ampullae, using a cathode ocillograph, and he put forward an explanation which was quite different to that of Dotterweich. According to Sand, the sensory functions of the ampullae of Lorenzini are restricted to perception of temperature changes – which seemed at first sight, even to Sand himself, to be a most unexpected and extraordinary result. However, he was able to show that sharks and rays are equipped with a thermometer of such precision that they are able to appreciate temperature variations of as small as $\frac{1}{10}°$ C. He also found that the lateral line nerve endings showed a similar but weaker response to temperature variations. Von Buddenbrock (1952) believed that Sand's work would be followed up and confirmed. However, Murray (1962 and 1967), using electrophysiological methods, has produced results which, in their turn, place Sand's findings in question. Thus Murray established first of all that the ampullae of Lorenzini are 'sensitive to weak tactile stimulation applied to the ends of their jelly-filled tubes', and later he found them sensitive to slight changes in the electrical field in the water surrounding the fish (of the order of 1 μV per cm²). The latter function would, of course, account for the ampullae being sensitive to changes in salinity. Dijkgraaf (1964) confirmed Murray's findings that the ampullae are electro-receptors in experiments on the Spotted Dogfish (*Scyliorhinus*). In a later paper, Dijkgraaf (1967) reported on his experiments using iron and glass rods. He found that the fishes would respond to the iron but not to the glass, a clear indication that the electrical field was being sensed. His fishes also showed a response to the very weak electrical impulses of biological origin, that is to say from the operation of muscles in another fish. This, he thought, was the biological significance of the ampullae, for they would aid in finding prey. The previous year, A.J.Kalmijn (1966) working with Dijkgraaf at Utrecht had shown that the Thornback Ray (*Raja clavata*) was capable of appreciating electrical stimuli of the order of $\frac{1}{10}$th of a microvolt per centimetre while the normal gill movements of a Plaice (*Pleuronectes platessa*) generated electrical potentials of as much as 1000 microvolts per centimetre. Kalmin concluded that the Thornback and presumably other selachians can not only detect these small electrical stimuli but use them as a means of homing on to prey at very close ranges. This would be especially important in the rays and also the more flattened bottom-living sharks since the snout obscures close range vision of the bottom.

To sum up, it appears that the ampullae of Lorenzini will react to a variety of stimuli (temperature, salinity, pressure, electrical potential) but that their most likely function is in the detecting of prey, at least for the bottom-living species, by detecting electrical impulses of biological origin.

(3) *Sensory pit organs*. These constitute the third category of sensory cutaneous sense organs. Unlike the sensory canals, or the ampullae of Lorenzini, the pit organs are almost always in close association with the dermal denticles (Budker, 1938). Exceptions to this have only been recorded in some Scyliorhinidae and small Topes (*Galeorhinus*).

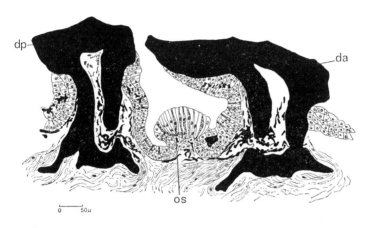

Fig. 33   Cross-section of a sensory pit in the Nurse Shark *Ginglymostoma cirratum*. Sensory cells grey. da anterior denticle. dp posterior denticle. os sensory organ (neuromast).

In sharks, the sensory pit has the following features: two modified dermal denticles lie close together, more or less overlapping and leaving between them a cavity, the sensory pit, at the bottom of which is a sensory papilla or bud (Figure 33). These papillae show a great similarity to the taste buds of higher vertebrates. Thus, there are supporting cells with sensory cells interposed, agreeing with the description which Cordier (1939) gives of a *neurogemme* (taste bud), i.e. tall sensory cells occupying the whole depth of the epithelium, their bases being at the same level as the support cells, suggesting a special sensory or a gustatory organ. The interior of the pit itself is lined with epithelial tissue which also on occasions has some sensory cells. The differentiated placoid scales, or paired protective spicules, are easily spotted in young sharks, where they produce a slight projection which catches the eye. But they are less easily found in larger individuals, and can be mistaken for ordinary denticles. They have often escaped notice

81

THE LIFE OF SHARKS

or again their true nature has not been recognized, as I found in a recent and on the whole excellent book where these denticles are carefully shown in a drawing of a Thresher Shark, but without any indication of their relation to the sensory organ itself.

The sensory pits occur in large numbers on the bodies of sharks, on the back, flanks, and in the region of the lower jaw. Their number and distribution vary considerably, but remain more or less constant within a species. Also, one finds that in the bottom-living benthic or semibenthic sharks, such as the Carpet Sharks (Orectolobidae), the pit organs are noticeably less numerous than in the open-water pelagic species. Almost certainly, there is a correlation between the ethology of the species concerned and the distribution of the sensory pit organs.

It seems somewhat paradoxical that these 'organs of taste' should occur on just those parts of the body where one would least expect them, i.e. on the back and flanks of the animal. The structure of the papilla, which strikingly recalls that of a taste bud, may give a clue to the function of the pit organs. One should be warned, however, that to try to deduce the function of an organ solely by reference to its morphology is, as Herrick (1903) pointed out, a particularly precarious approach to research. Tester and Nelson (1967), for example, in a comprehensive article on pit organs, state: 'The pit-organ, like the neuromast, is composed of two types of cell, sensory and supporting, whereas the taste bud is composed only of a single type.' This contradicts all accepted notions of the structure of taste-buds, in which two types of cell have been recognized, the sensory and the supporting cells (see Bouin, 1932, II, 318, fig. 250; Daniel, 1934, p. 276; Cordier, 1939, p. 12, fig. 3; and so on).

There is also the question of the presence or absence of the *cupula*. The cupula is a thin, gelatinous rod emerging from the top of a neuromast. The rod encloses fine hairs from the tips of the sensory cells. It is thought that bending of this rod as a result of movements of the water or mucus that surround it should be recorded by the sensory cells of the neuromast. Unfortunately, this rod is very difficult to detect in microscopic sections of neuromasts. Tester and Nelson (1967) claim to have found such cupulae in a few of their sections of pit-organs, which would suggest that the pit-organs are sensitive to mechanical stimuli. If this were in fact true, then the pit-organs might perhaps register important information on the state of the water layer bounded by the denticles. If, as suggested earlier (p. 48), this layer of water is held by the denticles at high swimming speeds, so that laminar flow is possible, then it would obviously be of advantage if the shark could determine the point at which this boundary layer of water no longer slips by but is held to the body. Equally, if Rosen's theory that fishes set up

82

a series of vortices as they swim is true, then the pit-organs could well serve to show the state of the vortices. The cupulae shown by Tester and Nelson, however, differ from those of normal neuromasts in that they are not free at the tip but appear to be applied to modified scales above them. This would seriously affect their sensitivity to water movements. One day the true function of the pit-organs will be found, but in the meanwhile science would be very dull without such controversies.

I have made rather summary experiments using Nuoc-Mam (a very sapid Vietnamese condiment made by macerating fishes in a strong solution of salt) on a Monkfish (*Squatina*), and the results are certainly suggestive of a gustatory function for the pit-organs. However, the results must be regarded as only indicative, and the trule role of the sensory pits must await investigation by electrophysiological methods. The difficulties inherent in this field of research can be judged by the case of the ampullae of Lorenzini, which are far more accessible.

The most recent and certainly the most extensive work on pit-organs is that cited above by Albert Tester and Gareth Nelson. These two authors studied in great detail the pit-organs in about twenty species of sharks. With excellent facilities and abundant material, they suggested that the sensory element in the pit-organ is a free neuromast and not a taste-bud; it is thus a mechano-receptor. They wisely added, however, that plausible as this might seem, it must remain a hypothesis until actually proven by electrophysiological and behavioural experiments – my own conclusion of some thirty years ago. The initiative must now lie with the physiologists, for they alone can provide the correct answer to this problem.

Finally, in addition to the various sensory functions of the cutaneous sensory organs, there is another important sense, that of olfaction. Dissection of the head of a shark shows the great importance of the olfactory apparatus which may account for two-thirds of the brain weight. The voluminous olfactory sacs, furnished with numerous lamellae, the Schneiderian folds, (Figure 34) are closely applied to the olfactory bulbs. The whole system is extremely well developed, and as Professor Perry W. Gilbert has remarked, in sharks, 'the sense of smell has long been regarded as the most acute; indeed, the shark has been described as a *swimming nose*'. The investigations made by Albert L. Tester (1963b) confirm this, as we shall see in the section dealing with current shark repellent work. In the majority of sharks (and rays) the nostrils are on the underside of the head, but in a few (e.g. the Hammerhead and the Whale Shark) they are situated along the anterior margin of the head.

The fact that fishes live constantly bathed in a liquid medium forces one

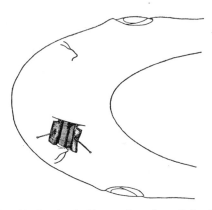

Fig. 34   Nostril of a shark dissected to show Schneiderian folds.

to reconsider the question of the chemical senses: smell and taste. In non-aquatic vertebrates, the distinction between the two is quite clear. In land animals the sense of smell is the means by which the source of a chemical stimulation is ascertained *in the air* and at a distance from its source; taste, on the other hand, is stimulated by substances dissolved in a liquid which is brought into contact with the gustatory organs lying within the mouth, i.e. the buccal cavity (Grassé, 1957).

In fishes, however, *all* stimulatory substances are dissolved in the water surrounding them, and passage through air obviously does not enter the question. Thus the term *olfacto-gustation* has been coined to define the ensemble of chemical senses in fishes. However, all authors who have studied this difficult question at first hand now agree that the separation of taste from smell in fishes is a perfectly legitimate one. As von Frisch (1941a) put it, smell is the chemical sense which provides information *at a distance* (presence of an enemy, proximity of food); taste, on the other hand, gives information principally about the animal's food, i.e. its chemical quality.

Finally, one can add Tester's 'the common chemical sense – the ability to perceive substances of an irritating nature – which is separate and distinct from the senses of smell and taste. . . . The irritant receptors are non-medullated nerve fibre endings, which terminate amongst the epithelial cells. . . . In fish they occur over all the body surfaces.' This recalls the trials made with the Nuoc-Mam on the Monkfish mentioned above. The re-actions observed may, perhaps, have come about through the action of the Nuoc-Mam on these non-medullated nerve fibre endings, for which we possess as yet little experimental data.

This very brief survey gives an idea of the complexity of the cutaneous sensory system in sharks, and also the extreme difficulty of studying this system. A.L.Tester, who himself carried out some very delicate experiments in this field, has insisted on the necessity of adopting the modern techniques of electro-dissection and electrophysiology for such research, and has also stressed the necessity to work on different species, the latter point being especially important. Modern research seems to be orienting in favour of such studies, e.g. the work of Gilbert and his colleagues in the United States, of the late Professor David H.Davies and others in South Africa, especially on the hearing of sharks, and R.H.Backus at Woods Hole in Massachussetts.

Vision

The cutaneous sensory apparatus in sharks is a well-developed system enabling the animal to maintain close contact with various aspects of the external medium in a manner which we ourselves are neither able to do nor fully appreciate. This said, there is another question to raise: what is the role played by vision in sharks? This is, or more correctly has been made to be, a controversial question. On the one hand, most skin divers insist that sharks can see very well, demonstrating their visual acuity in their behaviour in face of a prey, whether close to them or at a distance. On the other hand, anatomists are less certain. Verrier (1928) has said:

In general, the number of visual and ganglion cells in the retinas of sharks hardly corresponds even to the most peripheral areas of the human retina. The retina is above all concerned with the perception of moving objects; vision of forms can scarcely exist. Colour vision is nil . . . but the perception of light must be great, there being an abundance of rods. The dioptric apparatus is more defective than in any teleost fish.

A similar conclusion was drawn by Rochon-Duvigneaud (1943), who stated that in sharks 'visual acuity is feeble, but light sensitivity is well developed (rods long and numerous, retina purple, pupils capable of great dilation)'. He pointed out that sharks compensate for this by their ability to appreciate small changes in the salinity, temperature, pressure, etc of the water around them and are clearly sensitive to their environment in ways that man, the visual animal, can scarcely conceive. More recent work, however, has shown that the visual system in sharks is probably not inferior to that of man. In Lemon Sharks, Gruber (1967) found that the eye took longer to adapt to dark, but that the range of dark adaptation and the absolute sensitivity of the eye in these sharks was very similar to what has been recorded for the human eye.

The cells of the retina, which are responsible for reacting to a light

85

stimulus and passing the information to the brain via the optic nerve, are basically of two kinds. The rod cells are responsible for visual acuity, while the cone cells are associated with the perception of colour. At one time it was believed that cone cells were virtually absent in the shark retina, so that sharks must be unable to distinguish colours. More detailed studies have shown, however, that cone cells are definitely present in the Lemon Shark and may be more common in other species than was formerly suspected (Gruber, Hamasaki & Bridges, 1963). These authors found cone cells in the retinas of fifteen other species belonging to three different orders. The popular view that sharks are attracted by highly coloured bathing suits may in fact have some foundation.

In man and other mammals, as well as in birds and reptiles (except snakes) focusing is achieved by altering the curvature of the lens. In fishes, amphibians and snakes this cannot be done, and the lens must be moved. In the bony fishes (teleosts) and in the lampreys the lens is moved backwards to accommodate for seeing at a distance, whereas in sharks, as well as amphibians and snakes, the lens must be moved forward to accommodate for seeing near objects.

Another important peculiarity shared by almost all elasmobranchs is the possession of a chorioidal tapetum, or mirrorlike reflecting layer behind the layer of cells making up the retina (Figure 35). The tapetum is made up of a single layer of platelike reflecting cells which appear to be crystals of guanine (the pigment responsible for the silvery flanks of certain fishes, such as herrings). These tapetal plates evidently reflect light that has already passed through the retina so that it triggers off the retinal cells a second time as it passes out again. For this reason, the shark eye can appreciate very small amounts of light. It also causes the eyes to glow when light is shone into them. The arrangement of the tapetal plates is even more remarkable. Denton & Nicol (1964) have shown that the plates are set at various angles to the surface of the retina, the angles being such that light which is reflected back does not fall on another part of the retina, for this would result in a confused image. Obviously a shark that experiences bright shallow water and dark deeper water would be temporarily blinded on coming to the surface on a sunny day. It has been found that in many species there are small pigment cells at the bases of the tapetal plates and in bright light the dark melanin granules stream out between the plates so that they no longer reflect. In addition, the pupil of the eye also closes in bright light, leaving merely a pin-point or slit. Using Lemon Sharks, Gruber (1967) showed that after a period of eight hours of adaptation to dark conditions, the visual system in this shark was 1,000,000 times more sensitive to light. The tapetal plates

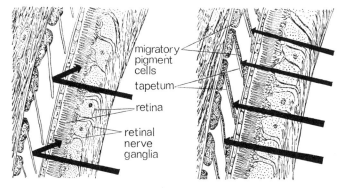

Fig. 35   Eye of Blue Shark *Prionace glauca* to show the tapetal plates responsible for reflecting light back into the eye in dark conditions so that the light sensitive cells of the retina are stimulated for a second time.

cannot be occluded in *Scyliorhinus canicula*, however, nor in deep-sea squalioid sharks and chimaeras (Nicol, 1961).

For man, vision is the most essential and important of our senses (hence phrases such as 'the apple of one's eye'). Human wickedness, which some-times seems boundless and thinks nothing of teasing or making fun of a deaf man, hesitates when confronted with a blind man. For us, loss of sight is the worst affliction, and one which inspires compassion and a kind of almost sacred respect on the part of those with sight. As Dr Rochon-Duvigneaud (1943) rightly says, a man without sight and on his own is doomed to perish.

It is most difficult, when approaching the problem of sense organs in other animals, to rid oneself of anthropomorphism, and it is unlikely that skin-divers are free from such bias. 'Observations on living sharks in their natural habitats,' wrote Professor Gilbert, 'and the use of their eyes in locomotion and predation, are limited and at best, subjective.' An intensive study of the structure of the eye in sharks, combined with well-controlled experiments carried out at the Lerner Laboratory at Bimini, led Professor Gilbert and his colleagues to state:

At distances greater than 50 feet, olfaction appears to be more important than vision in guiding sharks to their prey. At distances of 50 feet or less, depending on the strength and direction of the current, the clarity of the water, and the amount of light, vision increases in importance, and at very close range (10 feet or less), vision is probably the principal sense involved in directing the Lemon Sharks to food.

As a result of work on the Lemon Shark (*Negaprion brevirostris*), Professor Gilbert (1963c) found that 'when both vision and olfaction are obliterated simultaneously, an adult Lemon Shark swims helplessly about, subjects itself to serious injury and dies within 3 to 5 days'. This recalls Rochon-Duvigneaud's remark about a blind man on his own. Thus, it must be accepted that vision in sharks plays a not inconsiderable role in their general behaviour.

A further anatomical peculiarity of the eye in sharks is the nictitans or nictitating membrane (Figure 36), an additional eyelid whose presence or absence characterizes certain groups of sharks (see below). However, there seems so far to be no firm correlation between the presence of a nictitating membrane and the ethology of the species concerned. Amongst species lacking it, one finds pelagic forms (e.g. Mackerel Sharks, Isuridae), as well as benthic or semibenthic forms (e.g. the Carpet Sharks, Orectolobidae).

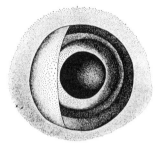

Fig. 36   Eye of shark to show nictitating membrane.

Again, in those that possess it, are many surface dwelling Carcharhinidae, whereas the Smooth Hounds (*Mustelus*) generally live near the bottom.

Professor Gilbert found, during his work on sharks, that in all the species of Carcharhinidae that he worked on, as also in *Scyliorhinus* and *Mustelus*, the nictitating membrane was not used to protect the eye from even very intense light. On the contrary, it covered the eye most completely at the approach of a strange object.

When present, the nictitating membrane shows various degrees of development, from a narrow fold scarcely impinging on the eye, to a membrane capable of covering the eye almost completely, as for example in the Brown Shark (*Carcharhinus milberti*) and the Hammerhead. This membrane would seem to afford protection to the eye, but there are many species which do not possess it and apparently do not appear to be unduly inconvenienced by its absence. One finds, however, that a nictitating membrane is present in the most highly evolved sharks (i.e. in the Carcharhinidae), but that it is absent particularly in certain primitive forms, such as the Hexanchidae. Five related muscles draw the nictitans obliquely backward and upward over the eye. The principal muscle is the *levator palpebrae nictitantis* (l.p.n. for short), a muscle that originally helped in opening the spiracle or first gill-slit. Sharks with a well-developed spiracle and spiracular musculature lack a nictitans, while those with the spiracle reduced or absent have a mobile nictitans. Gilbert (1963c) gives a convincing table of this correlation in sharks.

Hearing

In recent years, work has been in progress on the ability of sharks to hear and to use sound as a means of locating prey. This research is part of a general interest in underwater sounds which arose once electronic listening devices revealed that the 'silent world' of Jacques Cousteau was in fact a very noisy one. On one occasion during the last war, for example, a particularly vociferous chorus of Midshipmen (*Porichthys*) threw shore batteries and naval vessels into a state of tense alert until it was discovered that it was not enemy submarines entering the bay but the croaking and grunting of shoals of fishes. The human ear can appreciate almost nothing of this noisy world under the surface since it suffers a 40 to 60 decibel loss compared with sound reception in air. In addition, many underwater sounds are either in the infrasonic range (e.g. the 'noise' resulting from turbulence around a struggling fish) and are too low for the human ear, or they are in the ultra-sonic range and are too high to hear (e.g. the sonar pulses emitted by dolphins and other cetaceans for echo-location of objects or prey). Fishes of a wide range of families are now known to produce noises under water but curiously enough no sounds have yet been recorded from sharks or rays. Nevertheless, hearing is of prime importance to selachians, both as a warning of the approach of predators and as a means of locating their food.

Experiments have been carried out on the acoustic aspects of shark behaviour at the Institute of Marine Sciences in Miami, originally under the direction of Dr Warren Wisby and later Dr Arthur Myberg. They have shown that for Lemon Sharks (*Negaprion brevirostris*) the frequency range that can be appreciated is not much above 640 Hz (cycles per second) but that the animals will respond to sounds as low as 10 Hz. This contrasts with the human range, which is usually set at 20 to 20,000 Hz, although few people hear over the complete range. They also found that in the lower part of the shark's frequency range the hearing was remarkably sensitive and that the sharks possessed an extraordinary faculty for directional hearing. Since directional hearing is believed to be generally absent in bony fishes, it may be that the presence of a swimbladder, while increasing hearing sensitivity, at the same time destroys the ability for directional hearing.

The work carried out at Miami is described by Donald Nelson (1969). He

89

and his colleagues first recorded the sounds of a speared and struggling fish whose sounds were composed of very low frequencies, mostly below 100 Hz. These were analysed spectrographically and a series of artificial test sounds with controlled frequency ranges was put on to tape. A section of the reef was then chosen and the absence of sharks noted for fifteen minutes before the playback was commenced. After some twelve minutes of playback a large Tiger Shark (*Galeocerdo*) approached the speaker and gave every indication that it had been attracted by the noise. Subsequent experiments showed that a pulsed quality and a low-frequency composition were necessary for sounds to be effective in attracting sharks. The next problem was to determine the range of the shark's hearing and here the experimenters used an aeroplane to spot the shark and report its reactions while the men in a small boat operated the sound production. From nine separate observations it appeared that sharks could be attracted from as far away as 200 yards. Later experiments suggested that sharks became 'habituated' to the noises of the tape recording and would soon learn that they did not represent a wounded and struggling fish.

A more sophisticated project is the Bimini Video-Acoustic System used by the Lerner Marine Laboratory at Bimini in the Bahamas. The unit comprises a television camera capable of scanning 360°, a hydrophone array and a sound projector mounted on the reef bottom in 60 feet of clear water. Sitting in the comfort of the laboratory, it is possible to watch the effect of sounds, not only on sharks but also on other fishes. In his description of this project, Nelson (1969) notes that the results are all the more valuable because the behaviour of the fishes is not complicated by the presence of divers or boats. From work of this kind a great deal can be learnt of the role that sound plays in the life of sharks and perhaps one day it will be possible to find a 'repellent' noise that could be produced from a gadget small enough to be carried by swimmers.

Respiration

Without going too deeply into the subject, some comment must be made here on the mechanism of respiration in sharks since it differs considerably from that found in the bony fishes.

Anatomically, the selachians display an archaic type of gill arrangement, differing from that in all other fishes by the absence of an operculum or flap covering the gills (Figure 37). The group is thus characterized by the presence of gill-slits (lateral in sharks; ventral in the skates and rays). The term 'Pomatobranchs' has been used for all other fishes with an operculum (Greek, *poma*, a cover). In sharks, as we have already noted, there are five

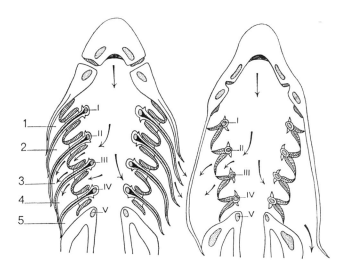

Fig. 37 Diagrammatic comparison between the gill chambers and method of breathing in a shark (left) and a bony fish (right). On the left of each drawing is shown the moment when water is drawn in, and on the right is the moment when water is expelled. I–V gill arches. 1–5 gill clefts.

gill-slits in the vast majority of species; in the Nurse Sharks (Orectolobidae) there are still five slits, but two of these are very close together. The only exceptions are members of the Hexanchiformes (6–7 gill-slits) and the Saw Shark *Pliotrema* (6 gill-slits).

In bony fishes the respiratory cycle has the appearance of two phases.

(1) *Inspiration:* mouth open, gill cover (operculum) closed.

(2) *Expiration:* mouth closed, gill cover opened.

Recent work has shown that two pumps are involved here, the mouth (a pressure pump) and the opercular cavities (suction pump), but that the two are slightly out of phase with each other. The result is a continuous flow of water over the gills, not an interrupted flow, as was thought previously.

In sharks, on the other hand, the cycle is slightly more complex, and is carried out in three phases:

(1) Entry of water through mouth; gill-slits closed so that water cannot enter there.

(2) Mouth and gill-slits closed; water filling the buccal cavity passes to the gills.

(3) Mouth still closed; gill-slits open, water expelled to the outside.

The following table summarizes these phases (from Bertin, 1958, p. 1329).

Sharks	Mouth	Bucco-pharyngeal cavity	Gill-pouches (parabranchial cavities)	Gill-slits
PHASE 1 (inspiration)	open	Dilation Suction	Contraction	closed
PHASE 2 (inspiration)	closed	Contraction Expulsion	Dilation Suction	closed
PHASE 3 (expiration)	closed	Contraction	Contraction Expulsion	open

It should be added, that this scheme only applies to the sharks, that is to say, to the Pleurotremata. In the Hypotremata, i.e. the skates and rays, the water enters the bucco-pharyngeal cavity by means of the spiracles in Phase 1, these being the only orifices on the dorsal surface. Such an arrangement is necessary in bottom-living forms in which the gill-slits are on the ventral surface since this would otherwise lead to clogging of the gills by sand or mud. In bony fishes, the alternate expanding and contracting of the mouth and opercular cavities to produce a pumping action is carried out by many different muscles acting on the jaws, the gill covers and the series of bones comprising or connected with the hyoid arch. In sharks, as Hughes and Balentjin (1965) have shown, the operation is more simple. Muscles close the mouth and contract the cavities, but certain tissues of the head are elastic and the opening of the mouth and expansion of the cavities is due to this elasticity. Since an elastic system begins fast and then slows down, the pumping action is probably not as smooth as in bony fishes.

Finally, in most fishes there are *buccal* or *respiratory valves*, simple folds of skin behind the teeth in the lower jaw (the *oral breathing valves* of Gudger, 1946). They are easily found in sharks, where they cover the rows of replacement teeth. These valves operate to seal the mouth against an outflow of water, but fold inwards as water is drawn in; they might merit the title of 'internal lips'. In the scheme shown above, their role occurs in the course of Phase 2, when water flows from the bucco-pharyngeal cavity into the gill pouches.

Light organs

Amongst the bony fishes, there are many examples of species with light organs, especially in fishes from the deeper waters. The light organs appear to serve in species and sex recognition, as lures for prey and to illuminate an area around the fish. Examples of sharks with luminous organs are fewer and the structure of these organs is simpler than in the bony fishes. In certain bottom-living species, such as *Etmopterus lucifer* and *Centroscyllium ritteri*, the lower surfaces of the fish are densely but irregularly scattered with tiny light organs. The organs are cup-shaped, with a group of photogenic cells inside and a backing of dark pigment underneath. In addition, there are two or three lens cells and an irislike structure of pigment cells that are presumably able to regulate the amount of light emitted. Hubbs, Iwai and Matsubara (1967) have contrasted this type of light organ with that found in the pelagic sharks *Isistius brasiliensis* and *Euprotomicrus bispinatus*, both members of the family Dalatiidae. The latter species is one of the smallest of all sharks, the largest recorded specimen being only $10\frac{1}{2}$ inches long and weighing $2\frac{1}{2}$ ounces. In this species, the light organs are spherical, with a single photogenic cell in the centre, a backing of black pigment and a lens overlying the light organ. These organs are very minute and form a rather uniform network over the entire lower surfaces of the body and head, a distribution which some workers believe will serve to eliminate the shadow under the body and thus make the fish less conspicuous. Carl Hubbs and his colleagues discussed the suggestion that a kind of light organ occurs in the Sleeper Shark (*Somniosus microcephalus*) but decided that the evidence was not sufficient to warrant the claim.

Chapter 4

Food and Feeding Habits

There is a widespread and popular notion that sharks are enormous eaters. It is not uncommon to hear that a shark can ingest in the space of twenty-four hours an amount of food equal to its own body weight. This idea is, however, quite without foundation, and merely a good example of the many 'categorical' statements which, with repetition, come to be accepted as true.

Work carried out in the last few years has shown how absurd this idea is, certainly as far as sharks kept in captivity are concerned. For a number of years now, sharks have been kept in aquaria or tanks of appropriate size, often in large pens in direct contact with the sea where the animals can live under conditions very similar to those they encounter in nature. As a result of observations on such fishes, some fairly accurate figures for feeding can be quoted (based here on the work of Eugenie Clark, 1962, 1963).

In captivity, sharks in good condition will eat, on average, a quantity of food equal to 3–14 per cent of their body weight *per week*, not per day. Juveniles show a greater appetite than do adults, which of course is a reflection on their greater needs (for growth and not merely for maintenance activities). For example, an adult Lemon Shark (*Negaprion*) of 9 feet in length consumes $3\frac{1}{2}$ per cent of its own weight per week, whereas an individual of the same species but small and immature may take in 10 per cent, which enables it to grow from 5 feet in length to 6 feet in a period of three months. On the other hand, the juvenile period may be considerably extended in some species. One can cite the case of the Tiger Shark, a species noted for its voracity, which in the Marine Studios of Miami, Florida, only started to feed at the end of the fifth month; it then ate 50 lbs of Blue Runner (*Caranx chrysos*) in a period of 36 hours and after that showed a preference for young sharks. In most cases, sharks in captivity are fed three times a week. It happens that, possibly as a result of temperature variations but sometimes for no apparent reason, sharks may cease feeding for some days, or for some weeks – even for some months – and then resume once more. Eugenie Clark noticed that this cessation of feeding occurred when the temperature dropped to below 20° C, but some variation was found in attempting precise correlations between water temperature and feeding activity.

Whatever the conditions, we are far from the formula 'daily intake = weight of animal', and this idea must be entirely discarded. To keep a Lemon Shark in good health in captivity, the average ration of food is 15 lbs of fish. As Eugenie Clark rightly remarks, the feeding requirements for sharks kept in captivity are perhaps lower than for those in nature, since the latter obviously expend far more energy in procuring their prey than do their domesticated colleagues. Also, there is the equally valid point that in nature sharks must search for their food and this search may often be greatly prolonged.

The ceaseless activity shown by sharks is consequent partly on their lack of a swim bladder (they tend to sink if not moving), but partly also on their need to ensure for themselves a meal. This latter is a peculiarity of most large carnivorous animals (except the lurkers). Their prey, often more swift or agile than they, flee at their approach, and the predator, to avoid death by starvation, must be in a constant state of readiness, living a life of perpetual ambush, pursuit and attack. In most fishes, however, and in sharks in particular, there is also their ability to fast for considerable periods. But in spite of this, sharks always appear to be actively engaged in the search for food. In this sense they resemble dogs, with their questing to right and left and their sniffing here and there, and 'dogfishes' are indeed appropriately named.

Certain sharks are more active than others, while some swim in a slow and idle manner; but all are capable of a sudden powerful dash, seizing whatever victim they come across. How then do they find their prey? We have seen that olfacto-gustation, perception of vibrations in the water, and vision all apparently assist the animal to locate its prey. But the relative importance of each of these senses and the exact part that each play in the various phases of the attack, from first awareness of the victim to the point at which it is gripped between the jaws, are still as yet little understood. Work is now being conducted along these lines and there is no doubt that interesting and useful conclusions will emerge (especially with regard to shark attacks on swimmers). Lineaweaver & Backus (1970) have concluded that as a general rule shark hearing operates at distances of some 1000's of yards from the source, the sense of smell at some 100's of yards, the lateral line canals and free neuromasts at about 100 feet, vision at about 50 feet in the most favourable circumstances, the ampullae of Lorenzini at a matter of only a few inches and finally taste only on direct contact.

According to divers who work in shark-infested waters, white or light colours are reputed to attract sharks. In the Antilles, Negro divers blacken the palms of their hands and soles of their feet (i.e. the light parts of their bodies) when they work in areas where sharks are known to be dangerous. It is to this practice that they attribute an almost total lack of accidents. Again, the Greek divers on the west coast of Florida wear dark colours for diving, and at the sight of a shark, tuck their bare hands under their armpits. Bernard Moitessier, the lone sailor, and also Henry de Monfreid (*Secrets of the Red Sea*) bear witness to this practice, which we shall discuss more fully in the section devoted to Man-eaters.

Nothing is more unpredictable than a shark's behaviour in face of food. This seems to be true of all fishes taken on a hook, and while it is agreed that hunger plays a dominant role in determining whether a fish will bite, yet there seem to be other factors also. With sharks, one never knows what will happen. Often a shark will approach the bait rather nonchalantly, sniffing at it, butting it with its snout, advancing and then retreating. The fisherman, watching all this, thinks, 'It isn't hungry . . . it has already fed . . . come on, bite!' Then, with an air of seeming infinite regret, the shark takes the bait; the fisherman strikes, brings it to gaff, hauls it aboard, cuts it open and finds a completely empty stomach. On other occasions or perhaps a little later on, another shark approaches and with a rush falls greedily on the bait, swallowing it at a gulp. 'Glutton,' thinks the fisherman, 'when did you last eat?' But this time the stomach is distended, stuffed full of fish heads and vertebrae. Stewart Springer (1967), citing such cases as his reason for suspecting that hunger is not very useful in describing a shark's urge to feed, concluded that 'I find no indication, however, that the kind of internal drive that men know as hunger operates or even exists for sharks'. Much of shark feeding behaviour thus remains baffling at present.

Amongst the popular misconceptions concerning sharks, perhaps the most widespread is that they are obliged to turn on their sides in order to seize their prey since their mouths are on the undersides of their heads (but nearly terminal in the Whale Shark). This formula rarely fails to appear in those adventure stories which involve an episode relating to shark attacks. Aristotle himself comments on this supposed habit.

Nature has thus arranged it, not only in order to preserve other animals, since thanks to the slowness of this obligatory movement other fishes have time to save themselves [from the sharks] which are all carnivors, but it is also to blunt their excessive voracity, since they surely perish quickly if allowed to gorge themselves with food.

This is an example of Aristotle's belief in the inherent wisdom pervading nature's ways. Besides sharks, Aristotle stated that dolphins and whales were subjected to this obligatory turning of the body, since in these animals the mouth is also ventral (*History of Animals*, 3).

The question does not arise in whales, but it is quite true that the mouth is underneath in sharks, and at first sight the idea seems sound. But it is enough to study Plate 8 (upper picture), for example, to see that this Grey Shark can very easily, and without contortion, snap up fishes which are swimming at its own level or *below it*; and such are, in fact, the normal conditions, as observed both in aquaria and in nature. There are only two occasions when sharks are inconvenienced by the ventral position of their mouths.

(*a*) When the shark wishes to take a bait attached to a hook. At the moment of seizing the bait, the snout of the shark strikes the line and it is quite impossible for it to take the bait into its mouth (Figure 38, I, II).

(*b*) When a shark wants to seize its prey and the latter is floating at the surface, that is to say, *above* it (Figure 38, III). However, in this case, sharks have often been seen to thrust their snouts out of the water, moving obliquely against the food object until it is within the range of the jaws (Figure 38, III). This does not seem to imply any very strong inclination to

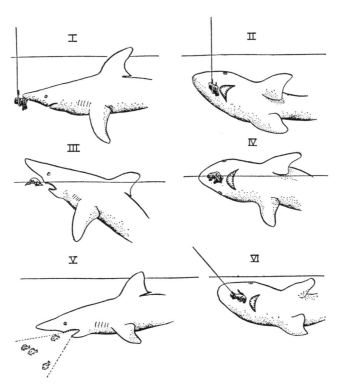

Fig. 38   Method of feeding in sharks.

turn on their sides. There is however the intermediate situation, when a bait is towed by a boat at a short distance below the surface, and on this occasion a shark may pivot its body to take the bait. These are unusual circumstances, and in the normal course of events sharks hunt prey which are on their own level or below them (Figure 38, V). This eliminates the need to perform an acrobatic roll every time they seize their prey.

If this popular belief in the roll performed by sharks is widespread, it is no doubt because the two exceptional cases when sharks do precisely this manœuvre are those observed from the deck of a ship or from the height of a jetty or pier. Men who frequently line fish for sharks cannot fail to notice this atypical movement of the fish at the moment when it takes the hook, and naturally will assume that this exceptional behaviour is in fact the normal one.

One is never told that skates and rays carry out this rolling movement and yet these relatives of the sharks have mouths which are even more ventral in position. The same thing applies to the Sawfishes (*Pristis*) and the Guitar fishes (*Rhinobatis*, etc). All of these fishes habitually feed on prey found on the bottom, or at least below themselves, seizing the prey without difficulty while still maintaining a perfectly horizontal position. However, if a ray, for example, decides to strike at a hook which is not lying on the bottom, it must of necessity tip its body to one side in a movement even more accentuated than in a shark.

In conclusion, it can be said that the numerous observations on the behaviour of sharks in captivity (by Gilbert, Davies, Eugenie Clark, and so on) amply confirm that an obligatory rolling of sharks to seize their prey is one of the many traditional misconceptions concerning the habits of these fishes.

The customary food of sharks encompasses almost all the living creatures found in the sea, from the surface to the bottom: fishes, crustaceans, molluscs, cetaceans, and so on. Neither do sharks disdain full cannibalism, that is to say, feeding on members of their *own* species, as well as on sharks of other species, often on a large scale. Cannibalism is most often found in sharks that have fed on their less fortunate companions entangled in nets. Russell Coles (1919), for example, recorded a Hammerhead of nearly 14 feet that had eaten most or all of six others of the same species (two swallowed whole) from Coles' net. Under such circumstances, however, natural checks to cannibalism (through visual or other recognition, behaviour, etc) are perhaps obliterated. Rays are also acceptable. With regard to 'man-eaters', more will be said anon (p. 107). Nevertheless, it has been found that certain species of shark appear to show a marked predilection for one particular fish or another. Thus, Coles (1919) reported that, in the shark fishery of Cape Lookout, North Carolina, the Hammerhead Sharks only went for Spanish Mackerel (*Scomberomorus maculatus*), scombroid fishes which grow to a length of about 2½ feet and are abundant in those waters. The same author noticed that older Hammerheads fed on rays of the genus *Dasyatis* and also on members of their own species. These observations are interesting, but generally speaking sharks do not always have the chance of exercising such a choice of diet and their stomachs often show a much more eclectic taste.

Here are some actual examples of the food found in the stomachs of various species of shark.

Nurse Shark (*Ginglymostoma cirratum*): prawns, lobsters, sleevefish, cuttlefish, sea urchin and some small unidentified fishes.

Cub or Bull Shark (*Carcharhinus leucas*): pieces of shark (probably *C. limbatus*), fragments of ray (almost certainly *Mobula*), shads, crabs, mackerel, the fin of a porpoise.

Tiger Shark (*Galeocerdo cuvieri*): head of a porpoise, a small Hammerhead Shark, a large but unidentifiable shark cut into seven or eight pieces, a large fragment of turtle. In another specimen of Tiger Shark: a complete Hammerhead of 5 feet length, large fragments of a turtle (*Thalassochelys caretta*), crabs, mackerel, and pieces of porpoise and unidentifiable sharks.

Sharp-nosed Shark (*Scoliodon terraeovae*) from the west coast of Africa: cuttlefish.

Mako Shark (*Isurus oxyrinchus*): a number of Bluefish (*Temnodon saltator = Pomatomus saltatrix*).

Dusky Shark (*Carcharhinus obscurus*) from the west coast of Africa: a complete small ray (*Dasyatis*), skull of a large unidentifiable bony fish.

Hammerhead Shark (*Sphyrna zygaena*): Menhaden (*Brevoortia*, a genus of shadlike fishes), mackerel, cephalopods, crabs and various other crustaceans.

Finally, Irving A. Field (1906) found in Smooth Hounds (*Mustelus canis*) caught by him in the summer of 1904 at the Woods Hole laboratories, Massachussetts, that 16 per cent contained the remains of lobsters, 34·7 per cent contained crabs, and 20·1 per cent contained spider crabs.

To sum up, it is perhaps truer to say that the stomach contents of sharks give a good indication of the marine fauna occurring in any specific area; sharks are probably less selective than Coles indicates, since one can find, for example, the remains of both pelagic surface-swimmers and bottom-living animals in the stomach of the same Hammerhead Shark.

LACY

Rays are frequently preyed on by sharks, particularly Stingrays (*Dasyatis*), Eagle Rays (*Myliobatis*), and Cow-nosed Rays (*Rhinoptera*). Stingrays have a barbed spine or 'sting' at the base of the tail which is a formidable means of defence but one which nonetheless does not seem to render them immune from attack by sharks. One often finds in the mouth of sharks or even in the jaws themselves, the spines of rays deeply embedded in the skin or sometimes actually passing through the cartilage of the jaw. Sharks do not seem to be unduly bothered by these spines. E. W. Gudger (1907) cites the case of a Hammerhead Shark which had fifty-four such spines around or inside its mouth, plus four spines in the pectoral fins which had come from Sea Catfishes (*Arius* sp.). It is well known that Hammerheads have a particular liking for rays, although this applies to other sharks also. In fact, one of the best baits for sharks is the flesh of a ray.

Fishes eaten by sharks are often found whole in the stomach. They are only cut when they are too large to be accommodated in the stomach whole or when, in the course of a struggle, it is necessary to cut them up to prevent them from escaping. Side by side with specimens of the herringlike fishes *Sardinella* and *Ethmalosa*, I have found other individuals in the stomachs of sharks which have distinct bite marks but have not been actually severed.

A list of stomach contents of sharks drawn up from fishery records does not perhaps give a good picture of the normal feeding habits of these animals in nature since net-caught sharks have the opportunity of attacking other fishes caught in the net and they rarely miss the chance. There are numerous cases of sharks being caught in nets and being partly devoured by their companions still at liberty, and fishery records alone would give the impression that this form of cannibalism is more common than is really the case. It is indeed common enough for large sharks to avail themselves of smaller ones; but it is much rarer to find line- or harpoon-caught sharks far from a fishery with large pieces of flesh taken from big sharks, whereas this is frequently true of those caught by net fisheries.

The search for prey is not always made at random. We have seen that the Thresher (*Alopias*) is considered a hunter, sometimes working in groups suggesting concerted action. R. J. Coles (1915) reported that Sand Sharks (*Odontaspis taurus*) are capable of indulging in manœuvres on a grand scale. Thus, he claims to have seen a hundred of these sharks encircling a shoal of the abundant tropical Atlantic Bluefish (*Pomatomus saltatrix*), driving them into shallow water and then charging into the middle of this boiling mass, a description which recalls accounts of the Thresher. On another occasion, in July 1914, the same author saw a large group of about two hundred Sand Sharks attack a netful of Bluefish, naturally destroying the net in the process.

However, these observations do not actually prove the existence of a predetermined plan on the part of the predators.

Another interesting observation was made by Harvey Bullis (1961), who was puzzled by the presence of 5 to 15 lb tunas in the stomachs of White-tip Oceanic Sharks (*Carcharhinus longimanus*), a lethargic species which would seem unlikely to be able to catch the fast tunas. During a cruise of the *Oregon* a little north of the Virgin Islands, Bullis noticed tuna shoals frenziedly attacking schools of small sardines. Amongst the tuna were many sharks of 3 to 6 feet 'swimming slowly in a rather erratic, sinuous course [each] with its snout protruding from the water, its mouth wide open at just about the surface level'. Bullis concluded that the sharks were waiting for tuna to swim or leap right into their mouths. A rather similar activity has been observed for the Whale Shark (*Rhincodon typus*), a species that feeds mainly on plankton but will also take small squids and fishes. Stewart Springer (1957) cited an observation from another *Oregon* cruise in which Whale Sharks were seen with their heads at or above the surface rising and sinking so that water and presumably small fishes poured into their open mouths. Schools of Blackfin Tuna (*Thunnus atlanticus*) were also after the small fishes and Springer saw several of them leap right into the mouths of the Whale Sharks, possibly to be swallowed.

Identification of stomach contents is not always easy. Frequently one merely finds a kind of mush containing vertebrae, skulls and other skeletal elements, mostly from bony fishes.

With regard to the actual mechanism of digestion, this poses a rather curious problem which, it would seem, has yet to be elucidated. As Coppleson (1962) has put it, a shark's stomach can apparently not only digest food, but on other occasions it can also hold and preserve food undigested for long periods, which at first sight seems to be a contradiction but is actually the case. The gastric juices in sharks are considered to be highly active, resulting in a very rapid process of digestion. Thus, off the west coast of Africa I have caught a Dusky Shark (*Carcharhinus obscurus*) which had part swallowed a small Hammerhead. However, it had not had time to swallow it completely and the tail of the latter was still between the jaws of the Dusky Shark and sticking partly out of the mouth. On dissection, I found that the whole of the posterior part of the Hammerhead lying within the buccal cavity and the entrance to the oesophagus, was still intact, while the head, now lodged in the stomach, had already been subjected to the processes of digestion to such an extent that it was almost unrecognizable.

Against this, there are the many examples cited by Coppleson (1962) of the undigested articles found in the stomachs of sharks. Perhaps the most striking example of this is the observation made by Sir Edward Hallstrom, chairman of the Taronga Park Trust in Sydney, on a Tiger Shark placed in a large pool at the Taronga Park Zoo on 23 August 1950. The shark died a month later, on 23 September, and at the autopsy:

> There was found in its stomach – whether it was a reserve compartment or a portion closed off I am unable to say – two dolphins about four feet long in a perfect state of preservation. These two dolphins were probably freshly taken by the shark before its capture but how they remained in the stomach uninjured and whilst other food was being regurgitated is a problem to which I am unable to give the answer.

Sir Edward's conclusion was quite categorical: 'The shark died of dolphinitis.'

Coppleson (1962) gives other incontestable examples which show that 'human remains appear capable of remaining for days and even weeks undigested in a shark's stomach'. In particular, there is a case of a young woman whose left arm was taken off by a shark which was then caught five days later. The arm was still in the stomach and 'showed few signs of digestion'. This is merely one of a number of cases of the same type. There is the well-known affair which came to be called the 'Shark Arm Murder' in Sydney. Here, a man's arm remained in the stomach of a shark for eight days at the very least and eighteen days at the most without being digested: a tattoo mark on the forearm was still perfectly visible and indeed was the principal means by which the victim was identified.

Records like these are troublesome, for the gastric juices in sharks are composed of mucus together with a secretion containing essentially pepsin and free hydrochloric acid (Bertin 1958b, Bernard 1952). The acidity of these juices is very high in sharks and rays, with an average of 1–2 per cent, but in exceptional cases (i.e. dogfishes of the genus *Scyliorhinus*) it may be as high as 15 per cent. In bony fishes on the other hand, the situation is quite different. The acidity of the stomach is much lower, and in certain cases the gastric juices may be neutral or even alkaline. In one and the same fish, however, the pH (acidity) of the gastric juices may alter according to the circumstances, i.e. depending on the nature and amount of food in the stomach, etc. As a general rule, digestion in fishes is very slow, no doubt a corollary of the low temperatures under which it proceeds. Periods of 2 to 6 days for the digestion of a meal have been recorded, while the highest figure for a dogfish (*Scyliorhinus*) was no less than 18 days. Naturally, the type of food is also a factor which must be taken into account. It has been found for example that a Rainbow Trout (*Salmo gairdneri*) will digest the flesh of fishes in 48 hours, but that it takes 72 hours to digest horseflesh. Should one thus conclude that the flesh of mammals is digested more slowly by fishes than is the flesh of other fishes? The observation cited earlier regarding the shark at the Taronga Zoo might appear to confirm this. Unfortunately in that particular case there is a little confusion over the word 'dolphin'. Was it a fish that was meant, that is to say, the Dolphin *Coryphaena hippurus*, or was it a mammal, a member of the family Delphinidae? The text gives no clue. In view of the length stated for the two dolphins (4 feet long), however, it seems more likely that it was the fish *Coryphaena*.

Sharks do not always confine themselves to prey which is edible. Very frequently they swallow quantities of odd things, and these are sufficiently striking for inventories to appear in the press. Some such lists are classic by now. For example, the stomach of a Grey Shark (*Carcharhinus*) of about 12 feet in length and caught near Port Jackson in Australia, was reported to contain 8 legs of mutton, half a ham, the hind quarters of a pig, the front half of a dog, the head and neck encircled with rope, 135 kg of horseflesh, a ship's scraper and a piece of sacking.

On 16 January 1948, Mr Couard, the director of the fisheries at Joal in Senegal, caught a Tiger Shark of about 500 lbs in the stomach of which he found a native tom-tom (Budker, 1948). I was able to examine this instrument on the spot. It was 10¾ inches high and its greatest diameter was just over 9¾ inches and it weighed 13½ lbs. It was made from Bimb wood (*Cordyna africana* [Lour]) and around the perimeter were wooden pegs to secure the skin to the drum. The skin itself had disappeared, presumably digested. At the bottom of the drum there was a compact mass of shark vertebrae, the remains of skeletons of bony fishes, some shells, sand, etc. The stomach itself showed strong traces of erosion due no doubt to chafing by the sharp edges of the drum and the wooden pegs. The drum had evidently been in the stomach of the Tiger Shark for some time, probably causing considerable discomfort.

Another Tiger Shark, of 660 lbs, caught on 11 March 1948 between Joal and Sangomar in Senegal, had in its stomach a fragment of human foot measuring 7 inches in length. The skin had been macerated in such a way that it was impossible to determine whether the foot had come from a European or an African. However, no accident of this nature had been reported in this area, but the shark may have come from some distance away (Budker, 1948).

Sharks which follow ships tend to seize anything that comes their way. In olden times, in the days of wooden sailing ships, when sailors did their washing they had a habit of rinsing their clothes by trailing them in the sea on the end of a line. Very often strong canvas trousers and shirts would disappear into the stomach of some shark which would also not stint itself on the salt bacon which the cook's boy might imprudently hang over the side to de-salt. Many an object falls overboard, whether by design or accident, and may later be retrieved from a shark's stomach. One can quote cases of sail canvas, the skin of a buffalo, tow, ends of rope, a cask of nails, a chest containing 'millions of pearls and jewels', and so on. In 1942, it was reported that the *La Junon*, a trawler from the port of Royan, caught a Blue Shark of six feet in length, and the trawler-men discovered 'in the entrails of this monster' a bottle of old and quite excellent Madeira. Further examples of stomach contents are given in Chapter 5.

One of the most colourful stories of this kind is the one often cited in shark books and apparently well attested. It took place in 1799 and concerned an American brig, the *Nancy*, under the command of Thomas Burggs, and two British ships, the *Sparrow* and the *Ferret*, under Lieut Hugh Wylie and Lieut Michael Filton respectively.

In the eighteenth century an American privateer was chased by a British man-of-war in the Caribbean Sea, and finding escape impossible, the Yankee skipper threw his ship's papers overboard. The privateer was captured and taken into Port Royal, Jamaica, and the captain was there placed on trial for his life. As there was no documentary evidence against him he was about to be discharged when another British vessel arrived in port. The captain of this cruiser reported that when off the coast of Haiti a shark had been captured, and that when opened the privateer's papers had been found in the stomach. The papers thus marvellously recovered were taken into court, and solely on the evidence which they afforded the captain and crew of the privateer were condemned. The original papers were preserved and placed on exhibition in the Institute of Jamaica in Kingston, where the 'shark's papers', as they were called, have always been an object of great interest. (Signed) A. Hyatt Verrill, New York, Nov. 20, 1915.

This case is not, however, unique. In 1915, certain documents, thrown into the harbour at Pernambuco (now Recife) in Brazil, were later recovered from the stomach of a shark and were subsequently used by the Brazilian Government in the course of some proceedings (the nature of which is not, however, recorded). McCormick (1963) describes the case in more detail.

One wonders what happens to all the inedible things that are eaten by sharks and which are not digested. Obviously, it is impossible for them to cope with a packet of tow or a tin box. On the other hand, such objects are too bulky to follow the normal course through the digestive tract and to pass through, for example, the duodenum or the spiral valve of the intestine. To rid themselves of such unwanted objects, it seems that sharks have a special ability, for it is often recorded that line- or net-caught sharks may come to the surface with the stomach everted through the mouth, the everted portion sometimes being quite large (projecting 9–12 inches). There is hardly a shark fisherman who has not noticed this at some time or another, and it was recorded as early as 1728 by Père Labat. This procedure would allow sharks to reject any indigestible objects, whether swallowed accidentally or not. The actual mechanism by which this is achieved has not been studied. One would think that the stomach – or the oesophagus – would, during this process of eversion, be prone to damage, and that those parts coming into contact with the teeth would risk abrasion. No doubt lesions caused in this way would heal quickly. At any rate, the phenomenon is very frequently reported and has been recorded in a number of species.

Finally, this account of the feeding of sharks would not be complete without mention of the phenomenon known as 'feeding frenzy'. Observations carried out at the Eniwetok Marine Biological Laboratory on Eniwetok Atoll (Marshall Islands) by Prof. Perry Gilbert, E.S.Hobson and Dr A. Tester have confirmed what has often been reported by shark fishermen. Thus, when many sharks are collected in a group round a prey, one may witness the sudden release of a kind of collective fury, a delirium of destruction which is reminiscent of what the Malays term *amok* and the Germans *beserker*. Gilbert (1962) aptly used the term 'feeding frenzy' to describe this state, in the course of which sharks attack indiscriminately and with great fury anything that comes their way – tin cans, wooden boxes, all are set on with equal determination. The attack over, the sharks return to their normal behaviour. It would indeed be useful to know the cause of such crises and whether they are manifested more often in some species than in others, and again, what is their frequency. One most interesting observation on a feeding frenzy is given by Nelson (1969). He and two colleagues were attempting to attract sharks in order to photograph some of the large reef species. They collected about 50 lbs of assorted fishes, together with a large Spotted Eagle Ray (*Aetobatus narinari*) with a wingspan of more than 5 feet. They slit the fishes to promote bleeding and left them in a heap on the bottom. It did not take long for the sharks to arrive. They included an 8-foot Hammerhead, a 6-foot Nurse Shark, another Hammerhead of 12 feet and a Tiger Shark of about the same size. While the divers were present, the sharks merely circled round, but when left alone the smaller Hammerhead 'turned in and snatched a fish from the bait pile. Then the larger Hammerhead came straight in, grabbed the dead eagle ray by one wing, and swam off with it, with the ray's body folded back over its head. About

15 metres (50 feet) away, the shark slowed down and shook the ray fiercely, tearing a large piece from it. Other sharks then dashed in to feed. As I watched, the frenzy developed and the sharks tore the remainder of the ray to pieces. In the hazy distance I could see a seething "ball" of shark bodies, pieces of ray, blood and sediment. I quickly returned to the safety of the boat.'

Current research on sharks held in captivity may throw more light on what releases this sudden frenzy, for it is certainly a most important aspect in relation to attacks on man.

Chapter 5

Man-eaters

'Guare! Voy le cy! O que tu es horrible et abhominable!
. . . Hoho! Diable Satanas, Leviathan!
Je ne te peux veoir, tant tu es ideux et detestable . . .'
(Rabelais, *Pantagruel*, Book IV, Ch. xxxiii)

Our felucca is moored at some distance from the shore off the Marine
Biological Station at Ghardaqa, whose grey buildings stand out sharply
against the yellow of the sand. Small waves lap against the sides of the boat;
all around us the Red Sea sparkles in the sunshine – deep blue paling to
silver. The 'Red Sea' can in fact be very blue indeed. On the horizon, to the
north-east, the Island of Shadwan sprawls its desolate bulk.

We fish. After trolling our lines for some hours between the outcrops of
coral we have thrown out the anchor and, with our lines paid out, we fish.
Above us, crystal azure, transparent and without equal, is the winter sky of
Egypt.

We catch some beautiful Groupers (*Epinephelus*), which are biting eagerly
and greedily. One feels the line suddenly spring to life. Quickly one must
strike and quicker still haul in the quivering line and snatch the fish from the
green freshness of the deep. In a shower of sparkling water the grouper
comes out of the sea, its huge mouth open on the hook, the gill-covers
dilated, the tail curved in a U, the fins expanded – a wonderful lustre of
marbled beige and black glinting in the sun. Let the identification of the
various species of grouper continue to perplex ichthyologists – for the
moment we fish in the incomparable morning light and how can one dwell
on such mundane matters?

Squatting on the gunwale, in a position which the rest of us would find
difficult, is the skipper of the felucca, the *Rahis*, Dakhil Allah Abdallah, who
is fishing also. He looks striking in his turban, like some kind of nautical
Haroun-al-Raschid. Something that Flaubert wrote comes to my mind:
the sight of a cornfield gladdens the heart of a philanthropist far more than
the sight of the Ocean, for agriculture embodies the best of honest motives.
But how pitiful is the ragged peasant compared to the noble sailor!

An observation which is valid also for the Red Sea, cornfields notwithstanding. . . .

The Director of the Laboratory, Dr H. A. F. Gohar, who had not forgotten my passion for sharks, asked while I was unhooking a fine grouper, 'You would prefer a shark, wouldn't you?'

'Certainly,' I replied, 'but this line would hardly hold a Tiger Shark, or even one of the smaller species, so we must content ourselves with groupers today . . .'

'Nevertheless, sharks never fail to appear round here. The Rahis was once bitten by one. Look . . .'

I approached the latter.

'Phew!'

Dakhil Allah Abdallah had extended a brown leg, thin and dried up, which bore down its length some paler marks, the scars of old and deep gashes.

'It was a long time ago. Some years now. The Rahis was over there, near Shadwan.'

He gestured towards the open water, where the island stood out in ochre against the blue of the sea and the sky.

'He was standing in the water. The shark suddenly rushed in to attack, biting deeply into his legs. See the scars . . .'

I saw that the other leg also bore clear marks of the teeth of the animal.

'The Rahis did not lose his head. He defended himself by digging his fingers into the shark's nostrils.'

'Nostrils? Surely you mean its eyes?'

'No, he told me the nostrils. The shark then left him alone and he was saved.'

'Was it a big one? What size was it, about?'

'He didn't have much time to take note of it. It all happened too quickly.'

Dakhil Allah Abdallah crossed his legs and resumed his former position, taking his line and casting it out with a precise and practised movement.

'Rahis, do you still hope to catch many more fish today?'

The reply came immediately and quietly.

'I will catch what Allah would like to send to me.'

I have transcribed here some notes taken down during a visit to the Red Sea, because they bear witness to the fact that a man was here attacked by a shark in shallow water. They also include a rather surprising fact: that the man disengaged himself by putting his fingers into the nostrils of the shark. It is not likely that this kind of thing would be effective in a struggle with a really large shark, and one wonders whether the assailant in this particular case was really bent on a mission of attack. Such paradoxical behaviour has led to some very exaggerated ideas. Some years ago there were certain naturalists who were convinced that sharks were in general inoffensive animals. One rather hair-brained ichthyologist even made a bet that he would, in front of witnesses, enter 'shark-infested waters' and, resolute in this belief, swim for several miles amongst the man-eaters, claiming that they would not attack him. Unfortunately, the story does not relate the location of the swim, nor does it tell us of the condition of the ichthyologist at the end of his experiment.

In opposition to this extreme and untenable view, one finds the equally extreme converse view, which usually finds expression in the following type of setting. A passenger boat pushes slowly through some tropical sea under a relentless sun. On deck, a well-travelled and evidently knowledgeable man is holding forth, surrounded by a circle of listeners.

'At this moment,' he pontificates, 'we are sailing through waters where, if by some mischance you should happen to fall overboard, it would be quite impossible for you to drown.'

The audience is intrigued. 'Really?' 'That's surely impossible,' and 'How do you make that out?' they chorus.

The knowledgeable man's face hardens momentarily. He narrows his eyes and says grimly, 'Sharks.'

The effect of this one word, coupled with a slight tightening of the line of the jaw, is infallible. The female passengers shudder, the men look bravely out across the sea. And for all of them, the ship is suddenly surrounded by a mass of thrashing monsters, snuffling at human flesh, ready to devour it without hesitation, ready to seize anybody unfortunate enough to fall overboard before they have even had time to gulp sea water. . . .

Of the two extreme views, one can without hesitation reject the first. With regard to the second, which paints the dangers of shark attack in somewhat excessive terms, it has for a long time been taken as Gospel Truth. However, the experience accumulated by skin-divers in the last twenty years together with marine biological research in that period, enables us to approach the problem with more scientific certainty.

Obviously it is absurd to think that an animal that is capable of devouring the skin of a buffalo, or of attacking a porpoise or a seal or a swordfish, would not occasionally take a man in the water. On the other hand it would be ridiculous to think that sharks go for human flesh in preference to any other kind of food which they may encounter. Such a diet would end in sheer starvation since opportunities for eating *Homo sapiens* are comparatively rare, and a large White Shark for example would require a quantity well beyond anything that would in fact be available. For sharks, man-eating can at best be only an accidental supplement resulting from fortuitous circumstances, for the shark, that is!

Nevertheless, the tradition persists, expressed in the simple statement that sharks are filthy, man-eating beasts. Pliny, for example, in Book 9 of his *Natural History*, gives a pathetic description of the dangers of *'canicules'* (that is to say, dogfishes or sharks) to the sponge fishermen. Thus he speaks of

the cruel battle they have to wage against the *canicules*; the latter make for the groin, the heels, and for all the whitest parts of the body. The only way to deal with this is to go straight for them and frighten them, since *they fear man no less than he fears them*. At the bottom of the sea the advantage is equal, but once at the surface, the diver has much to fear since, in order to leave the water, he must make movements which are the reverse of advancing upon his enemy. He needs all the resources of his companions, who pull on the ropes attached to his arms. First of all they pull him up very slowly; but when he gets close to the boat, if they did not pull him in quickly he would be devoured by the monster. Often, when he is already out of the water, he is even snatched from their hands, unless he contributes to their efforts and rolls his body into a ball. During this time the others threaten the *canicule* with a trident, but the shark instinctively lies underneath the boat. One thus takes the greatest care to look out for this deadly animal.

In this passage one finds, besides certain observations which I will deal with later, a tradition which appears to have persisted in the Mediterranean area right up to the 18th century amongst the men plying small coastal vessels, who dreaded sharks. According to common belief, a shark only attacked a man if pressed by hunger, and most of the time it was enough to appease it by throwing it some bread. 'If that was not enough, there was only one thing to do. By means of a rope, a member of the crew was lowered to the surface of the water: his unselfish act was rewarded provided that he looked at the monster with a menacing air. Otherwise the latter would seize hold on the boat with its teeth, placing both the boat and the sailors in danger.'

This apparent blend of ferocity and timidity is surprising, and one doubts the efficacy of a mere 'look', however menacing, to put to flight a hungry shark. This method is certainly less effective than that of the Rahis at Ghardaqa. But it is interesting to find that in Pliny's opinion the *canicules* are as frightened of men as men are of them. We shall see further on more recent and equally unexpected evidence of the timid nature of sharks, so apparently out of keeping with the ancient image of 'tigers of the sea'.

However, this was not Rondelet's (1558) opinion. When speaking of the inoffensive Tope (*Galeorhinus galeus*), he mentions the

great battle that this fish is wont to have with men, which is still today feared by the fishermen and those who live by the sea shore. This fish so longs to wound men in the thighs, the groin, the heels, or any exposed part, that it some-times leaps on to dry land when it sees men with bare legs near the water, which is done by no other dogfish but the Tope, nor is there any other which has a pillow-slip (*taie*) on the eyes but this one.

The 'pillow-slip on the eyes' evidently refers to a nictitating membrane, which in fact the Tope possesses. Such aggressive behaviour in a dogfish, which is generally considered to be most peaceable, seems to show that Rondelet is quite ready to attribute to sharks ('despicable to look at and rough, all covered with harsh skin') the most belligerent of instincts. And he does not stop there. His 'Chien de mer bleu' (the Blue Shark) has, accord-ing to Rondelet 'such daring against men, like the preceding [i.e. the Tope], that it too hankers after the flesh of humans. I have seen the experience of a lackey who walked along the beach and was followed for some time by this fish, and it did not hesitate to take him by the legs and kill the said lackey.'

Actually, there are a few claims of sharks leaping out of the water and seizing men who are walking along the shore. The French naturalist Lacepède (1798) cites the case of a shark which succeeded in tearing limb from limb the corpse of a Negro which had been hung more than eighteen feet above the surface of the water; this represents a quite astonishing athletic performance for an animal so large and heavy. If true, this record probably relates to the Mako Shark (*Isurus oxyrinchus*), a species noted for its ability to leap clean out of the water, reputedly to a height of 15 to 20 feet. Lacepède himself did not witness this, but quoted it from the manuscripts of the naturalist Philibert Commerson, who had sailed round the world with Bougainville. Still, it is more reasonable than the idea of a shark hunting a man along a beach (which brings to mind Alice's puzzlement at the anklets round the feet of the Knight's horse. 'To guard against the bites of sharks,' the Knight replied. 'It's an invention of my own.').

The Great White Shark (*Carcharodon carcharias*) made a deep impression on Rondelet, who called it the *Lamie*. He referred to one 'so large that when laid on a cart it could scarcely be pulled by two horses. I have seen a medium-sized Lamie weighing 1000 lbs. The stomach and gullet are wonderfully large and spacious. Extremely glutonous, it devours men whole, as is known from experience, since at Nice and at Marseilles they have on occasion caught Lamies in whose stomachs were whole men in armour.' At the time Rondelet was writing, that is to say in the first half of the 16th century, men still wore armour – but very much heavier than in the preceding century as it was more often put to the test. Thus, a fully armoured man would represent a pretty cumbersome and heavy prey which could only be accommodated by a stomach of unusual proportions. At Marseilles again, Rondelet assures us that he found in the stomach of a shark 'two tunny and a fully-clothed sailor'; another shark contained 'a soldier with his sword'. Again, Müller and Henle (1838–41) claimed that a 'shark of 750 kg [1650 lbs] captured near the Isles of Sainte Marguerite contained a complete horse'. John Barrow saw, in a 'Chien de mer' harpooned near the island of Java 'a large number of bones, some fragments of a large turtle, a head of a cow buffalo and a calf'. To his previous claim, Rondelet adds the following:

> For this great voracity of Lamies, I believe that they call certain Lamies witches, which have a great desire to eat human flesh, attracting by every trick of pleasure and ribaldry good-looking young men, afterwards eating them. I have seen a Lamie at Saintonge with a throat so big that a large and fat man could easily enter it, such that if one held the mouth open dogs could easily go inside to eat what they might find in the stomach.

Witchcraft, together with well-documented details, are happily mingled in the observations of this ancient author. Although the name *Lamia* has also been used for a shark of the family Carcharhinidae, i.e. the Cub or Bull Shark (*Carcharhinus leucas*), it is certain that the *Lamie* that Rondelet refers to is the Great White Shark (*Carcharodon*), of which he had certainly seen some large specimens. Mythical and theological ideas have been engendered by these monstrous creatures. Incidentally, Müller and Henle (1838–41), in their work on the 'Plagiostomes', honoured Rondelet by calling this species after him (*Carcharodon rondeletti*, a name which is, however, predated by *C. carcharias* of Linnaeus).

It has been said that man-eaters show some discernment in their choice of victim. According to Père Labat (1728), the flesh of white men is less attractive than that of Negroes (and, in reference to a barracuda, that an Englishman is taken more readily than a Frenchman!). Such ideas were evidently commonly held at the time, for Sir Hans Sloane (1707) remarked that the barracuda feeds on 'Blacks, Dogs, and Horses, rather than on White men, when it can come at them in the water'. Lacepède (1798) sounds an indignant note when dealing with this subject, declaring vehemently:

> When white men and black men bathe together in the ocean, the black men, who smell more strongly than the white, are more susceptible to the ferocity of

sharks and are sacrificed first to these voracious animals, giving the white men time to escape their sharp jaws. To the shame of humanity, one is forced to believe that white men can still forget the sacred laws of Nature to the extent that when they go down to the water they station around themselves some unfortunate negroes to face the sharks.

In the days of the slave trade, the slave ships had a particular reputation for being followed by sharks, which the sailors claimed 'sensed' the presence of the Negroes packed on board. It was said also that sharks 'sensed' the presence of a dying man, and collected round a ship where men were on the point of death.

This speaks highly of both the olfactory acuity and the cunning of sharks. We have indeed seen that their olfacto-gustatory sense is particularly well developed. Tester (1963a), for example, showed that sharks are able to sense human blood in the minute proportion of 1 part dissolved in 10 to 100 million parts of sea water. Obviously this sense is quite inoperative for objects out of water. Supposing that a shark really was able to 'sense', first that there was a sick man on board, second that his illness was a grave one, and third that in the near future the ship would hove to in order to cast the dead man overboard . . . this would be to attribute to sharks a quite amazing medical and nautical knowledge!

In the tropics there was almost always in the wake of a sailing ship, one or more sharks ready to fall upon anything which was thrown overboard – including, of course, a clumsy or unlucky sailor. One can understand the feeling which would come over the crew of these ships when they saw the 'triangular fin' of their undesirable followers. Nevertheless, it has been noticed that sharks scarcely pay any attention to the body which is slid over the side, heavily weighted and slipping down to the depths in accordance with the simple and beautiful words: 'We therefore commit this body to the deep.'

Granted this it follows, however, that the slavers must have contributed in large measure to the keeping up of a taste for human flesh amongst sharks. The slaves were transported under the most revolting conditions – conditions which, to the shame of humanity, have been not only repeated but even exceeded by the Nazis when transporting political prisoners during the last war. The only difference is that, for the Nazis, the goods wagons took the place of the "'tween decks' where the 'Black Ivory' was stacked. One can only be struck – and sickened – by the complete similarity of the two procedures, separated by a hundred years (see for example the medical reports on Buchenwald by Dr Charles Richet, 1945).

Here, as in the case of the Nazi victims, the mortality rate was high. Those log books which have come down to us (for such compromising documents naturally do not figure in the official archives) bear witness to this. For example, here are some notes extracted from the journal of a slave trader who wrote of the trade between Mozambique and Bourbon in about 1828 (cited from Bertaut, 1837).

The trip was long and full of misfortune: the bloody flux carried off ten hundred heads; and in a sudden gust of wind we lost 10,000 piastres with [the loss of] fifty Negroes that we found suffocated in a day of tempest when we had to batten down the hatches. We threw all to the sea, and each officer lost so much per head: the sailors only cursed at this additional work; but thirty sinewy hands had soon thrown fifty corpses into the water. A good windfall for the sharks.

On the slave ships, it was not rare for revolts to break out. Bertaut (1837) studied the subject and gave details of one particular case. The miscreants were reprimanded with very great severity, while the ringleaders were executed on the spot and thrown into the water. 'They rent the waves with a large splash, and we saw how, in the distance, a group of sharks disputed over their prey.'

Finally, there is a telling phrase, commonplace and typical of that period: it became necessary to make a decision that the cargo should be thrown into the sea in order to save the ship, and this was done.

But in this case, the cargo was three hundred Negroes. This jettisoning of the cargo took place also when the slave traders, pursued by an observant man-of-war, were afraid of not being able to beat a swift enough retreat and having to submit to a formidable visit. Again, suicides were also frequent amongst the captives, some even jumping into the sea during a momentary inattentiveness on the part of their guards. Thus, the losses were great during the transport of the Negroes, and the sharks surely had their share – since their 'wickedness' knows no bounds. . . .

The old-fashioned whaling ships also attracted sharks, particularly at the time that the whale carcasses were cut up. This operation was at that time carried out alongside the ship, the whale being trussed and held by pulleys, lying in the water while the men cut off slabs of blubber and carried them to the boiler fitted up on deck. All around the ship would hang an oily cloud of debris and blood. The sharks would arrive in enormous shoals, which some authors have estimated to number many thousands, feasting and gorging themselves on the flesh and entrails of the whale, which at that time were not utilized, but merely thrown overboard. Some sharks, more audacious than the others, would even attack the body of the whale while it was secured to the ship, and men often had occasion to give them a blow with their 'blubber-spades', narrow scoops used for removing the blubber.

Somewhat similar scenes occur nowadays at the tropical whaling stations. Thus, at Port-Gentil during season 1949–51, the whales that were caught (mostly Humpbacks) were frequently attacked by sharks while they were being cut up alongside the ship *Jarama*. Many of the whales were so badly eaten as to render them useless, and the whalers fired guns in attempts to frighten off the unwelcome guests. The sharks were so abundant in the bay off Cap Lopez that a shark fishery was later established, and it operated throughout the whaling season. In the Antarctic it is different, for there the whaling industry uses huge factory ships, into which the whales are hoisted, and utilization of almost every part of the whale ensures that there is little left over. Furthermore, the icy waters of the Antarctic are practically empty of sharks.

In view of the evidence of the preceding pages, one might be led to think that there is nothing more dangerous than to fall into the open sea from a ship that is being escorted by sharks. But when such accidents happen, there is no set rule on what will occur. For example, on 15 May 1895, the steamship *Comorin* left Marseilles bound for Tonkin with 1500 troops on board belonging to various branches of the armed forces. Towards the end of the same month the ship was in the southern part of the Red Sea. Following a mechanical breakdown, it was only making four knots. One morning, at about eleven o'clock, a sailor was suddenly taken by a fit of madness and leapt overboard. A lifeguard (a regular sailor) cut the rope securing the life buoys, seized one and plunged over the side to help the stricken man. Because of the damage to the machinery, the *Comorin* was not able to stop, for fear of being unable to get underway again. The captain then put the helm about and went in circles while launching a lifeboat. Unfortunately, the latter was not in good order, the securing of one of the pulleys broke during the launching and the crew of the boat, about a dozen men, were precipitated into the sea. It was now essential to stop the ship and send another boat out to the rescue of the two men, whom the passengers could see quite distinctly clinging to the lifebuoy. There were numerous sharks swimming round the two men, but not one touched them although it was by now four hours that they had been in the water. Similarly, the crew of the lifeboat were also rescued without incident.

The Red Sea, especially the southern end, is particularly full of sharks; this area is even considered to be one of those where death by drowning *is* impossible. . . . But here are two men remaining in the water for *four hours*, clinging to a lifebuoy, that is to say, with the lower parts of their bodies submerged, while the 'Tigers of the Sea' prowled around them without doing the least harm. Moreover, the twelve sailors who fell into the water remained together and splashed around for some time, well exposed to attack, to the apparent indifference of the sharks whose behaviour (fortunately for the sailors) was quite the reverse of what is normally believed and expected.

One can only repeat what was said earlier in connection with shark fishing: *one can never tell what a shark is going to do.* The uncertainty is quite absolute. Doubtless, one could say that, in the case of the *Comorin*, perhaps there were no 'man-eaters' in the vicinity. However, this is not really an explanation since it fails to grasp the precise meaning of the term.

For the last twenty years, biologists, doctors, fishermen and skin-divers have delved into the problem of man-eaters. Some important conclusions have already emerged; others cannot fail to follow since this whole problem is being pursued relentlessly by numerous teams of workers who have first-hand experience of the factors involved, combining field studies with laboratory research. There are three countries in the forefront of this research: the United States, Australia and South Africa. All are well placed for this kind of work, having shark waters of one kind or another on their doorsteps.

It is not possible here to list all the details of the work in progress, nor all the results and research projects, but a brief outline can be given.

Above all, research is concentrated on finding out which species of shark are the most addicted to man-eating. For this purpose, sharks can be classified in the following way:

(1) Those which are well known as being inoffensive.

(2) Those which, notoriously, are considered dangerous.

(3) All other species, not particularly prone to eating human flesh, but which are perfectly capable, should the circumstances arise, of taking a bite out of a bather or a man who has fallen into the water.

It must be clearly understood that we are here referring to *unprovoked* attacks on men by sharks – this is most important. In the first category then, one can include the two giants, the Whale Shark and the Basking Shark, both of which are peaceable plankton feeders and of these one has nothing to fear provided that one does not pick a quarrel. Garrick and Schultz (1963) report two cases of provoked attacks on boats, both occurring off Scotland. In each case it was merely defensive reflex on the part of the shark. There are also certain other sharks which, because of their small size, must be classed in the category of 'inoffensive species', although they can attack if handled without due care.

In the second category, it is not always easy to draw the line between those which *are* dangerous and those which are *perhaps* dangerous. Captain Cousteau, in his well-known book *The Silent World* (1953), gives a striking example of this.

During an encounter with a shark in the Cape Verde Islands, at a distance of 40 feet there appeared from the grey haze the lead-white bulk of a 25-foot *Carcharodon carcharias*, the only shark species that all specialists agree is a confirmed man-eater. Dumas, my bodyguard, closed in beside me. The brute was swimming lazily. Then the shark saw us. His reaction was the least conceivable one. In pure fright, the monster voided a cloud of excrement and departed at an incredible speed.

Captain Cousteau described this incident to me when he returned from his cruise. In commenting on it, he used the phrase common to all who have studied or have had dealings with sharks – *one never can tell what a shark is going to do*, a saying that cannot be repeated too often when dealing with the relation between sharks and men. The incident related by Captain Cousteau also shows that a species which is justly reputed to be ferocious and blood-thirsty, such as the White Shark – the man-eater *par excellence* – can show an unexpected and truly disconcerting timidity and cowardice.

Nevertheless, it must not be accepted blindly that all sharks with a bad reputation will behave as did Captain Cousteau's *Carcharodon*. There is a great deal of evidence to the contrary. For example, the Nurse Shark (*Ginglymostoma cirratum*) has long been classed as 'inoffensive'. Along the coasts of Florida the fishermen force these fishes into shallow waters, then leave them on the beach, throwing them back into the sea when they have been examined and measured, in due course, by naturalists. But, probing more deeply into the study of the behaviour of this apparently harmless species of shark, one finds to one's surprise, that it has been responsible for many attacks, a large number of which were quite unprovoked (Garrick and Schultz, 1963).

It is, therefore, wise to distinguish between those sharks which are aggressive and those which are not. Prudence is always necessary when dealing with any shark, dangerous or not. Circumstances, locality, and so on, play an important role, as also the habits of the sharks of the region. Alexander von Humboldt (1814) recorded that, at Le Guayra, a port close to Caracas, one had nothing to fear from sharks although they were plentiful in the harbour. On the other hand, amongst the islands opposite the coast of Caracas, the sharks were dangerous and blood-thirsty. I recall that, in one of his books, William Tatham tells of his astonishment at Charleston, South Carolina, on seeing a boy fall from a bowsprit and brought back on board again whole and safe in spite of the presence of two or three sharks in the spot where he fell.

Another incident is that related by Gudger (1941). Apparently, a sailor, seeing a shark at the surface alongside the ship, made a bet that he could jump on to the shark's back. Gudger did not take the bet but was assured that such disrespect for sharks was by no means unjustified.

When one compares sharks with the large terrestrial carnivores, it is always the tiger that comes to mind. Sharks are the 'Tigers of the Sea'. The very name 'tiger' suggests cruelty and voracity carried to their limits. There are three species of shark in particular which, by their vernacular names, conjure up an image of Shere Khan of the *Jungle Book*. First, *Rhincodon typus*, the Whale Shark, which around Acapulco in Mexico is named the 'Tiger of the Sea'; second, the Zebra Shark, *Stegostoma varium*, which Pierre Broussonet referred to as '*Tigre*', and which scientists have referred to as *Squalus tigrinus* (Pennant, 1769) or *Stegostoma tigrinum* (Günther, 1870); finally, there is the true Tiger Shark (*Galeocerdo cuvieri*).

One should note, however, that the reference to tigers is not based here on the habits of the sharks in question, but on their coloration. It is well established that the first two species are quite harmless. The third has, however, a vicious reputation and is classed amongst the man-eaters, but again, its name derives from its very tigerlike appearance in the young fishes. With growth, this colour pattern fades until in older individuals it almost disappears, leaving a uniform dark grey colour with some blackish markings on the flanks faintly recalling the tiger stripes of the juvenile. The same thing happens in other species, notably in the Zebra Shark (*Stegostoma*) and the Nurse Sharks (*Ginglymostoma*).

For many years – one can say for many centuries – there has been only sparse and fragmentary evidence regarding the problem of the relationship of sharks to men, and then often imprecise and unreliable. Fortunately, thanks to research undertaken in recent years, a clearer picture is beginning to emerge.

Notoriously dangerous sharks

It is not always easy to identify the species of shark responsible for a particular attack, especially as there is a wide choice amongst the 250 or so species known. In fact, Garrick and Schultz (1963) report that only 27 of these species are definitely known to have been responsible for unprovoked attacks on men or boats (the latter being very rare). The classic man-eater (which is one of its vernacular names) is *Carcharodon carcharias*, the Great

White Shark, White Shark or White Pointer (Plate 7 and Figure 2d). This is a pelagic species, but one which sometimes comes close inshore, where its presence is made known by accidents which are generally very serious. It is above all a 'lone-wolf' and is never found in schools – fortunately! It has a world-wide range, in tropical and temperate waters, reaching as far north as the British Isles (but no records more recent than the middle of the last century). Records from the Mediterranean and from Australia suggest that it regularly migrates with the seasons. Normally it reaches about 20 feet in length. The largest specimen known, whose jaws are preserved in the Natural History Museum in London, measured 36 feet 6 inches in length, undoubtedly a giant individual. Its teeth measure 3 inches in length (Norman and Fraser, 1948). Even a specimen of 20 feet, with jaws lined with triangular cutting teeth, is a creature one would not care to meet. In the Paris Museum there is an individual of 17 feet 4 inches and this too is an imposing monster. However, this is nothing in comparison with the truly gigantic *Carcharodon megalodon* of Tertiary times, a species now extinct but known from its enormous fossil teeth (Plate 4). Judging by the size of their teeth, these leviathans must have approached the size of a large whale.

The incident related by Captain Cousteau must be counted as a happy exception. Thus 'more attacks on men and boats have been accredited to the White Shark than to any other species' according to Garrick and Schultz (1963), and the list of all such attacks, many fatal, of this mainly tropical species, would indeed be lengthy. The White Shark does occur, however, in temperate waters.

In the matter of aggressiveness, the prize undoubtedly goes to the White Shark, but thereafter it becomes much more difficult to establish a gradient of aggressiveness. A list of those species to which unprovoked attacks can be attributed runs the risk of being incomplete, but a few of the better known can be mentioned here.

The Mako Shark – a Maori name – (*Isurus oxyrinchus*), known also as the Blue Pointer, Bonito Shark or Sharp-nosed Mackerel Shark, is a second man-eater with a curious predilection for attacking boats (Plate 5 and Figure 3a). Another well-known species is the Tiger Shark (*Galeocerdo cuvieri*), which is considered second only to the White Shark for ferocity (Figure 5c). Regarding the various species of Hammerhead, only three reach a size rendering them dangerous. The extraordinary shape of the Hammerhead gives it a rather forbidding, even repulsive appearance; one can expect no good from such an odd-looking creature and it has always been considered a notorious man-eater. However, the Hammerhead's record, although including incontestably unprovoked attacks, is not particularly bad, and in fact its teeth are noticeably feeble in comparison with those of the White Shark or the Tiger Shark. The Blue Shark (*Prionace glauca*) is also held to be responsible for many of the accidents which occur in open waters. It is a pelagic species, often accompanying ships, and is considered by sailors to be a definite man-eater. But study of statistics shows that it is probably not so bad as its reputation would suggest. Garrick and Schultz (1963) have cited ten attacks, of which three were against boats and one was provoked; others were a question of 'unauthoritative identification'.

On the other hand, the reverse may be the case for one most abundant pelagic shark, the White-tip Oceanic Shark (*Carcharhinus longimanus*). Spending almost all its time in open waters, its habits are poorly known, and if it is accused of being a man-eater, the evidence for this is rare. It was a White-tip Shark which attacked Captain Cousteau in open water off the Cape Verde islands, and again it was a White-tip Shark which followed Alain Bombard's tiny inflatable dinghy for some time during his famous trip across the Atlantic. Lineaweaver & Backus (1970) quote an account by John Randall of an experience off Puerto Rico. Circled by a White-tip Shark, Randall made an aggressive gesture towards it but, unlike the common sharks of the Pacific, this one did not swim away and Randall was thankful to reach the safety of a canoe. The White-tip is well known for its persistence. However, in the family Carcharhinidae, there are many species which have 'something on their conscience'. For example, the Bull Shark (*Carcharhinus leucas*) and many related species of the genus *Carcharhinus*, as also the Lemon Shark (*Negaprion brevirostris*), are probably not completely innocent. Finally, under the name 'whalers', there are the many Australian species of Carcharhinidae, of which a number are dangerous. Dr Gilbert Whitley (1963), by the way, has given the following explanation of the way in which these Australian sharks got this name. 'The term *whaler* for a shark goes back to the days when there was a whaling industry at Twofold Bay, New South Wales, in the 1840s when these sharks were observed to attack the carcasses of whales being towed into port. They are still a nuisance to whalemen in eastern and western Australia.' To which one can add that they are just as troublesome in other parts of the world where there are whaling stations.

Things that attract sharks

We return now to the question of what impulse drives a shark to attack a man. Hunger, naturally, is a factor. Sharks are out and out carnivores and the search for prey must be their constant objective. Nevertheless, one can see that certain of them show a curious propensity for attacking boats. The Mako in particular, seems to be particularly addicted to this type of aggressiveness, although it is known too in the Tiger Shark and the Whale Shark, if not to the same extent. What can it be that impels a shark to attack an object so inedible as the hull of a boat? It is unlikely that its sensory equipment, olfactory or otherwise, persuades it that it has chanced on a good prey to eat, for this type of encounter often ends badly for the shark. It may leave some teeth implanted in the wood or else knock itself senseless on impact, for sharks have been observed to swim headlong and at full speed straight into a boat, damaging rigs and planking. In his excellent book *Shark Attack*, Dr Coppleson (1962) devotes a whole chapter to this kind of aggression and he makes many most interesting observations.

(1) It seems that, at least along the Australian coasts, attacks on boats take place in areas where attacks on bathers are practically unknown and where, however, the White Shark abounds.

(2) It is believed that, above all, it is the fishing boats which attract the sharks because of the presence of fish on the ends of lines or even on board (which is all the more strange since the fishes which have been caught are out of the water and sharks must thus have especially good 'noses' to detect them). But Dr Coppleson records that racing skiffs, canoes and even a racing eight have all been the objects of characteristic attacks. Such cases are frequent, sharks going for the blades of the oars or even jumping out of the water as if to try to get on board – all this has been observed.

D.S.Stead (1906), writing on shark attacks on small boats, has expressed the following views:

It is clear that these are not always attacks in the proper meaning of the word. Reviewing a considerable number of cases that have come under my notice in the last fifty years or so, and after closely studying a number of others from various records, I would say that these seem to fall into three general categories:

(1) Boats are fishing at sea, with sharks taking the fish (especially snappers) off hooks. The sharks (chiefly Blue Pointer or Mako) impetuously dash up to the surface, sometimes shoot out of the water, and occasionally collide with the bottom of the boat. (One actually leaped right into the boat off the New South Wales coast on one occasion.) Under such circumstances, boats have been smashed or upset and their occupants cast into the water; but though the sharks were all around the swimming men, they did not attack them.

(2) Leaky or old fishing boats, in which fish are stacked, and the gurry from the fish was leaking into the water and into the wake of the boat.

(3) Small launches with tiny whirling propellers which attracted the actual

attack of the shark, but there was no further attack when the propeller was stopped, and none on the man or men if thrown into the water.

In short, I would say that there is no evidence whatever that any attack on a fishing boat by a shark has been made to get the man or men in it.

One may well question whether it is hunger that drives sharks to attack boats. The comparison might be made with a mongrel dog chasing a bicycle, barking at it like mad; it is unlikely that the mongrel intends eating the cyclist. There is no doubt that hunger is not the only possible explanation, although it certainly must rank top of the list from time to time. However, there is another factor to consider: an aggressive reflex which occurs as a response to a feeding impulse. Thus, the salmon for example, does not feed during its migration up rivers, but nonetheless it readily takes artificial lures when these are presented to it. Professor Fontaine (1953) at the Natural History Museum in Paris, has suggested that in the salmon, high concentrations of thyroid hormone present in the blood during the first part of the fishes life in freshwater and of gonadial hormone thereafter, can explain this aggressive reflex. Possibly, sharks in a state of sexual activity are more irritable, more aggressive. The problem does not seem to have been tackled from this point of view, although experimental studies would be extremely difficult to carry out.

When one carefully examines all the evidence relating to shark behaviour in relation to man, one finds amply confirmed the already twice-quoted statement that you never can tell what a shark is going to do. Thus, Alain Gerbault in one of his books tells how in the Marquesas he was swimming back to his boat the *Firecrest*, which was anchored a little distance from the shore, when he was followed by a shark. He frightened it off by splashing the water vigorously, applying the theory that the movement of the feet in the crawl (a style of Maori origin) had the double object of both propelling the swimmer and of putting off sharks. Fine. But here we encounter a completely contradictory opinion, equally widespread. Dr Conrad Limbaugh, during his visit to Clipperton Island, says specifically: 'As we moved the boat from one area to the next, we tried to frighten off the following sharks by splashing, *but this only attracted more.*' (Dr Limbaugh disappeared on 20 March 1960 during a dive in the Mediterranean off the Provençal coast.)

Dr Limbaugh's observation, however, is corroborated by the circumstances of a fatal accident which occurred in Buzzards Bay, Massachusetts, on 25 July 1936. A boy of sixteen was swimming in the company of an adult some 150 yards from the shore. The man was using the side-stroke, whereas the boy was using the crawl and hence splashing more than the man. They were about ten feet from each other when suddenly a White Shark appeared and went for the left leg of the boy, who died eventually, after an amputation. Therefore, do not count on the splashing of the crawl to frighten off sharks, for it would appear that one risks the reverse result. Dr Limbaugh, à propos his diving at Clipperton, reported having seen some cases of 'feeding frenzy' in the course of which sharks, in full fury, went for anything that they encountered, including the ropes of the buoys and the hull of the boat. He also noticed that the White-tip Reef Shark (*Carcharhinus platyrhynchus*) was definitely attracted by the green swimming fins of some divers but was indifferent to the brown and black fins of other divers. He also noticed that light coloured bathing suits seemed to attract the sharks (off Saipan), while darker trunks did not. The Japanese pearl-diving women known as *ama* wear a jacket, skirt and hood of shining *white*; they believe that white repels sharks and jellyfishes (McCormick, Allen & Young, 1963). Dr Wisby for his part, confirms the fact that brilliant objects exert a certain attraction for sharks. In Australia it is not unusual to find shiny objects in the stomachs of sharks, and swimmers wearing bangles have had their arms bitten off. Which brings us back to the observations made in Chapter 4 on the attraction exercised by light coloured objects on sharks.

We are indebted to Dr Coppleson for the introduction of an idea that is now generally accepted, that of the 'rogue shark'. This is a solitary shark which for some reason or other has developed a particular taste for human flesh and turns up unexpectedly along coasts where, for periods of variable length, it carries out terrible ravages, attacks on bathers sometimes following one on another at quite short intervals. The shark then leaves the area or else is finally captured, and peace returns. Dr Coppleson furnished many examples of these kind of accidents in Australian waters, in the Antilles and along the eastern seaboard of the United States. He distinguished between the 'local' rogue and the 'long-range cruising shark'. It is not always possible to identify the killer, but in many cases it seems to have been the White Shark. One can thus compare the rogue shark to the tiger or lion that has turned into a man-eater by taste and habit.

Stewart Springer (1963), who for many years has studied the sharks of the Florida-Caribbean region, recognizes two groups amongst the total population of each migratory species of large shark in the temperate and sub-tropical Western North Atlantic region: on the one hand, the *principal population*, and on the other, the *accessory population*. The former constitutes the main breeding population, the latter that which is 'lost, and usually permanently lost, either through wandering from the usual geographical range of the species, or through disorientation in seasonal movements, which puts it out of phase in the reproductive cycle'. Springer came to the conclusion that it is amongst the accessory populations that one most often finds Coppleson's 'rogue sharks', which the Florida fishermen refer to as *bank loafers*. He adds that what is known of White Sharks along Florida coasts agrees well with this idea of accessory populations. However, it must be admitted that the general biology of the White Shark is still as yet little known.

There is a very important factor in the aggressive behaviour of sharks, and that is the water temperature. With thirty years' experience in careful study and assessment of attacks by sharks in Australian waters and throughout the world, Dr Coppleson has come to the following conclusions:

The critical temperature appears to be 70° F (Davies, 1963; Coppleson, 1963). In parts of the world where sea temperatures are above this, attacks may occur throughout the year, that is to say, in the zone roughly between 21°N to 21°S. In the Northern Hemisphere, between latitudes 21° and 42°N, the dangerous months are from May to October; in the Southern Hemisphere between latitudes 21° and 42°S, the dangerous months are November to April. In other words, attacks are most frequent in the warm summer months. In Europe, accidents have been reported in the Mediterranean at Genoa and at Pola (respectively 44°24′N and 44°52′N). The White Shark itself is known in Mediterranean waters. Dr E.Postel (1958) has reported its regular appearance along Tunisian coasts in the latter half of May and in 1964 a report on the radio stated that a White Shark had been caught on the Italian coast just as it was devouring a juvenile Sperm Whale – an observation which has a double interest but requires confirmation. There are some cases where confirmation is indispensable, as in the following instance which took place in the Mediterranean.

In the month of August 1934, a report in the daily press gave the following information to the general public: while swimming in the sea at Fiume, a young Yugoslavian girl, a Miss Printz, was attacked by a shark which, having cut her in two with a snap of its jaws, proceeded to gulp her down before the horrified eyes of those who had come to help, amongst whom, wringing her hands and crying out to heaven, was the girl's mother. . . . And then came a rather disquieting detail: the unfortunate mother had, some time previously, had a premonitary dream in which she had seen her daughter devoured by a 'sea monster'.

As told, and apart from the dream episode which was obviously added for dramatic affect, this account could well take its place amongst the list of well-authenticated cases of shark attacks. Nothing is missing – neither the name of the place where the attack occurred, nor the name of the victim and her approximate age. Unfortunately – or rather, most fortunately for the young woman – a cable from Havas arrived which contradicted this story in the most categorical terms. Under the headline 'Young Girl Devoured by Shark is All Right' the newspaper *L'Oeuvre*, for 2 September 1934, inserted a small paragraph.

Belgrade, 1st September. It is reported from Kraljevica in the Avala District that the news published by certain foreign papers according to which a young Yugoslavian girl, Miss Printz, was attacked and eaten by a shark off the Italian coast, is without foundation. Miss Printz is actually at her parents' home in Ljubljana and intends to spend the coming month taking examinations for admission to the university of this town (i.e. Havas).

This is an excellent example of a 'shark story'. There are numerous others, unfortunately not all so definitely contradicted. It would be most interesting to know how they start. In the above case the beginnings are not clear and, lacking pictorial assistance, it seems to have necessitated a little preliminary publicity.

But things do not always turn out as happily as they did for Miss Printz. Again in the Mediterranean, there was the tragic death of Maurizio Sarra, a 28-year-old Italian diver, a case which shows that the danger is indisputably present in this area, which is well within the zone indicated by Dr Coppleson. Maurizio Sarra dived in a diving-suit off the coast of San Feliceo Circeo, between Rome and Naples on Sunday, 22 September 1962. He was attacked and severely wounded by a shark which appears to have been a Porbeagle (*Lamna nasus*) but which did not appear at the surface since the attack took place in thirty feet of water (*L'Aventure Sous-Marine*, No 41, Oct.–Nov. 1962, p. 254). Maurizio Sarra was wearing a compact iso-thermic suit. All these circumstances make one reconsider, since one is given to understand that the greatest danger is *at the surface*, and that a completely submerged swimmer, in a horizontal position, is much less at risk, particu-larly if he is wearing a dark suit. However, it must be stated that Sarra was at the time harpooning and manipulating a Grouper, whose blood and mucus were spread all over him. Also, the site of the accident may have been important, since a half mile from where Sarra met his death another diver, Golfredo Lombardo, had been attacked six years previously, in September 1956, but in that case the accident was not fatal. It can be noted too, that these attacks occurred at latitude 41°17′N, i.e. very close to the limit of 42° mentioned by Dr Coppleson.

This possibility of being attacked by sharks in temperate seas has been doubted, and one particular instance deserves mention. In 1890, an American called Hermann Oelrichs made it known through the press that he was offering a reward of 500 dollars to anyone who reported a duly authenticated case of a man attacked in the water by a shark along that part of the United States coast lying to the north of Cape Hatteras, North Carolina, at 35°15'N. It was a case of finding out whether attacks occurred in the temperate zone. This proposition having been published by the New York paper, *The Sun*, I wrote some years ago to the editor for more details. Here is the substance of the reply he sent me (I must acknowledge his promptness, for he answered on 27 September to my letter of 14 September 1934).

Mr Hermann Oelrichs died on 1 September 1906. In the obituary notice published in *The Sun* at this time, it was said that Mr Oelrichs had great confidence in his opinions. Talking one day about swimming in tropical waters, he declared that there were no man-eating sharks north of Cape Hatteras, and in support of his claim, he offered, through a letter published in *The Sun*, a reward of 500 dollars to anyone who could give an authentic case of a man killed by a shark to the north of this point. He received thousands of letters from correspondents who had not taken proper note of the geographical conditions he had specified and no one got the money. A short time before his death, Mr Oelrichs took back his offer, satisfied that he had been proved right.

In fact, some 25 years elapsed from the date of Mr Oelrichs' offer without a single accident being reported from the specified area and it was assumed that man-eating sharks truly did not penetrate so far north. Then, in 1916, on 2 July, at Matawan Creek, near Sandy Hook, New Jersey, and well to the north of Cape Hatteras, a young boy who was swimming a short distance from the beach was attacked and killed by an unseen animal; a man who went to his rescue was in turn so badly wounded that he died shortly after; and, some minutes later, another boy received such severe wounds in his leg that it had to be amputated subsequently. As usually happens in these tragic circumstances, nobody had identified or even seen the attacker. But two days after this accident (on 14 July) a medium-sized White Shark (*Carcharodon*) was caught nearby, and it was considered, no doubt justly, to have been the culprit. The incident had wide repercussions. Holiday-makers, terrified, abandoned the famous New Jersey beaches, including Atlantic City, the 'Blackpool' of the eastern seaboard, and this led to losses of many thousand dollars by the proprietors in the area. The affair received wide publicity and was even raised and discussed by the President.

Some very thorough studies have been made throughout the world on the wounds caused by sharks. Such wounds are always serious, often ghastly. Dr Coppleson (1962) and the late Dr Davies (1964), amongst others, give numerous examples and details. The percentage of fatalities is high: Dr Whitley rates them as high as 80 per cent in Australia. According to Halstead (1963) and Davies and Campbell (1963), mortality resulting from shark attacks occurs in 49 per cent of cases as an average for all countries.

Certain wounds are immediately fatal. In other cases the wounded person dies on the way to hospital or shortly after being admitted. Dr Davies made one extremely important discovery (Davies and Campbell, 1962, 1963). He noticed that, from a study of the statistics, people often died after being wounded by a shark even though the wounds themselves were neither serious nor mortal; this occurred, he found, when the wounds had not received medical or surgical treatment immediately. From this idea, Dr Davies set up a programme of research into the pathogenic bacteria of the teeth and mouth in sharks. Some samples were taken from live sharks and were studied by a pathologist. He discovered in the cultures derived from the samples 'a particularly virulent haemolytic organism in the mouth of every shark examined'. There is no doubt that it is this organism which is responsible for the otherwise inexplicable death of those who had been wounded but had not received prompt medical aid and, in particular, any form of antibiotic treatment. One can see the importance of such studies, which are at the present time being followed up. For it is known that other marine animals, for example the Moray Eels, are reputed to have a venomous bite but the operative factor has not yet been definitely isolated and identified. Thus the research initiated by Dr Davies has wide and important applications.

Defence and protection against sharks

A swimmer, even one equipped with aqualung (Scuba) and a harpoon or gun, finds himself at the outset in a vulnerable position when faced with a large shark bent on attacking him. And since the Golden Rule is 'one never knows what a shark is going to do', there is almost complete uncertainty of the best tactics to adopt. Frogmen and skin-divers have acquired, little by little, some knowledge on which to base their tactics, and this is very far from the sort of advice handed out in former times.

The manœuvre which was recommended at one time for dealing with a shark was this: pass underneath the monster and cut open his belly with a thrust of your knife, neither more nor less . . . the body cavity of the shark will then fill with water and the animal will die instantly. This performance looks all very well on paper. Seizing a pectoral fin with one hand as the shark passes close to you, you trail along holding your breath and when the opportunity arises, you slit open its belly. On the face of it, this is child's play – with the small reservation that such a manœuvre can only be carried out by a swimmer of more than average ability, blessed with imperturbable *sang-froid* plus an extremely sharp knife. However, even granting these qualities and granting that the operation is carried out successfully, the swimmer's situation is hardly improved, for other sharks cannot fail to be attracted by the blood gushing from the wound of the first shark. Again, it is by no means certain that this disembowelling will put the shark out of action. Such a recommendation should be relegated to the chapter dealing with shark myths and legends, for the vitality of sharks is truly amazing; one sees eviscerated sharks thrown back into the water and sculling along feebly, still showing definite signs of life. One shark has even hooked itself on a hook baited with its own entrails, which is surely the height of voracity and insensitivity! The story is related by Norman & Fraser (1948) and a similar experience is recounted by Lineaweaver & Backus (1970) who watched sharks attempt to swim after removal of jaws for souvenirs and inspection of guts and gonads for recording purposes, the animals then being heaved overboard presumed dead. Murphy (1947) during his cruise on board the whaler *Daisy*, saw a Blue Shark which had been horribly mutilated by a sailor with a blubber-spade, the skin being cut to shreds, hurling itself afresh at the whale, devouring great pieces of it and dying literally with its mouth full and under circumstances in which no other animal would have shown any appetite. This exceptional vitality has always been a source of astonishment. Kemp Welch reported that, having extracted the heart of a shark, this organ did not cease its contracting and dilating, beating in a perfectly regular manner for *four hours*, after which the movements slowly stopped. This is the kind of experience that all shark fishermen have come across, and one that writers of adventure stories frequently use to give a dramatic effect. Kemp Welch also records that the jaws of the same shark snapped shut violently when the head was touched after the latter had been separated from the rest of the body. Such things are not restricted to sharks, however. One finds them in a number of lower vertebrates, in turtles for example. I myself have seen a shark of about six feet brought on to dry land and apparently quite dead, suddenly make a brisk jump of about $4\frac{1}{2}$ feet into the air; by good chance there was nobody near to it, for no femur, tibia or skull could withstand a blow from a tail capable of bouncing off the ground a weight of more than 200 lbs.

It should be pointed out that not only are the jaws armed with teeth; the tail also can be dangerous. It is wise, therefore, to remember that sharks are dangerous at both ends and that the lashing of a body armed with placoid scales can result in deep lacerations on a person's body. Thus, sharks combine many of the dangers enumerated in the classic advice tendered by the old sea dog to his son: if you want to get on in life, distrust dogs from the front, horses from the rear, and women from all sides; shorten your sails when the wind rises, look out for squalls and give a wide berth to headlands.

The problem of the protection of bathers on beaches has been studied intensively. In South Africa (Durban) and in Australia (Sydney) the problem has been largely solved by the use of protective nets. The nets do not form a continuous barrier but they are so arranged that there is no straight route through them. This system, known as 'meshing', is expensive but effective, for since its introduction there have been very few reports of attacks within the protected area (one or two cases in South Africa and Australia). Bubble-barriers have also been considered, i.e. a curtain of air-bubbles, following on the supposition that the escape of air bubbles from a diver frightens off sharks. Gilbert & Springer (1963), however, have shown that sharks will pass unperturbed through such a curtain, which is thus quite useless. This is yet another example of our formula 'you never can tell what a shark is going to do'. For in the bubble-curtain experiments at Bimini, Gilbert noticed that 'one tiger-shark out of twelve was repeatedly turned back by the bubble curtain, while the other eleven tiger-sharks promiscuously swam back and forth through it'.

It is possible, nevertheless, as we shall note later on in the section 'Advice to skin- and Scuba-divers', that a sudden discharge of bubbles may make a malevolent shark hesitate. For work on the sea floor, skin-divers use cages, of which many kinds have been designed and used satisfactorily. For cast-aways, Lineaweaver & Backus (1970) describe recent work by the United States Navy on the development of a protective bag, known as the John-son Shark Screen after its inventor C. Scott Johnson. The bag, made of plastic and most successful if black, is supported by three inflatable buoyancy tubes round the top and should be filled with water before the castaway clambers in. The man is thus invisible to the shark, cannot be smelt (an important factor if he is wounded), to some extent conserves his heat and finally derives considerable psychological comfort from being covered. Tests have shown the bag to be most successful with sharks of about 6 to 7 feet but it remains to see what a 20-foot *Carcharodon carcharias* would make of such a floating object.

Finally, a few words on 'shark repellents' and 'shark chasers', which naturally have been the object of considerable research since the war

(Springer, 1954; Springer & Gilbert, 1963). During the war, the problem was acute for airmen and sailors operating in tropical parts of the Atlantic and Pacific. 'Fear of sharks' was an important factor in the morale of men who faced the risk of being plunged into shark-infested waters.

The initial experiments showed that three materials had possible shark repellent properties: maleic acid, copper sulphate, and decomposing shark flesh. The principal chemical substance released by the latter was found to be ammonium acetate, and it was decided to combine this and copper sulphate to make copper acetate, which should, by this token, have a 'double-barrelled' effect (Tuve, 1963). The results seemed encouraging, and a black nigrosine type dye was added, thus simulating the protective device of the octopus or squid. All divers operating over the Pacific were equipped with shark repellent kits, whose use continued for some time after the end of the war. Australian airlines have developed a shark-chaser. Thus the question of protecting men in the water appeared to have been solved satisfactorily.

Nevertheless, over the years, the results have not been very convincing and have thrown doubt on the effectiveness of these 'shark repellents'. At the present time, work in progress (notably by Gilbert & Springer) on different types of repellent, shows that in fact none of them can be considered infallible, although certain of them have proved efficient under specific conditions. It is sincerely to be hoped that this line of research will quickly lead to a final solution of the problem.

The Shark Research Panel

Founded in 1958, this organization was attached to the American Institute of Biological Sciences (AIBS), and with Professor Perry W. Gilbert as President, it had the following aims (see Gilbert, 1963b).

(1) To keep an up-to-date record of shark attacks throughout the world, and to compile annual statistics of these accidents, published as a list with an analysis of the attack and the conditions under which it occurred.

(2) To promote and to follow up all basic research by co-ordinating studies carried out in all parts of the world on the systematics, migrations, general biology, anatomy and physiology of sharks.

(3) To study the methods and results of shark repellents.

In close co-operation with the Shark Research Panel was the Shark Research Committee in Van Nuys, California, under the Chairmanship of Ralph S. Collier.

The classical method for following the movements of fishes is by marking individual specimens. The Shark Research Panel set up an International

Shark-tagging Programme, in which Stewart Springer was particularly active. Marking has above all been carried out in the waters off South Carolina and southern California. Regarding the technique of marking, which can only be done by taking the fish out of water, it can be noted that sharks are surprisingly sensitive to such handling. They show such a delicacy that it has been strongly recommended that one must not be brutal since 'fatal internal injuries [to the shark, that is!] may follow merely lifting a very heavy shark from the water'. This is quite unexpected and seems to contradict what is known of the extraordinary vitality of sharks, as discussed earlier. As Springer has rightly remarked, the tagging programme should at least give most useful data 'on the abilities of sharks to withstand stresses'.

This huge programme is an excellent scheme and the recent collection of papers published together as *Sharks and Survival* (edited by Professor Gilbert) gives an impressive account of the remarkable results already achieved. This basic work is quite indispensable to anyone who wants to go more deeply into any topic concerning sharks. I reproduce here Gilbert's summary entitled 'Advice to those who frequent or find themselves in shark-infested waters'. A chapter on man-eaters would be incomplete without it.

The following statement has been prepared in response to requests from bathers, skin and Scuba (aqualung) divers, and Navy and Air Force Personnel. In addition to the numerous publications listed in the bibliography, advice has been solicited from a number of experienced skin and Scuba divers and scientists familiar with the behavior of sharks. For the sake of clarity and brevity, the advice presented here is arranged in outline form. It must be remembered above all that sharks are unpredictable. Moreover, we know relatively little about their behavior patterns, about the environmental conditions that cause them to attack, and about what actions of a swimmer may provoke a shark to attack. The AIBS Shark Research Panel is currently gathering documentation on all shark attacks throughout the world, and, from an analysis of this, it expects to learn more about the environmental conditions in which shark attacks take place and the behavioral patterns that attract sharks.

Advice to Bathers and Swimmers

(1) Always swim with a companion. Do not become a lone target for attack by swimming away from the general area occupied by a group of swimmers and bathers.

(2) If dangerous sharks are known to be in the area, stay out of the water.

(3) Since blood attracts and excites sharks, do not enter or remain in the water with a bleeding wound.

(4) Avoid swimming in extremely turbid or dirty water where underwater visibility is poor.

Advice to Skin and Scuba Divers

(1) Always dive with a companion.

(2) Do not spear, ride, or hang on to the tail of any shark. To provoke a shark, even a small and seemingly harmless one, is to invite possible severe injury.

(3) Remove all speared fish from the water immediately; do not tow them in a bag or on a line cinched to the waist.

(4) As a rule a shark will circle its intended victim several times; get into a boat or out of the water as quickly as possible after sighting a circling shark, before it has time to make an aggressive 'pass'. Use a rhythmic beat with the feet and do not make an undue disturbance in the water as you move toward the boat or the shore. If wearing Scuba, it is best to remain submerged until you have reached the boat.

(5) If a shark moves in and there is not time to leave the water, try not to panic and keep the shark in view. A shark can often be discouraged by releasing bubbles or, at close range, by deliberately charging it and hitting it on the snout with a club or 'shark billy'. Since the hide of a shark is very rough and may cause serious skin abrasions, hit the shark with your bare hands as a last resort. Shouting underwater may or may not discourage a shark.

Advice to Survivors of Air and Sea Disasters

(1) Do not abandon your clothing when entering the water. Clothing, especially on the feet and legs, is your only protection against the rough skin of a shark.

(2) Place wounded survivors in a life raft; all should use the raft if there is room.

(3) Remain quiet – conserve energy.

(4) If you must swim, use regular strokes, either strong or lazy, but keep them rhythmic.

(5) Do not trail arms or legs over the side of the raft.

(6) Do not jettison blood or garbage, for this attracts sharks.

(7) Do not fish from a life raft when sharks are nearby. Abandon hooked fish if a shark approaches.

(8) When a shark is at close range, use Shark Chaser (US Navy Repellent) if available – the black dye will repel many species of sharks.

(9) If your group is threatened by a shark while in the water, form a tight circle and face outward; if approached, hit the shark on the snout with any instrument at hand, preferably a heavy one; hit a shark with your bare hands only as a last resort.

Advice to All

(1) Always swim with a companion.

(2) Avoid swimming at night, or in extremely turbid or dirty water, where underwater visibility is very poor.

(3) Remain calm when a shark is sighted; leave the water as quickly as possible.

(4) If an attack does occur, all effort should be made to control hemorrhage as quickly as possible – even before the victim reaches shore. If the wound is serious, the victim should be treated by a physician as soon as possible.

(5) Adopt a sensible attitude towards sharks. Remember that the likelihood of attack is less than that of being struck by lightning. Attack is almost assured, however, when one deliberately grabs, injures, or in some other way provokes even a small and seemingly harmless shark.

In this very pertinent advice (which should be engraved in large gold letters wherever there are bathers, swimmers, skin-divers or seamen), there is one phrase which deserves further comment: *Remember that the likelihood of attack is less than that of being struck by lightning.* This statement, from one of the greatest experts on sharks, should, at the end of a chapter on man-eaters, help to place things in their proper perspective.

Amongst marine animals, however, it is not only sharks that are to be feared. There is another fish, a teleost, which is classed, if not actually as a man-eater, then at least amongst possible attackers. This is the Great Barracuda (*Sphyraena barracuda*), which attains a length of 6 feet and a weight of up to 100 lbs. In certain places the barracuda is quite as feared as are sharks. On the other hand, many skin-divers declare that its reputation is over-rated, and that in spite of its menacing appearance and formidable jaws, the barracuda is fairly inoffensive. In his study of the Great Barracuda, Donald DeSylva (1963) found records of only twenty-nine attacks on swimmers since 1873, all except one taking place at the surface (eight of the records were possibly barracuda but not confirmed). As Lineaweaver & Backus (1970) point out, this is a very small figure compared with the average of about fifty shark attacks per year documented by the Shark Research Panel. The attacks differ from those of sharks: the barracuda attacks only once whereas the shark, apparently stimulated by the smell of blood, continues to attack. The wounds inflicted by the two fishes can in principle be distinguished fairly easily by a trained observer, those of the barracuda consisting of two nearly parallel rows of tooth marks, while those of a shark tend to be parabolic with jagged tooth marks (DeSylva, *loc. cit.*). It is possible, however, that sharks have sometimes been blamed for barracuda attacks and vice versa.

There is another fish, freshwater, and only to be mentioned here, which is certainly the most aggressive and ferocious of all aquatic animals: this is the Piranha (*Serrasalmus piraya Cuvier*) of the Amazon. Its powerful teeth, its

133

voracity, and also the fact that it lives in shoals which attack in concert, make it an animal that is greatly feared even though it does not grow to a large size.

But to return to sharks, here are some of Coppleson's conclusions, given in *Shark Attack*:

The fear of Shark attacks is out of proportion to the risks. Australia, for instance, has a bad reputation for shark attacks. Yet Bondi, Australia's most popular beach has not had an attack for over thirty years. Out of more than 100,000,000 bathers there, only three have ever been attacked and there is good reason to believe that they were attacked by the same shark. . . . The idea that the sea is full of savage sharks swimming around seeking what humans they may devour has little to support it. . . .

The risk is less than walking across a road or playing cricket or football. More people are killed by snakes, bulls or spiders than by sharks, three times as many are struck by lightning, and many more are killed by horses. . . . More people are killed every day of the week by motor cars than sharks account for in years.

Yet, despite these figures, a horror of being eaten alive constantly lurks in people's minds. The fear of shark attacks, based apparently on a primitive cannibalistic fantasy, has become an almost universal phobia.

Dr Coppleson then cites a letter written by Dr D.G.Campbell to the *South African Medical Journal*:

In spite of the fact that twenty people are killed on the roads of this country almost weekly, one single shark attack on the Natal coast, is enough to empty every hotel within miles. Tourists stream back home on the roads, where they face an astronomically greater risk of being hurt than if they were to bathe for years in the most 'dangerous' surf.

These conclusions deserve quoting *in extenso*. They agree with the confirmed view of all those who have seriously studied the problem of shark attack. To be sure, danger undoubtedly exists, for we have the proof of it. But the total number of accidents is relatively small (although this is poor consolation to the victim who contributed to this small percentage). Bernard Gorsky, of the *Moana* Expedition, believed the risk to be no more than that of being bitten by a dog in the streets of Paris. But once again, we must repeat that one never knows what a shark is going to do, which is why the sane and prudent advice quoted earlier should always be uppermost in one's mind when one exposes oneself to the possibility of meeting with a shark.

It only remains to say that, amongst the causes of premature death, and leaving aside the toll of war, sharks must be ranked far below motor cars,

Plate 5. Record catches of the Porbeagle (*Lamna nasus*) (*upper*) and the Mako (*Isurus oxyrinchus*) (*lower*). The Porbeagle, weighing 271 lbs, was caught by Mrs Betty Eathorne off Looe, Cornwall; Charles P. Meyer landed his Mako off Montauk, New York, using only a 12 lb test line.

Plate 6. The culmination of a periodic shark hunt off Kyushu I., Japan. Having netted the sharks and brought them to the shore, considerable skill is required to lassoo and drag them up the beach since they are still capable of snapping or lashing out at legs.
(*Below*) A horrifying example of damage inflicted by a shark. Remarkably, the wounds had healed four months later, without the need for skin grafting. Michael Hely was attacked while swimming in murky water at Inyoni Rocks near Amanzimtoti (South Africa), probably by a Zambezi Shark.

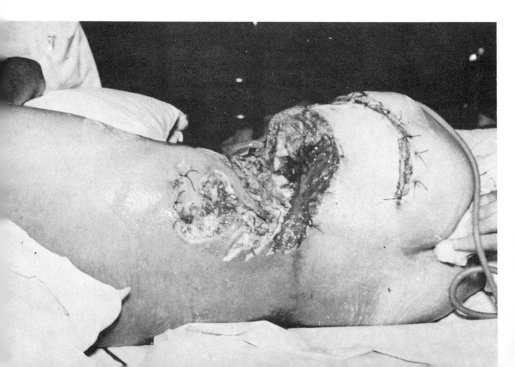

Plate 7. The largest fish ever taken on rod and reel, a Great White Shark (*Carcharodon carcharias*) of 16 ft 10 in with a girth of 9 ft 6 in and a weight of 2,664 lb caught by Alf Dean of Victoria, Australia, in 1959.

Plate 8. Small Pilot Fish (*Naucrates ductor*) hover round a Grey Shark (*Carcharhinus* sp.) (*upper picture*). Experienced divers sometimes take risks with sharks (*lower picture*) – but sometimes regret it. *This shark is dead but to provoke a shark, even a small, seemingly harmless one, is to invoke possible severe injury.*

motor cycles, bathing which culminates in drowning without the aid of sharks, alcoholism, excessive smoking, the vagaries of heat and cold, mountaineering accidents, rabid dogs (before Pasteur), runaway horses (before the motor car), narcotics, air or rail traffic . . . And if one turns to the animal kingdom – fleas, lice, mosquitoes for the diseases that they transmit, all these are infinitely more to be feared than are sharks.

Chapter 6

Freshwater Sharks

I have already mentioned some sharks from the Ganges which, without being confirmed man-eaters, nevertheless have the reputation for attacking human beings. It may seem surprising that representatives of a group such as sharks, which are thought of as being so characteristically marine and pelagic, should live not only in freshwater but even some distance from the sea. However, this is indeed the case, for there are species of both sharks and rays which are perfectly adapted to life in freshwater.

Above all, there are the Stingrays which live in rivers and streams. In South America, in the Amazon, the Plate and their tributaries, there are many species of *Taeniura* (= *Potamotrygon*) and *Trygon*. These are the much feared *arraias de fuego*, stingrays with a barbed and poisonous spine at the base of the tail with which they can inflict a painful wound and one which does not heal easily. Stingrays occur in rivers of other tropical regions, for example in Florida, Senegal, India, Australia, and so on. In all, there are about a dozen species.

There is another selachian which is widespread in freshwaters, the Sawfish (*Pristis*), known from Lake Nicaragua and from rivers of South America, Senegal, and from India to the Philippines. Again, there are two members of the genus *Raja* and a Rhinobatid known from Indian freshwaters. All these forms are rays (Order Hypotremata – see p. 10) and are of interest here only in that they have close ties with the sharks.

It should be made clear at the outset that, while marine sharks may stray far from their normal habitat in the tropics, there are no sharks known in the rivers of the temperate zone. Freshwater sharks mainly occur within latitudes 30°N and 30°S. The extreme limit is probably about 35° on either side of the equator, although Schwartz (1959) reported the presence of two eight-foot Bull Sharks (*Carcharhinus leucas*) in Chesapeake Bay on the US eastern seaboard (latitude 37°N), which is seemingly the most northerly limit, but this record was in brackish water (salinity 10–14 parts per thousand). Sharks are unknown in European freshwaters, nor have they been found in the large rivers of northern Asia.

Amongst others, Pausanius comments on this in his *Description of Greece* (Book 4, Messenie, Ch. 34):

136

The rivers of Greece harbour none of those murderous monsters which infest the Indus, the Nile, even the Rhine, the Danube, the Euphrates and the Phasis [now Rioni]. Indeed, in those rivers one encounters monsters which are most eager for human flesh, and which are larger and blacker than the Glanis[1] of the Hermus and the Meander, although having the same shape. . . . There is nothing to fear of this kind in the rivers of Greece, since the dogs (οἱ κύνες) which are found in the Aoüs, a Thesprodite river, come from the sea and are not fishes born in the river.

Here the word 'dog' should be taken in the sense of 'shark', and Pausanius is quite explicit on their occasional presence in the eastern province of Thesprotides on the Ionian Sea.

Englehardt (1913) explained the absence of sharks from northern freshwaters by the fact that only in tropical regions can freshwater sharks find an environment where annual temperature fluctuations do not exceed 5–10° C. This is an interesting suggestion, but it would be useful to have it verified.

Freshwater sharks are found in two types of habitat. Firstly, they occur in coastal rivers or in large rivers and their tributaries, that is to say, in places where there is direct access to the sea. One can easily envisage a marine species becoming progressively acclimatized to brackish water in the estuary and then, bit by bit, working its way upstream until it is in perfectly fresh water. Secondly, there are sharks which are found in lakes which have little or no direct contact with the sea.

Rivers and streams

One of the best known members of this group is the Ganges Shark (*Carcharhinus gangeticus*). As its species name implies, it is found in the Ganges and also known in the Hooghly, the arm of this river on which Calcutta lies. We have already noted that this species can be quite aggressive, and that this behaviour would be encouraged by the Hindu custom of committing bodies to the waters of this sacred river. Accidents involving sharks are not rare, it would seem, in the neighbourhood of Calcutta. Another species has been recorded from this river, *Hypoprion hemiodon* (M. & H.), the type species of which came from Pondicherry. This species is also known at Calcutta. This, however, is an example of a marine shark which is occasionally capable of entering freshwater. The Ganges Shark, on the other hand, is exclusively freshwater.

---

[1] This is not the Wels of the Danube (*Silurus glanis*) but Aristotle's *Glanis* of Greek rivers (*Parasilurus aristotelis*), the two being confounded and Aristotle's accurate data doubted until 1890 when Garman recognized the latter as distinct (Gill, 1911).

In their classic treatise on the Plagiostomes (selachians), Müller and Henle (1838–41) described the type specimen of *Carcharhinus gangeticus* as a small individual of five and a half feet, and the type locality as '*In Ganges, 60 Stunden oberhalb des Meers bei Hougly gefangen*' (in the Ganges, caught 60 leagues from the sea, in the Hooghly – a league being 2½ miles).

In the Muséum National d'Histoire Naturelle in Paris there is a paratype[1] of *C. gangeticus*. It is a small male specimen (25 inches in length), from the lower reaches of the Ganges (Figure 39). Garman (1913) placed *C. gangeticus* close to the Bull Shark (*C. leucas*) and there has been some discussion as to whether *C. gangeticus* is not merely an Asian form of *C. leucas*. In the Paris specimen there are thirteen teeth on each side in both jaws, but in addition, there is a continuation of four or five irregular teeth towards the angle of the

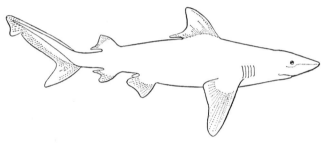

Fig. 39   The Ganges Shark *Carcharhinus gangeticus*, drawn from the specimen in the Muséum National d'Histoire Naturelle in Paris.

mouth, bringing the total for each jaw to at least thirty-five, as against only twenty-five to twenty-seven in the Bull Shark (Figure 40). This kind of problem often arises when one is trying to establish the identity of a species by reference to the type specimens. Is the Paris specimen merely a freak, or are the extra teeth characteristic of the species? Boeseman (1964) examined this question and reported that Garrick had sent him details of two other specimens of Ganges Shark in which these extra teeth are present. Boeseman concluded, therefore, that the appearance of the extra teeth in specimens from three different collections, made at quite different times, must surely indicate that the Ganges Shark is distinct from *C. leucas*.

[1] *Holotype*: the unique specimen on which a new species is founded, or a specimen selected by the author from amongst those actually used for his description.

Paratype(s) : all other specimens used in the original description. Type specimens are usually kept in the larger museums where they are accessible for study since they stand as the ultimate reference to the identity of a species. Their occasional loss or destruction can pose difficult systematic problems.

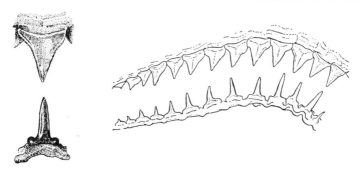

Fig. 40   The teeth of the Ganges Shark *Carcharhinus gangeticus.*

The Ganges Shark is reported from other localities besides the Ganges and Hooghly Rivers. There are records from several of the large rivers flowing into the Indian Ocean, as well as from rivers in Japan, the Philippines and the Fiji Islands (especially Viti-Levu). Since there is as yet no evidence that these also have the extra teeth at the side of the jaw, Boeseman felt that these records probably referred to the real *C. leucas.* The Ganges Shark does not seem to reach the large size of the Bull Shark. Most of the recorded specimens are about the size of a large dogfish, so that in spite of their reputed ferocity, the sharks of the Ganges are perhaps less formidable than their close relatives elsewhere. Nevertheless, Lineaweaver & Backus (1970) cite reports of twenty attacks (mostly fatal) in the Hooghly River during 1880 and thirty-five attacks (five fatal) in the Devi River in 1959 during the months of July to September only, all presumably due to *Carcharhinus gangeticus.*

In Africa, the freshwater species is the Zambezi Shark, formerly known as *Carcharhinus zambezensis* (Peters), the type specimen of which came from Tete, 120 miles up the Zambezi. This specimen is only 2½ feet in length. Some authors, such as Barnard (1925), were inclined to regard this species as identical to the Ganges Shark, but *Carcharhinus gangeticus* now appears to be a quite distinct species. Garrick & Schultz (1963) and Boeseman (1964) identified the Zambezi Shark as yet another freshwater member of the *Carcharhinus leucas* group, i.e. the Bull Shark. The Zambezi Shark is also known from McCarthy I. on the Gambia, about two hundred miles from Bathurst and thus in absolutely fresh water. Svensson (1933) caught three specimens there, all of them small (about 2½ feet in length). This species is also well known apparently to the natives of Basse and Fattatenda, localities that lie upstream from McCarthy I. Boeseman (1964) examined a specimen from the Ogooué River in Gabon and found that he could not distinguish it

139

from *C. leucas*. The Zambezi Shark has a reputation for ferocity and many unprovoked attacks have been attributed to it by Davies (1963) and J.D. d'Aubrey (1961, 1964), both in freshwater and in the sea. In reviewing ten attacks in the Natal area almost certainly attributable to the Zambezi Shark, Davies & Campbell (1962) brand the shark as 'a particularly ferocious species which will attack large fish without apparent provocation and not for food'.

The freshwater sharks of Africa and India are reasonably well known, even if ichthyologists are not yet entirely agreed on the relationship of one to the other. There are, however, other places where river sharks have been recorded, but with no indication of the species. In Australia, for example, they are known in the Fitzroy River and its tributary the Margaret (N.E. Australia; confluence of the two rivers at 18°30′S, 125°30′E). Hardman (1884) has seen some sawfishes and sharks at 170 miles from the mouth of this river. Again, in Borneo, sharks have been reported many times from the *upper* reaches of the Sarawak River. The sharks in the Margaret River are found so far from the sea that it seems certain that they live permanently there and are not merely chance visitors. For this does sometimes happen. Thus Homer W. Smith and his wife, physiologists from America, stayed at Teluk Anson in Malaya and carried out certain studies on the freshwater sharks. The village of Teluk Anson lies on the Perak River, a small coastal river that discharges into the Straits of Malacca. The place that they chose was about 40 miles from the sea, so that the water there was perfectly fresh. There, Smith caught sawfishes, stingrays (*Dasyatis uarnak* [Forsskål]) and a shark, *Carcharhinus melanopterus* (Q. & G.). The latter is normally a marine species, widespread throughout the Indo-Pacific region; I have myself caught one specimen in the Red Sea, near the Jubal Straits.

According to Smith (1936), three species of shark at one time or another ascend the Perak River to well above the limits of saltwater and penetrate far into freshwater. Some individuals were very large apparently, but he did not see them himself. Following the reports of the fishermen, who gave a very clear description of eggs and young, Smith believed that one species bred in freshwater, although he did not say if this was *C. melanopterus*. There are other examples of positively identified marine species being caught in fresh or brackish waters. For example, in the rivers of South America, the Lemon Shark (*Negaprion brevirostris*) has been recorded, although it is an Atlantic Ocean species (type locality, Cuba) known also from the west coast of Africa; also the Great Hammerhead Shark *Sphyrna mokarran* (*Val*), whose normal habitat is the coasts of tropical America.

Lakes and lagoons

The presence of sharks in Lake Nicaragua (Figure 41) and its effluent river the San Juan was reported in 1526 by Oviedo y Valdez shortly after the discovery of the country. These sharks belong to a single species, formerly known as *Carcharhinus nicaraguensis* (Gill & Bransford) and they occur with three other normally marine fishes, the Tarpon *Tarpon atlanticus* and two species of the Sawfish *Pristis*. The sharks reach about four to six feet in length and according to Bigelow & Schroeder (1948) have a reputation for ferocity.

Garman (1913) believed that the Nicaraguan Shark was identical to the Brown Shark (*Carcharhinus milberti*), a species which is very common in the tropical Atlantic, especially in the Gulf of Mexico, along Florida coasts and

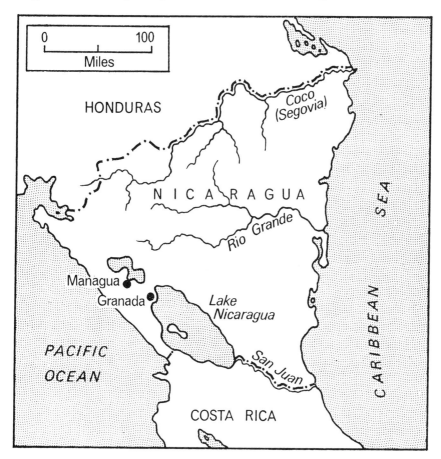

Fig. 41   Lake Nicaragua, showing its connection to the sea via the San Juan river.

in the Antilles; it is also found in the Mediterranean and the tropical Pacific, and is not rare in temperate regions, reaching as far north as New York. Growing to a length of about six feet, the Brown Shark is reputed to frequent estuaries and rivers and to ascend into freshwater.

Bigelow & Schroeder (1961) disagreed with Garman and identified the Nicaraguan Shark as merely the well-known Bull Shark (*Carcharhinus leucas*). Stewart Springer (1960) agreed and felt that the Nicaragua fishes probably represented an 'accessory population' (see p. 123) of the Bull Shark that has penetrated into the lake via the San Juan River. Garrick and Schultz (1963), in their study of potentially dangerous sharks, probably took the best course by relegating the Nicaraguan form to what they termed the '*Carcharhinus leucas-gangeticus* Group' – a tacit recognition of the fact that far too few specimens have been properly studied as yet. Many more comparisons from widely separated areas are needed before the true status of these freshwater sharks can be clarified.

The origin of the Lake Nicaragua shark population is a puzzle that has been well described by Lineaweaver & Backus (1970), largely on the field studies reported by Thorson et alii (1966b). Thomas Thorson and his colleagues first satisfied themselves that sharks caught from the far end of the lake down to the river mouth were identical and that all could be identified as *Carcharhinus leucas*. They then showed that even when the river level was low, their party was able to navigate the eight rapids along its course and so too were loaded barges some thirty to fifty feet in length. Clearly, there was nothing to prevent sharks reaching the lake or leaving it. Thorson also noted that sharks occurred both above and below the worst of the rapids. He concluded that 'there is no real basis for the belief that the shark population in the lake is landlocked', although he cautioned that in spite of strong circumstantial evidence there was still no definitive proof that the sharks actually pass between lake and sea. The proof can only come through a programme of marking individual fishes at either end and seeing whether they arrive at the other end. This may eventually confirm what the natives of the area have always asserted, that the sharks of Lake Nicaragua are of two kinds: the *tintoreros* or permanent dwellers in the lake, which have a reddish tinge to the belly, and the *visitantes* or *immigrantes*, sharks which have come up from the sea and have a more whitish belly. There is also the problem of why the Lake Nicaragua sharks do not make the further migration up the intermittent Tipitapa River into Lake Managua, where sharks are as yet unknown. Sharks and sawfish also occur in the Lake Izabel-Rio Dulce system in Guatemala and have been studied by Thorson et alii (1966a).

In the Philippines, the Lagoon of Bay near Manila contains perfectly fresh water. Referring to it, Gironierre wrote in his *Aventures d'un Gentilhomme breton* (1857) the following observation: The Shark and the Sawfish. The first is fortunately rare, but the second is very abundant. The sawfish was *Pristis perotteti*, of which Meyer said that he saw a specimen of almost twenty feet in the market, although most individuals were smaller than that. The sharks he said were 'small dogfishes and quite inoffensive'. Boeseman (1964) identified sharks from this lagoon as '*C. gangeticus* = ? *C. leucas*' and he records them also from the Agusan and Sang Rivers and also Lake Naujan in the Philippines.

The list of freshwater records given here is by no means exhaustive. For example, a shark has been reported from near Iquitos (Peru), some 2300 miles up the Amazon and sharks may well occur in many other of the little explored South American waterways (McCormick, Allen & Young, 1963). Sharks occur in the Tigris and Euphrates and the latter authors cite a non-fatal attack in the nearby Karun River involving a soldier standing in water only a foot or two in depth, the twenty-seventh attack (of which about half were fatal) in this river between 1941 and 1949. Smith (1936) recorded a small shark in the Patalung River of Siam and also in the Tale. He identified it as *Scoliodon walbeemhi* (Bleeker) – which Springer (1964) re-identifies as *Carcharhinus acutus* (Rüppell) – a species which had not been reported from freshwaters before. Further observations are given by Boeseman (1964). Reviewing the literature, there is no doubt that sharks, and also rays, invade or live in many fresh and brackish water localities throughout the tropical world.

The list will no doubt be enlarged, but it shows that sharks, normally thought of as stenohaline (unable to withstand drastic changes in salinity) can apparently, and with no undue inconvenience to themselves, abandon the sea for freshwater. From direct observations, one might conclude that members of this otherwise marine group of selachians have subsequently migrated from the sea to colonize freshwaters. However, certain American physiologists (E.K.Marshall, H.W.Smith and Carlotta Smith) believed that the earliest selachians lived in freshwater or slightly brackish water. It is thought that the Elasmobranch fishes emigrated to the sea in the middle of the Devonian period or a little later, and although penetrating frequently into freshwater since then, the subclass as a whole is today predominantly marine (Black, 1957).

These authors base their argument partly on the study of the glomeruli of the kidneys, which are more developed in freshwater fishes than in marine fishes. They admit, however, that the subject presents numerous difficulties, as much in its geological as its palaeontological aspects, leaving room for controversy.

H.W.Smith (1936) pointed out that all hitherto published research on selachians had been on animals living in saltwater (freezing point $\triangle$ 1·5–2·3° C) – somewhat naturally, since the group is mostly marine and the freshwater species mainly occur in regions far from the main centres of research. Now that there is some reason to believe that the marine habitat is a secondary one, there is urgent need to study the physiology of the freshwater species. The selachians of the Silurian and Devonian may well have lived primitively in freshwaters, and there is no reason why some, when faced with appropriate ecological conditions, should not have made the migration back to their ancestral home.

Marine bony fishes (teleosts) are known to drink frequently and abundantly; they have a daily intake of about 4–22 cc of seawater per kilogram of body weight. Marine selachians, on the other hand, do not drink or do so very little. Their internal salt concentration is hypertonic (higher) in relation to the external medium (saltwater), and by osmosis there is a tendency for their bodies to absorb water. So, by simple osmotic uptake, sharks are pro-

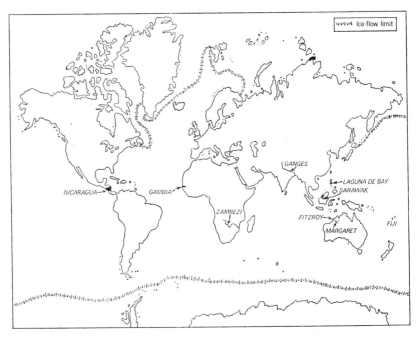

Fig. 42   Principal localities where freshwater sharks have been recorded.

vided with water, and this is thought to take place in the gills, the mouth (buccal mucosa) and the anterior part of the oesophagus. This mechanism is found also in freshwater selachians. In this respect, sharks and rays, whether marine or freshwater, resemble freshwater bony fishes, which also do not swallow water, or at most only a little accidentally. Thus, of all fishes, only the marine teleosts actually drink water normally and regularly (see p. 64).

The freshwater selachians pose problems for the physiologist, the palaeontologist and the geologist, problems which in some cases remain as yet untackled. But whatever the history and mechanics of freshwater colonization by sharks, the following is a summary of what facts are established:

(1) Certain well-known marine species can enter estuaries and ascend into completely fresh waters.

(2) Apart from those species which make incidental incursions into freshwater, there are those which live normally in a freshwater habitat (rivers, streams, lakes). All these sharks are found in tropical or subtropical regions (Figure 42).

(3) Three sharks have been described as living permanently in freshwater: Carcharhinus zambezensis, C. nicaraguensis and C. gangeticus. The first two are closely related to, if not identical with, the Bull Shark, C. leucas.

(4) Certain sharks, not yet identified, are frequently reported from tropical freshwaters. They have in common their small size (about 3 feet).

(5) The freshwater sharks of the Ganges, Zambezi and Lake Nicaragua have all been implicated in attacks on men.

Chapter 7

Pilots and Remoras

'... I say a remora
For it will stay a ship that's under sail.'
(Ben Jonson, *Poetaster*, III, i)

The name 'pilot' has been given to a number of species of fish which are found frequently in the company of sharks and whose behaviour suggests an association such that the smaller fishes lead the shark as blind people were once led by children. Geoffroy Saint-Hilaire, who was professor at the Muséum National d'Histoire Naturelle in Paris in the early part of the last century, described the relationship thus:

It is written that sharks have taken into their employ a very small fish of the cod tribe, that it precedes its master in its travels, that it shows him the places where most fish abound, discovers the trail of fish of which he is most fond, and that in recognition of these services so reported, the shark, in spite of its gluttony, lives in harmony with a creature which is so useful.

This is a fair description of the beliefs commonly held concerning sharks and pilots. Here, however, is Geoffroy Saint-Hilaire's (1807) account of his own observations:

On the 6th Prairial, in the year VI [25 May 1798], I was on board the frigate *Alceste* between Cap Bon and the island of Malta. The sea was calm: the passengers were tired of this long period of calm, when their attention was drawn to a shark which was coming towards the ship. It was preceded by some Pilots which kept at an even distance from the shark; two Pilots swam towards the stern of the ship, visited it twice, and having satisfied themselves that there was nothing there from which they could profit, resumed the course they had held to previously. During all these activities, the shark did not lose sight of them, but rather he followed them so exactly that one would have said that he was towed along by them.

Having seen the shark, a sailor on board prepared a large hook, baiting it with a piece of fat and throwing it into the sea, although in the interval the

146

fishes had had time to draw away to a distance of about 20 to 25 yards from the ship. Geoffroy then continues:

The brute which had occasioned the throwing out [of the line] remained at some distance. Our travellers were astonished and arrested: the two Pilots detached themselves and went to investigate the stern of the ship. During their absence, the shark played in a thousand ways at the surface: it turned over on to its back, turned back on to its belly, dived down into the water, but always re-appeared at the same place. The two Pilots, reaching the stern of the *Alceste*, passed close to the fat and no sooner saw it than they returned to the shark with more speed than when they had come. When they reached the shark, the latter began to continue on its way: then the two Pilots, swimming one on its right and one on its left, made every effort to direct it; scarcely had they done this than they turned round and returned a second time to the stern of the ship: they were followed by the shark which, thanks to the sagacity of its companions, thus came to see the food which was intended for him.

Geoffroy Saint-Hilaire emphasized further the fact that the shark did not appear to be aware of the fat 'until the moment when his guides had, so to speak, indicated it to him'. The shark then rushed forward to seize it, and was caught and hauled on board. On this occasion, the 'guides' had rendered it a bad service.

A little later, a specimen of one of the shark's 'guides' was caught, which Geoffroy Saint-Hilaire recognized as 'belonging to the *pilote* or *fanfre* of sailors, and to the *Gasterosteus ductor* of naturalists'.

The pilotfish or pilot is in fact *Naucrates ductor* (Linnaeus), a member of the family Carangidae (Figure 43 and Plate 8), which Linnaeus had placed in the genus *Gasterosteus* (together with the stickleback) (*Naucrates* = Greek, ruler of ships). These fishes certainly accompany sharks frequently, although not always. In fact, *Naucrates ductor* seems to have a particular tendency to come close to all kinds of floating objects, such as boats and large marine animals. The pilot is abundant in the Mediterranean and was well

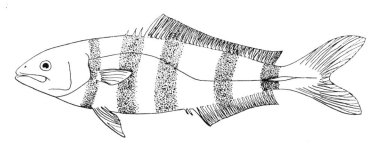

Fig. 43   The Pilotfish *Naucrates ductor*.

known to the ancients, who knew it as a habitual companion of whales and dolphins. It was this fish which, under the name of *Pompile*, followed ships while they were at sea and which, by its sudden disappearance, announced the proximity of land. The term *Pompile* did not necessarily apply to *Naucrates ductor* only, but was given to other fishes which accompanied ships. Pliny says that 'some call Pompiles the tuna that thus follow vessels'.

Of species other than *Naucrates ductor* which are reputed to act as pilots to sharks, there are certain members of the genus *Seriola*, and in particular *Seriola zonata* (Mitchill). The distinction between this species and *N. ductor* is not always obvious at first glance. *Naucrates ductor* has four to five free spines in front of the dorsal fin, the spines not being joined together by a membrane in the adult (but thus connected in juveniles). In *Seriola zonata*, on the other hand, there are seven spines, joined by a membrane. There are also certain less obvious characters separating these two apparently closely related species.

Such an association with sharks is not, however, limited to *Naucrates ductor* and *Seriola zonata*. Limbaugh (1963) has identified two further species which play the role of 'pilots' to sharks. These are the Rainbow Runner (*Elagatis bipinnulatus*) and the Starry Jack (*Caranx stellatus*). These two species frequently escort two common sharks of the Galapagos Islands, the White-tip Reef Shark (*Carcharhinus platyrhynchus*) and another member of that genus, *C. galapagensis*. Apparently they shoal in such numbers that 'sometimes it was impossible to see the shark hidden in the dense school surrounding it'. But, although there are other bony fishes which are found to associate with sharks, it is the Pilotfish (*Naucrates ductor*) that is the classic example.

What can be said of the interpretation put on the shark-pilotfish association by Geoffroy Saint-Hilaire and others before and after him?

His observations are interesting enough, but one cannot help wondering whether, impressed by stories told him beforehand, and then actually seeing the two pilotfish accompanying a shark, he did not approach the behaviour of the trio with preconceived ideas. For sharks have neither better nor worse sensory equipment than other fishes. On their own, and unaccompanied by pilotfish, they are quite capable of searching for and catching their prey without the aid of a 'guide'. With C.Bosc, Geoffroy Saint-Hilaire suggested that perhaps the pilotfish feeds on the leavings of the shark, and that in order to find 'security and protection in the proximity of so voracious a species' it imposes on itself 'the painful duties of domesticity'. In fact there is something picturesque, even a little fabulous, in this association between the blood-thirsty shark and the frail, obliging and harmless little fish. Geoffroy

Saint-Hilaire gave prominence to this case in his *Observations on the natural affection between certain animals, and particularly in the services rendered to a shark by a Pilot.*

That sharks and pilotfish (or other species) are often found together is unquestionably a fact. That sharks should need a scout to search for their prey is very doubtful, to say the least. But it is too much to believe that sharks accord to pilotfish, as a reward for their pains and troubles and recompense for their good offices, on the one hand help and protection, and on the other the remains of their meal, either before or after digestion, the whole constituting a 'gentleman's agreement' whose tenets are always respected. Nevertheless, the existence of a 'treaty' between sharks and pilotfish is believed by some, especially on the Atlantic coast of tropical America, where *Naucrates* is apparently more numerous than elsewhere.

Limbaugh (1963), however, reports an observation made in the Galapagos Islands: 'On one occasion a large rainbow runner bumped a small shark, causing it to disgorge some food which the more agile runner promptly swallowed.' This is a strange type of commensalism and one that was only able to occur because this Rainbow Runner (*Elagatis bipinnulatus*) was much larger than the shark – an exceptional circumstance. This author also noticed that when the same rainbow runners found a prey that was too large for them to eat, their school would sometimes attract a shark 'which would move in and feed'.

Also, local conditions must play their part. Off the west coast of Africa, where sharks are abundant, I have never seen *Naucrates ductor*, either alone or in its supposed association. The pilotfish is not mentioned in the lists of fishes from this region, although it is known from Madeira and the Canary Islands. Fowler (1936) records it, but gives no actual African localities. It is not included in the fine collections made by President Theodore Tissier during his cruise in 1936, in which there are many examples of Remoras (*Echeneis*). The same is true of the Red Sea and the Indian Ocean; although sharks are very common, this reciprocal association with pilotfish has not been observed. *Naucrates* has a widespread distribution, occurring in all tropical and subtropical seas, although the distribution is naturally not even, the fishes being more numerous in one place, rare or absent in another. And in the latter areas the sharks appear to be perfectly able to get along without them.

This tendency to seek shelter or to be attracted to larger creatures is also found in young *Naucrates*, who frequently shelter amongst the tentacles of jellyfishes, a feature common to other species in the family Carangidae, (for example the Common Horse Mackerel (*Trachurus trachurus*) which shelters under the belly of the Sombrero Jellyfish (*Cotylorhiza borbonica*). In the adult, such an attraction may reach almost absurd lengths. Thus, one of the members of the *Siboga* Expedition wrote:

> Near to Kabaena (an island to the south of the Celebes), when we had hooked a large specimen of Blue Shark (*Prionace glauca*), and when the animal was already half pulled out of the water, three specimens of *Naucrates ductor*, the 'shark pilot', swam unceasingly round the tail of the captive. We tried, without success, to catch them in a small handnet; pilots indeed, they made no attempt to save themselves, and we finished by catching them in a vertical Hansen net. It was a sign of remarkable devotion to the shark that they accompanied.

Van Beneden (1870) examined the stomach contents of many specimens of *Naucrates ductor*. They contained pieces of fishes, small crustaceans, some fragments of the skin of fishes, debris of the alga *Fucus*, and some potato peelings – which shows that the specimens in question had followed a ship and eaten some of the rubbish thrown overboard. Van Beneden deduced that pilotfish are fish-eaters or even omnivorous, and that, living in the same waters as sharks, they eat the same type of food as the latter, 'each on the look-out for food proportionate to its size'. Bosc's supposition, reported by Geoffroy Saint-Hilaire, does not seem to have been verified. At the very most, the pilotfish is sometimes in a position to snap up food particles dropping from the sharks jaws when the opportunity arises, but this cannot be the general rule, for we have seen that sharks, in the normal course of events, mostly seize their prey and swallow it whole or cut it up into small pieces neatly and without spilling it. The regurgitation observed by Limbaugh is probably an isolated or extremely rare case.

Regarding the immunity which the pilotfish enjoys with regard to sharks, it can perhaps be attributed to the great agility of *Naucrates*, which is a small, lively and fast-swimming fish; or perhaps more simply to the fact that pilotfish are not to the taste of sharks. We have already seen that the latter can be quite selective in their choice of food, although the absence of pilotfish from sharks' stomachs cannot be taken as final proof. Nevertheless, taking into account the case of the remora (see below), one must conclude that it is more likely to be the agility of *Naucrates* that keeps it out of harm's way.

There is a second companion to sharks which has earned the name of 'pilot', albeit somewhat derisively. This is the remora, a more frequent companion to sharks than the pilotfish and one which is extremely unusual (Figure 44). Here again one must use the plural, remoras, for there are a number of species. These bizarre fishes belong to the family Echeneidae, the

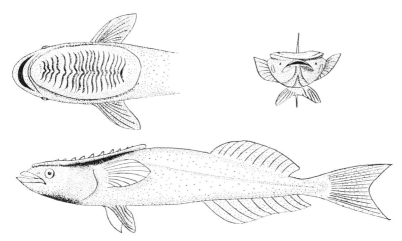

Fig. 44   A Remora or Shark Sucker, showing the 'upside-down' appearance of the
fish and the extraordinary modification of the dorsal fin to form the sucker, the
transverse plates or lamellae being derived from the dorsal finrays.

only family in the order Echeneiformes. The family is very homogeneous
although containing many different species. The essential character in this
group is the presence on the dorsal part of the head of a flat elongate 'disc', a
kind of oval sucker, furnished with transverse lamellae, the whole having
much the appearance of a venetian blind. The edge of each lamella is lined
with sharp denticles which, together with the vacuum action of the sucker,
ensures a firm grip. By means of this organ the remora attaches itself to
floating bodies and often rides for considerable distances. Many remoras are
not exclusive in their choice of host. They adhere to all floating bodies:
hulls of ships, turtles, whales, swordfishes – and also to large pelagic sharks.
In this way they are perfect examples of the phenomenon known as *phoresis*
(from the Greek, to carry, i.e. the carrying of one animal by another of a
different species). Phoresis is known in a number of animals.

The cephalic sucking disc has evidently evolved from nothing less than a
highly modified dorsal fin, the lamellae being the left and right halves of the
dorsal finrays. This is a most remarkable example of the way in which one
body part can become specialized to fulfil quite another function, although
what possible selection advantages the early stages in this evolution would
have conferred on their owners is difficult to imagine.

In the absence of animals or floating objects, remoras freely attach themselves to any flattish surface available. At the aquarium at Vincennes in
Paris, numerous remoras have been kept in a large tank of sea water for some
years, and there is always at least one that is attached to the glass of the

aquarium. The operation is done extremely rapidly, taking only a fraction of a second; one scarcely has time to see the sucker applied to the glass, the lamellae lowered – and the remora is firmly attached. On such a smooth, hard surface, the denticles play no part, but adhesion to the shell of a turtle or the belly of a shark must be even firmer when the denticles are also brought into play. In fact, it is extremely hard to prise a remora loose by pulling it by the tail, i.e. pulling it backwards. On a smooth surface such as glass one can slide the animal but not lift it off. On a rougher surface, where the grip is even stronger, one can go so far as to tear the disc off the fish if the latter, as often happens, does not voluntarily release its hold.

Lutken (1880) believed that only a single species attaches itself to sharks, *Remora remora*. It has since been found that all species of the genus *Echeneis* can temporarily adhere to sharks and then transfer from the latter to another floating object, or merely swim off independently. A sportsman (M.V.), who enjoyed underwater fishing along the West African coast, told me of his surprise when one day he found himself almost a host to a remora. M.V. was in the N'Gor Channel, near Dakar, gliding along near the bottom when an *Echeneis* made a number of attempts to attach itself to him. He was obliged to chase the little fish away by striking out at it, but the remora was in no way intimidated, and kept returning to its prospective host. To rid himself of it, M.V. had to return to the beach. And even until he was in water only six inches deep, the remora kept swimming close to him and trying to attach itself to his ankles. The behaviour of the *Echeneis* was exactly like that of a domesticated animal, like a cat or dog demanding physical contact.

Most remora which are seen belong to the species *Echeneis naucrates*, particularly in the tropical Atlantic. The different species are distinguished mainly by the number of lamellae on the cephalic disc; these range from 10 (in the genus *Phteirichthys*) to 20–28 (in *Echeneis*), with 16–20 in *Remora*. Some species are elongate and fusiform, while others are more stubbily built. The belly and the back are about the same colour, which is rather rare in fishes. In *Echeneis* the lower jaw is very prominent, extending well beyond the tip of the upper jaw. This, coupled with the elongate but symmetrical body and the more or less uniform body colour, gives the impression that the remora swims belly uppermost (from which it receives its Spanish name of *Reverso*). But observations made at the aquarium at Vincennes has shown that, away from their attachment, *Echeneis* swims like any other fish, back (and disc) uppermost. Many photographs taken at the New York Aquarium show remoras lying on the bottom of their tank, without any marked tendency to turn over; and when they attach themselves to sharks, it is mainly to the ventral surface of the animal.

In describing the relationship between sharks and remoras, the terms symbiosis and parasitism have been used; both are incorrect in this context. The shark and the remora are correctly termed 'commensals' (from the Latin, to share a table). If one can put it that way, the shark and the remora eat at the same table, but no more. The remora does not live at the expense of the shark, neither does it render it any particular service. It demands nothing more than a means of transport from place to place. Perhaps it may profit accidentally from food dropped by the shark, but this is the exception. Remoras feed on living fishes and even on molluscs. Van Beneden (1870) examined many *Echeneis* and found in their stomachs fragments of shells (*Haliotis*) and, most remarkably, whole specimens of the Pilotfish *Naucrates ductor*, as well as other fishes.

With regard to the remora itself, it may run some danger from the shark that it accompanies. For example, Springer (1963) reported finding fairly large *Echeneis naucrates* in the stomachs of Sand Sharks (*Odontaspis taurus*). When it is attached to the flank or the belly of its host, it is evidently quite safe. When it is freely swimming, its agility and nimbleness (as observed and recorded by Gudger, 1919) may usually enable it to remain beyond the reach of the shark's jaws. Like the pilotfish, the remora is probably not a habitual prey for sharks. Further, audacity and impudence are sometimes carried to the extent that *Echeneis*, when size allows, will seek refuge in the gill openings or even in the mouth of a shark. This is rare, but it has been seen a number of times in both sharks and large bony fishes, and there can be no doubt that small *Echeneis* will even shelter in the branchial cavities of large marine animals, including sharks. They can attach themselves by their sucker to the inside of the mouth, regaining their liberty either by escaping through the gill-openings, or simply by taking advantage of the next opportunity that the host opens its mouth. Gudger (1922) has published a photograph of a Manta Ray (*Manta* sp.) with a small remora attached to the upper jaw inside the mouth. Some *Echeneis* have been seen to pass with impunity through the jaws of a Hammerhead Shark (*Sphyrna*), a Tiger Shark (*Galeocerdo*) and a Blue Shark (*Prionace glauca*). A Whale Shark, harpooned and brought aboard the research vessel *Vettor Pisani* (in the Gulf of Panama, 1883) contained in its buccal cavity many remoras of about 12 inches in length attached to the palate. The same has been recorded for a whale, and American sport fishermen are well acquainted with the fact that remoras are frequently found to have entered through the gill-openings of Swordfishes (*Xiphias*), Marlins (*Tetrapturus*), Barracuda (*Sphyraena*) and Sailfishes (*Istiophorus*). In this, they resemble the well-known 'cleaner fishes', small species which enter the mouths or branchial chambers of

153

larger fishes, in this case to remove parasites on the gills, etc. However, there is no evidence that remoras perform this function. There are eight species of remoras, placed in two genera, *Remora* and the more elongate *Echeneis* within the family Echeneidae (although some authors recognize more genera depending on the number of lamellae in the sucker). Some species choose a variety of hosts, but others are more particular. *Remora brachyptera* and *R. osteochir* choose billfishes, *R. albescens* favours manta rays, while *R. australis* is found on cetaceans.

The remoras are certainly most curious fishes, but quite as remarkable is the use to which they are put by fishermen. Having discovered that the remora can adhere with considerable force, native fishermen in various parts of the world have made this fish play the role of fisherman. This technique is used in Singapore, in Zanzibar, in Central America, in Australia (Cape York particularly), in Cuba – in fact almost everywhere that the remora occurs. What is especially striking is the fact that in all these areas, which are widely separated from each other and as far as the native fishermen are concerned, not in direct contact with each other, the *same method is used*. James Parsons (1962), in his excellent book on the green turtle and its exploitation, speaks of the possibility of remote transoceanic cultural contact to account for this, but it may merely be a case of convergence since there is virtually only *one* way in which a remora could be used for fishing. A fine line is attached to the base of the tail (caudal peduncle) (Figure 45). The fisherman in his dug-out or other craft keeps his remora either in some kind of container filled with sea water, or in the bottom of his boat with enough water to cover it – or more simply, he tethers it alongside the boat, where the fish often attaches itself to the hull. When the fisherman spots his quarry, he throws the *Echeneis* overboard in that direction. The latter attaches itself to the animal in question – turtle, porpoise, large fish, or whatever it may be. Then the fisherman has only to haul in the line tied to the tail of the remora

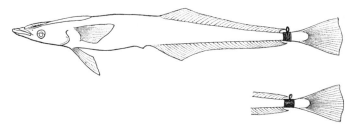

Fig. 45   Two methods used by the fishermen of Zanzibar for the attachment of a line to the caudal peduncle of a Remora. Peduncle wound with wire or cord (upper) or with a metal ring attached (lower) (redrawn after Holmwood).

to bring aboard the catch so obligingly caught by his little fisherman. A blow with a club or knife ends the affair, and the remora is returned to its post to await further work.

The only variation found in this technique is the means by which the line is attached to the remora. Certain fishermen insert the end of the line through the muscles of the fish. Others, and this is more commonly practised, tie the line to a buckle on a small metal collar round the caudal peduncle, or pass it through an eye of wire held in place by whipping (Figure 45).

This is indeed a most extraordinary fishing technique, and when Lady Anne Brassey (1885) gave a precise and circumstantial account of it, she was met by a number of disbelievers. She had, however, been able to observe this kind of fishing under excellent conditions while her yacht, the *Sunbeam*, was moored off La Guayra in Venezuela in 1885. Since then, numerous other observations have been made and some ichthyologists and European fishermen have themselves successfully tried out the technique in the company of native fishermen. In his *Industrie des Pêches à Madagascar*, G. Petit (1930) relates that this method of fishing is used on the coast north of Nossi-Bé (Madagascar) as well as in the Comoro Islands. He states that the Comorans of Moroni pierce the posterior part (of the remora) right through the muscle, inserting a small round peg of wood to prevent the wound closing up and then passing through a small cord to form a ring. This cord is made from the bark of the baobab tree. It even appears that the natives of Pemba and Zanzibar have domesticated their remoras, the latter coming to the fishermen and allowing themselves to be handled when the fishermen whistle in a special soft manner.

A good account of remora fishing is given by C. Ralph DeSola (1932) who helped to catch turtles in this way off the coast of Cuba (where remoras are known as *pega-pegas* or *pegadores*, i.e. stickers). Normally, in a light canoe and with the remora firmly attached to a turtle or shark, the strain placed on the line as the fisherman hauls in his catch is not very great and well within the capabilities of the remora's sucking disc. One cannot, of course, lift the catch out of the water by means of the line. If the strain is too great, the remora is damaged, usually by tearing the sucker and in this event the animal is allowed to rest until healed. The strain that the sucking disc can withstand is surprisingly large. One early experiment was that carried out by Dr C. H. Townsend. He placed the head of a 2-foot remora in a bucket of water and the remora immediately attached itself to the side of the bucket. He then lifted the fish by its tail and it was quite able to support the weight of both bucket and water, the whole weighing 21 lbs. A similar experiment on a slightly larger remora showed that it could lift 24¼ lbs. More recently, Bonnell (1961), in an excellent description of the mechanism of the sucker, has considered the sucking disc to be as efficient as anything yet produced by man and thus capable of a sucking power of some 15 lb/sq. in. He pointed out that since some suckers may cover 8 sq. in. in area, then the fish would be able to suck with a power exceeding 100 lb. Experiments in the New York Aquarium have met with some success: a turtle has been raised to the surface and some large fishes lifted right out of the water. In air, however, the remora relinquishes its hold.

The earliest record of remora fishing dates from the voyages of Columbus and is given by Pierre Martyr d'Anghera, a prominent figure at the Court of Ferdinand and Isobella. From him we have an account of Columbus's second voyage to the New World in 1494. It was off the coast of Cuba, at a place named Jardinellas de la Reine, that the travellers first saw natives in canoes practising this curious fishing technique. In his description, Pierre Martyr (1511) speaks of the remora as an eel-like fish with a kind of pouch or cowl on its head with which it seized its prey. Drawing on this description, Conrad Gesner (1558) published a woodcut showing an *Echeneis* in the act of catching – before the startled eyes of a turtle – an animal that one can only assume to be a manatee or sea cow (Figure 46). This picture was reproduced, with some modifications such as the removal of the boat and the fishermen, by Aldrovandi (1613). Several centuries elapsed before this curious method of fishing was rediscovered by Europeans, in the same area from which it was first described.

Fig. 46   Remora fishing, from Conrad Gesner, 1558. Woodcut illustration based on the report of Pierre Martyr on this method of fishing in the Antilles. An eel-like Remora projects a kind of cowl from its head on to a manatee. One can clearly see the line tied to the Remora by native fishermen (who wear European clothes).

Using this method, the natives catch turtles, large bony fishes, and also sharks, although the latter can give trouble sometimes. Charles F.Holder (1905) relates how, having tried to catch a shark with a remora, the latter was instantly seized and devoured by the shark. This is a most interesting observation, for one almost never finds *Echeneis* in the stomachs of sharks, no doubt because remoras are endowed with agility and fast reactions which render them uncatchable by the larger and less manœuvrable shark. In Holder's case, on the other hand, it would seem that the remora's movements were seriously hampered by the line tied to its caudal peduncle and that it was thus an easy prey for the shark.

Finally, and although this takes us even further from the subject of sharks, I cannot leave out the very ancient belief concerning the ability of remoras actually to stop ships to which they are attached. Pliny the Elder (23–79 AD) wrote:

There is a very small fish, customarily living amongst rocks, which is called Echeneis. It is believed that, attaching itself to the bottoms of ships, it retards their progress; from this it derives its name. According to this belief, it is used to make potions for damping down love, for prolonging legal proceedings and for slowing down the course of justice. It redeems these bad features by having the fortunate ability to arrest ageing in old women and to bring a child to term.

Aristotle (384–322 BC) was, in fact, the first to mention the remora:

A small fish which lives amongst rocks and has received the name Echeneis or Remora; it is used sometimes for conspiracies in legal proceedings or for philtres.

One must suppose that Aristotle had never actually seen a specimen of *Echeneis* when he wrote these lines.[1] He was a keen observer, and the cephalic disc, so characteristic of this animal, could hardly have escaped his notice. The same applies to Pliny who, while stating that the remora

---

[1] This quotation (*Historia Animalium*, 2: 14) continues: 'The creature is unfit for eating. Some people assert that it has feet, but this is not the case: it appears, however, to be furnished with feet from the fact that its fins resemble those organs.' Günther, Gudger, and other authors think it probable that Aristotle here was referring to a Blenny or Goby. Elsewhere, however, Aristotle says: 'In the seas between Cyrene and Egypt there is a fish that attends on the dolphin, which is called the "dolphin's louse". This fish gets exceedingly fat from enjoying an abundance of food while the dolphin is out in pursuit of its prey.' (Book V, 31.) This seems much more likely to be the remora, and as D'Arcy Thompson points out, Hasselquist and Forsskål, pupils of Linnaeus, record arabic names for the remora as *Chamel al Ferrhun* (louse of the terrible one) and *Kaml el Kersh* (louse of the shark). This is discussed in more detail by Gudger (1918).

attaches itself to the bottoms of ships, does not say by what means. Like Aristotle, he does not mention the sucker, such an obvious and exceptional feature that it would certainly have merited comment and description.

It is interesting to note that the magic attributes of the remora which Pliny reports, are all those of a retarding nature; the philtres made from *Echeneis* all have the action of a brake, slowing down and creating an obstacle to advance – in fact all recalling the ability of the remora to stop ships.

There are also the lines from Oppian's *Halieuticks*, Book I (translation of Diaper & Jones, 1722).

> Far from the Shore the wily *Sucker* waits
> The coming Ship, but him the Sailor hates.

and later:

> The *Sucking-Fish* beneath with secret Chains
> Clung to the Keel the swiftest Ship detains.
> The Seamen run confusèd, no Labours spar'd,
> Let fly the Sheets, and hoist the topmost Yard.
> The Master bids them give her all the Sails,
> To court the Winds, and catch the coming Gales.
> But tho' the Canvas bellies with the Blast,
> And boist'rous Winds bend down the cracking mast,
> The Bark stands firmly rooted in the Sea,
> And will unmov'd nor Winds, nor Waves obey.

There are some celebrated examples of the braking action of *Echeneis* to be found in other ancient writings. For example, at the battle of Actium, the flagship which bore Antony, was suddenly stopped short by a remora. As a result, Antony was not able to harangue his troops as the battle commenced, and he even had to transfer to another ship – which, as it turned out, had an unfortunate influence on subsequent events. Again, Caligula's quinquireme, on its way to Antium from Astura, was brought up sharply and was unable to proceed, in spite of the exertions of the 400 oarsmen. When the hull was examined, there was found attached to it a remora – indisputable proof that this small animal had held the galley back.

In the Middle Ages and during the Renaissance, this myth was revived, and there is not a scientific author who does not mention the extraordinary power of the *Echeneis*, whose ability to stop ships in mid-course does not appear to have been doubted by anyone. The earliest known figure of a remora holding up the progress of a ship is that found in Cube's *Hortus sanitatis*, published in 1475. Rabelais mentions this fish on two occasions in

Pantagruel; once in Book 4, Ch. 62; and, on the occasion quoted below, Book 5, Ch. 30.

I saw there a Remora, a small fish, called *Echeneis* by the Greeks, near a big ship which did not move although it had all sails set on the high sea: I believe it was this small fish which stopped Periander the Tyran in spite of the wind.

As might be expected, all naturalists of the 16th century mention the remora, as also many of the poets. Du Bartas, in his *Sepmaine*, for example, has a stanza describing the '*arreste-nef*' (ship-holder):

> La Remore fichant son debile museau
> Contre le moitte bord du tempesté vaisseau
> L'arreste tout d'un coup au milieu d'une flote,
> Qui suit le vueil du vent, et le vueil du pilote.
> Les resnes de la nef on lasche tant qu'on peut,
> Mais la nef pour cela charmée ne s'esmeut,
> Non plus que si la dent de mainte ancre fichée
> Vingt pieds dessous Thetis la tenoit accrochée.

In Spenser's *World's Vanity* comes the following:

> When suddenly there clave unto her keel
> A little fish that men call Remora
> Which stopped her course and held her by the heel
> That wind nor tide could move her thence away.

Following a custom which in some spheres is still practised today, each of these early authors took the affirmations of his predecessors and reproduced them more or less faithfully for the benefit of future generations. Aldrovandi (1613), who nonetheless gave a good figure of an *Echeneis*, showed no advance on Pliny regarding the remora's ability to retard ships. It was not until the end of the 17th century that the abilities of the remora began to be seriously doubted. Until then, there was even a distinction made between the 'Sucez' (*Echeneis*) which attaches itself to the helm in order to slow down the progress of the ship, and the remora, which stopped a ship completely, '*à ce que l'on prétend faussement*' (Le Maire, 1696).

The curious thing is that this legend of a fish able to stop ships is not merely limited to the Mediterranean basin. On the River Leeba, a tributary of the Zambezi, the Barotse believe that there is an enormous but invisible aquatic monster which stops canoes in spite of the efforts of those paddling. Also, Captain Slocum (1948), in the Cocos Keeling Islands, had to carry out a propitiatory ceremony in order that the *kpeting*, a large crab which held his boat by the keel, would be persuaded to let go.

The Discocephali (Berg's order Echeniiformes) are not the only animals held to be responsible for holding back ships. Other marine creatures were also believed to have this power. Pliny cites Gaius Mucianus, who speaks of 'a *Murex* larger than a porpoise, with a head neither uneven nor round, and a snout which is not bony. Its shell is simple and folded inwards on both sides.' He says that this murex attached itself to a ship which, under Periander's orders, bore children of high birth to be made eunuchs; the ship, which was in full sail, suddenly became immobile. He adds that 'the shells which rendered this good service to humanity are honoured in the Temple of Venus at Cnide' (Pliny). So, according to the ancients, these shells can also act like remoras, but this concept did not become widely accepted and it is *Echeneis* which was almost always blamed, until the end of the Middle Ages. The word 'fish' is always expressly used. Certain authors are more precise, specifying a type of *Anguilla* or *Muraena*, i.e. some kind of eel (Abbé A. Fortis, 1778). Some reputedly trustworthy authors have reported seeing lampreys attached to boats.

Having said all this, the incontestable fact remains that on a number of occasions ships have, suddenly and without apparent cause, come to a stand-still, no longer responding to the helm and giving the exact impression that an irresistible force had taken hold of the hull and prevented it moving forward even though the sails remained full and the wind had not dropped. Many explanations have been given to account for this phenomenon.

(1) That the hull was weighted by algae and attached marine organisms. Obviously this could slow down the progress of a ship, but under no circumstances could it bring the ship abruptly to a halt.

(2) That the remora, attaching itself to the rudder, pushes against the boat. One cannot see how. Rondelet's argument was that an *Echeneis* or *Remora* might put its mouth or snout against the rudder and move it back and forth, and this movement would then be communicated to the prow and the ship would be stopped in its tracks. This is not very convincing.

(3) That a large number of remoras attach themselves simultaneously to the bottom of the ship. This is not unknown; E.W.Gudger (1919) has cited examples of it, but in his observations it involved rather small craft whose reduction in speed would be very noticeable if half a dozen large remoras attached themselves to the bottom of the boat. On a ship of moderate or large size the effect would be negligible. In any case, it is here a matter merely of a slowing down of the boat, not its complete stoppage. Again, such con-certed action on the part of *Echeneis* is very rare. According to all other authors, it is just *one* remora that is involved and the problem to consider is how one small fish could exert such power as to counteract the force of the wind or the strength of numerous oarsmen.

(4) 'Dead-water.' The direct action of remoras cannot therefore be seriously considered, even where small craft are concerned. All the evidence points to there being 'something', some other factor that early authors were not able to deduce nor even suspected. Thus DuTertre (1667–71), like many another writer of that time, resorted to the miraculous, in order to explain the unknown in the physical world:

As there are such a great number of Remoras around the Western Isles, there is hardly a boat that does not have many attached to its bottom: and, moreover, since for a century or more these islands have been frequented, yet [it is curious that] it has not been noticed that a single boat has been stopped. This makes me believe that the two or three ships that are said to have been stopped by remoras have been detained by some *miracle or charm*, and that at the time remoras have been found attached as usual to these ships, to which the cause of the stoppage has been falsely attributed.

It is from northern waters, however, that light is finally thrown on the problem. There is a phenomenon known as *dödvand* or 'dead-water' by Norwegian sailors, and it was well known to the Scandinavian navigators. For a long time they had noticed that sometimes, without apparent reasonable cause, a boat would suddenly stop, failing to respond to the helm, and to all appearances held by some irresistible force. The Norwegians have a well developed 'feeling' for, and knowledge of, the sea, leaving fabulous explanations to excite the imaginations of the Mediterraneans. Instead of placing the blame on an inoffensive remora, they merely observed that this phenomenon of 'dead-water' only occurs where fresh or brackish water comes into contact with seawater. This was a most illuminating observation, and one that was eventually destined to provide the solution to the mystery.

During his voyage in the *Fram* in 1893–6, Dr Nansen many times experienced this effect of 'dead-water' along the coasts of northern Siberia. Professor V. Bjerknes of Stockholm passed this problem over to his illustrious pupil, V.W.Ekman, indicating the direction in which he thought Ekman should investigate it. Ekman made a thorough study and published his findings in an important paper which I would strongly recommend to readers interested in hydrodynamical problems. I will here give an account of the general conclusions reached by Ekman (1906).

Ekman first proceeded to an extensive study of the places where the phenomenon of dead-water had been reported, which confirmed his opinion that it was only where fresh and saltwater met that it occurred. The *dödvand* is so frequent off the Norwegian coast that Ekman was able to map the places that were particularly prone to it. It occurs, however, in other parts of the world. Ekman collected evidence regarding the coasts of Sweden and Denmark, the Mediterranean, the mouth of the St Lawrence, the Gulf of Mexico, the mouths of large South American rivers, and so on.

The phenomenon of 'dead-water' has been reported off the coast of France, for example, at the mouth of the Loire where it is known by the name of '*bournes*' (a boat thus being *embourné*). It occurs also near Bordeaux, where it is said that the waters are 'heavy', and sometimes also in the bay of Arcachon. In fact it seems to occur wherever a layer of fresh or brackish water overlies seawater.

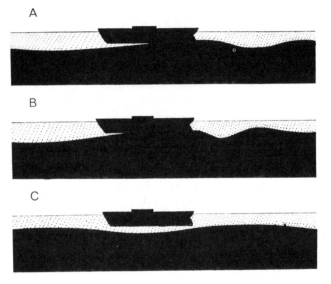

Fig. 47   The phenomenon of 'dead water'. Diagram to show Ekman's experiments on a model of the *Fram*. Sea water shown black, freshwater stippled. The ship is retarded in A and B but not in C.

From this evidence, Ekman went on to make a series of experiments which confirmed the hypothesis originally put forward by Professor Bjerknes. Into a glass tank containing seawater which had been coloured black with Indian ink, he poured a certain amount of freshwater, but in such a way that it lay in a layer on top of the seawater. He produced in this manner a fair representation of the natural conditions found at the mouths of rivers or at the outlets of fjords, i.e. in those places where the phenomenon of dead-water occurred. He then had a model of the *Fram* made (for the research had been initiated by Dr Nansen), and towed the model across the tank at various speeds. The results fully confirmed the ideas suggested by Professor Bjerknes.

When the model boat moved on a layer of freshwater overlying the coloured seawater, it set up at the interface between the two liquids a series of waves often of quite large amplitude. The waves would be invisible to an observer on the ship since there was no sign of them at the surface. It was precisely these waves which brought about the phenomenon of dead-water. When the wave of saltwater rose high enough to touch the hull of the ship, the boat slowed down and then stopped (Figure 47, a and b).

Ekman found that there was a critical speed at which the slowing effect was greatest. Above this critical speed waves were no longer formed between the freshwater and the seawater and the effect of dead-water disappeared; the boat then regained its freedom to manœuvre.

This is the reason why dead-water was above all encountered by sailing ships and slow steamers. The *Fram*, which with its engine attained $4\frac{1}{2}$ to 5 knots, had its speed reduced to $1\frac{1}{2}$ or even 1 knot in dead-water. On another occasion, it took 8 hours to traverse a distance of barely 8 miles, with the engine working at full power. With sailing ships, the situation is made worse by the fact that in dead-water they would not respond to the helm. A sudden slowing down of the ship, almost to a standstill, and consequently the failure of the ship to respond to the helm – this is a set of circumstances which would be quite inexplicable and would certainly astonish ignorant and super-stitious sailors. It would only need the discovery of an innocent remora attached to the hull for the explanation to seem clear. So it was that for centuries the remora was blamed for this curious hydrodynamic phenomenon.

It is noticeable that the cases in antiquity in which the remora is accused of holding back ships, all occurred in areas where the presence of freshwater at the surface of the sea is more than probable. The battle of Actium took place at the entrance to the Gulf of Arta, where many rivers discharge – conditions which are comparable to those found along the coast of Norway, at the entrance to fjords or the mouths of large rivers. Caligula's galley, on the way to Ostia, could, thanks to the discharge from the Tiber, have encountered all the conditions necessary for the phenomenon of dead-water.

If the remora has no retarding action on ships, there is still some doubt regarding its effect on sharks. When many remoras attach themselves by their suckers to the belly or flanks of a shark, they must surely provide a certain amount of resistance and thus reduce the speed of a shark, particu-larly at that moment when it rushes in to seize its prey. Similarly, when the shark is swimming fast, they must have a noticeable retarding effect.

Normally, however, sharks tend to cruise rather slowly, and the presence of even a number of remoras would be hardly apparent. But whatever inconvenience the remoras may be, the shark is obliged to put up with it, since it is not in its power to rid itself of these 'passengers'.

Chapter 8

Shark Myths and Legends

The giants of the animal kingdom are all found nowadays in the seas. The largest of elephants makes a poor showing against a Blue Whale of a hundred feet in length and weighing a hundred and twenty tons. There are, in fact, cetaceans, sharks, even large bony fishes in Neptune's Kingdom, whose enormous size is enough to impress any shore dweller. The 'sea monster' is a classic figure. Out of the dreaded watery unknown, full of mystery and at the same time full of wonderful beasts, a strange animal is suddenly seen, of prodigious size and thus quite certainly sent by the Gods to terrify and punish men!

The men of antiquity provide us with many types of sea monster. There is, for example, the monster sent by Theseus to avenge the incestuous love between his wife Phaedra and his bastard son Hippolytus. The monster's role was indirect. It rose from the sea as Hippolytus was driving his chariot from Athens; mad with terror, the horses reared, the reins caught on a tree, and Hippolytus was dragged to his death. Usually, however, the classical sea monster ravages the shores of a country until it is finally paid tribute, preferably annually. It has a marked predilection for young maidens, and in particular for unmarried girls of royal parentage. The unfortunate victim, in tears, is offered sacrificially to the beast; but at the last minute the brave hero arrives and full of courage and daring, saves the maiden from the fate apportioned her. Thus Andromeda is saved by Perseus, and Hesione by Hercules. The story ends in marriage (in the case of Perseus and Andromeda), in accordance with a tradition that had been maintained for thousands of years. Or again, in the case of Hercules and Hesione, at a much later date, with the battle of Troy. . . .

Whatever the origin of these fables – sun myth, eastern tradition, symbolism, etc – the sea and its inhabitants play an essential role. The result is a theme which runs through some of our greatest tragic literature, and one that appears time and again in our painting and sculpture. But the monster which forms the basis of these stories is never figured, or at best is such a vague and fantastic creature that it would be impossible to identify it. So vague in fact, that one cannot tell if it is supposed to be a cetacean, a shark or some other marine animal.

The Cachalot or Sperm Whale (*Physeter catodon*), males of which reach 60 feet in length, is found in the Mediterranean: perhaps it was more common in the heroic epoch than it is nowadays, and one can imagine the effect that this enormous beast would produce on the minds of men sailing in small ships and with a slender knowledge of the sea (and perhaps no great confidence in their craft). A large White Shark, although less imposing, could also be quite frightening. Sharks have always lived in the Mediterranean, contrary to the absurd view of those who assert that they have only entered since the opening of the Suez Canal; Aristotle, Pliny, and many others have attested to the presence of sharks off the coasts of Egypt, Italy and Greece.

There is now no means of knowing what was meant by the term 'sea monster' used in so many of the ancient fables. But Keller (1909–13) thinks that the *Bul* (that is to say 'The One that Devours') of Babylonian legend, which periodically left the sea to ravage the countryside and to devour young girls, and who was finally killed by Izdubar, might well have been a large shark or grampus (or Killer Whale (*Orcinus orca*), the only cetacean habitually preying on other mammals). However that may be, the Chaldean Bul was closely related to the Mediterranean monsters and perhaps directly ancestral to them.

Sharks often form the basis of highly sophisticated legends of marine peoples living in close touch with these 'tigers of the sea'. Captain Young (in McCormick *et alii*, 1963), for example, records numerous Polynesian myths relating to sharks, to a shark-god, and so on. Curiously enough, the shark is not always depicted as the villain. The shark-god shows a certain spirit of justice, and even the ordinary sharks play the part of pilots, guiding lost canoes and boats towards the land, in the dark or in a mist, with perfect precision.

Leenhardt (in Levy-Bruhl, 1938) tells the story of a Kanaka or South Sea islander at sea in his canoe who is attacked by a shark. The animal, jumping out of the water, falls right into the boat and seizes the gunwhale in its teeth. The Kanaka, who is alone with his wife in the boat, picks up an axe and prepares to kill the shark; but at that moment he is struck by the 'look' of the shark, which fixes him peacefully with his red [*sic*] eye. The man lays down the axe, empties the ballast out from the boat and proceeds to capsize it. The shark is thus returned to the water, where it swims off, while the couple right the boat and make for the shore.

Commenting on this remarkable story, L.Levy-Bruhl (1938) links it to the general significance that is attached in primitive eyes to any encounter with an animal whose behaviour seems a little different to that of its fellows. The Kanaka knew that there were two kinds of shark: the first were simply the animals that they appeared to be, but the second were men who had taken on this form, usually after death. Just as he was about to strike the shark, the Kanaka discovered that the animal had a curiously human look in its eye. One recalls that the eye in certain sharks does indeed have an almost human look (*l'œil d'almée* of Rochon-Duvigneaud). If this man went through the delicate operation of overturning his boat in order to set the shark free, it might not only be compassion that prompted him; it could be as much a desire not to remain for too long in the company of a supernatural being. Moreover, the story-teller asserts that the shark was quite certainly one of the man's parents!

It is in the story of Jonah and the Whale that a shark makes its most remarkable appearance. In his description of the Great White Shark (*Carcharodon*), Rondelet (1554) shows with precise detail the enormous capacity of the stomach and the size of the throat (see p. 112). He adds:

On considering carefully, I felt that it was a Lamie [i.e. White Shark] in the stomach of which Jonah, by Divine Providence, remained for three days, whence he emerged safe and sound, which is not against the Holy Scriptures: for it is written that Jonah was in the belly of a cetacean, a name which is general to all large fishes and chiefly to those giving birth to live young and not eggs according to Aristotle. This being so, it need not be that by the word cetacean, a whale is understood rather than any other large cetacean fish, seeing that the whale has a wind-pipe and lungs which are so placed that the stomach and throat cannot be so large as in the Lamie, in which one sometimes finds whole men.

Rondelet used these anatomical facts to put forward his hypothesis, all the time giving good reasons to show that he was not erring from the word of the Scriptures. This was prudent in the 16th century; in this period of fanaticism it was wise to take certain precautions. The impossibility of passing a man down the narrow throat of a whale led Rondelet to search for a marine animal capable of swallowing such a large prey and of bringing it up later on. *Carcharodon*, the White Shark, was not a bad choice. However, Rondelet was not alone on this view. As Lineaweaver & Backus (1970) point out, several other writers chose a shark rather than a whale, one of them being Heinrich Herman Frey in his *Biblisch Fischbuch* or *Ichthyobiblia* of 1594. Concerning the Jonah legend, there is a drawing in a 14th-century manuscript showing the prophet at the moment that he is re-gurgitated (Figure 48). The 'monster' shows the fantastic and unidentifiable appearance with which the artists of the Middle Ages drew whales and other large marine animals. But Jonah himself is completely naked and unclothed; moreover, he is totally bereft of hair. Possibly the artist wanted in this way to show the corrosive effects of the gastric juices of the 'whale', which would

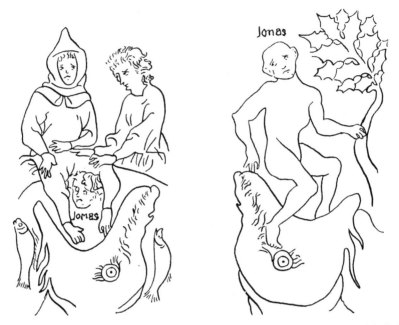

Fig. 48   An old print illustrating the Jonah story. In the first picture Jonah is being swallowed by the 'sea monster'; in the second Jonah emerges after his sojourn in the stomach of the beast.

have had time to act on Jonah's hair and clothes in the three days that he was incarcerated. Another picture shows Jonah as he is being seized by the monster. The prophet wears a cloak and has long curly hair. The comparison between *before* and *after* is quite striking. . . .

Linnaeus (1758) took up Rondelet's hypothesis, and in the section on *Carcharias*, that is to say, the White Shark *Carcharodon* (definitely identifiable as such by the description of the teeth as *Sq. dentibus triangularibus serratis*) he wrote: '*Jonam prophetam, ut veteres Herculem trinoctem, in hujus ventriculo tridui spatio, haessisse vero simile est.*'

Such is the formula given by Linnaeus in the 10th edition of the *Systema Naturae* of 1758, the starting point of modern zoological classification and nomenclature. In subsequent editions, and particularly in that of 1788 by Gmelin, this formula is preserved and amplified. One should, therefore, substitute 'shark' for 'whale' in the story of Jonah, and even, for the sake of complete accuracy, *Carcharodon carcharias*. In the 1611 translation of the Bible the word whale is not used in the original story: the animal is simply referred to as a 'great fish' – a direct translation from the Hebrew words *gadol* and *dag*. In the New Testament, however, where the story is retold in

Matthew (12 : 40), the word 'whale' is used (from the Greek *kētos*). Elsewhere in the Old Testament (Genesis, 1 : 21; Ezekiel, 32 : 2; and Job, 7 : 12) the Hebrew *tanhim* (a great sea monster) has been rendered as whale, suggesting that those who first recorded the Jonah story wanted to emphasize that it was not a monster that swallowed Jonah but a fish, albeit a great one.

In the olden days, the capture of a shark on a sailing ship was taken to be an omen. In the 16th century, to come across a Hammerhead Shark was thought to bring bad luck. Sharks are frequently mentioned in the predictions of the '*Calier*'. In the days of wooden ships, the *caliers* were sailors on French merchantmen or frigates who travelled in the hold, where they were constantly engaged in handling the numerous things indispensable to daily life at sea. They hardly came on deck, living almost entirely in the dark bowels of the ship, amongst the noise of the water and the creaking of the timbers, and producing like magic the articles required by the top-men. In the eyes of those on deck, this cavelike existence conferred on the *caliers* a certain amount of prestige, for they were thought of as seers, with the ability to see into the future. (In passing, it can be noted that darkness, such as that provided by the long Scandinavian winters, seems particularly conducive to story-telling and myth-making – leading naturally to soothsaying where a few men are isolated from the rest of the community.) The *caliers*, of course, exploited the sailors' credulity for their own ends, since it brought them, in return for their prophecies, the most cherished thing of all – a quart of wine whenever the top-men or gunners wanted to know what Fate held in store for them.

The *caliers* never committed themselves too far – a technique common to all soothsayers – and their vocabulary was sufficiently imprecise that the prophecies could not be pinned down with certainty. Here is an example (de la Landelle, 1842) of some predictions made by a *calier* to a young and gullible newcomer on board a frigate at the beginning of the 19th century.

> There will be on board a great destruction three days hence. The day after taking a large female shark, which will be caught on a thundery morning, there will be a battle: and as for you, if you are not done for, I shall be surprised. . . .

Armed with this information, the sailor could await the battle with as bold a heart as he could muster. There were enough sharks in the sea, and enough English men-of-war, for the *calier*'s predictions to turn up one day or another. For the young sailor, the prophecy was sufficiently vaguely framed that he could not say that it had failed.

The catching of a female shark was thought to portend major events, either good or bad, particularly if the female carried a full-term foetus. This superstition would have been perpetuated by the 'Down-Easters', the large American sailing ships which made the voyage from San Francisco to New York in the days when Cape Horn had to be rounded. On French ships, the catching of a shark, either male or female, had a particular significance in these later years. Moreover, it was traditional that a sailing ship carried, nailed to the bowsprit, the tail of a porpoise. Failing this, the tail of a shark would do. Thus, in 1908, the four-masted barque *Avenir*, which for many years was to be the training ship of the Belgian navy, was at Antwerp ready to make her first voyage to the South Seas. But, just as it was about to depart, many of the sailors, mostly Scandinavian, Irish and German, pointed out that the ship did not have the traditional porpoise or shark's tail on the bowsprit. The ship had nonetheless 'sailed', since it was built in Bremen. Many refused to go on board, and it had to be pointed out to them that the *Avenir* had not sailed in the strict sense; a tug-boat had taken it to Bremen on leaving the shipyard and had brought it to Antwerp, without the ship being rigged or moved in any other way than by towing. This persuaded them, but as soon as the ship was under way, all equipment was checked and watched, and when a shark first appeared, everything was done to catch it. Finally, the luck-bearing tail was nailed to the bowsprit, greatly to the relief of all concerned.

Modern cargo and passenger ships do not give much scope for the retention of these old superstitions, for most of them are too fast for sharks to be caught by trolling a hook over the stern and it is doubtful whether sharks care to follow ships at this speed for long. Thus, one can travel many times on passenger lines nowadays without seeing the 'triangular fin' in the wake of the ship or alongside, the sight of which was so commonplace to the men aboard the slaving ships, the whalers and the old sailing ships. Nowadays, it is also true to say that on a multi-decked modern liner, with its indoor pool, gymnasium, lounges and bars, one hardly sees the sea itself for long periods, except by chance.

Shark stories! They would fill a huge dossier, which could well be labelled 'Absurdities', although even this is too mild for some of the naïveties and errors, often stated categorically, which besprinkle such a collection. Sharks have always acted as a stimulant to men's imagination.

There is a quite distinct vocabulary used for sharks: they are referred to as ferocious monsters, fearful, dreaded beasts, and so on. These are formulae such as the standard clichés 'distinguished economist', 'trim chamber-maid', 'confirmed bachelor', etc, which one merely notes in passing. There is nothing very remarkable about this. Shark's teeth are always 'razor sharp' and the tail is usually 'powerful'. In a word, the shark vocabulary is unrelievedly banal and one is pleasantly surprised by the rare use of a new epithet.

Less banal however, is the 'new' information given on these 'sea monsters', details of the manner in which they were caught, the use to which they are put and their behaviour. The Press's contribution to this collection of observations is important. For the most part this comprises reports and short news items, but also there are documentary articles with all the appearance of being serious writing. If the old sailors' traditions concerning sharks are near to dying out, the literary and journalistic counterparts are showing a remarkable vitality and tenacity.

In taking a look into this dossier of 'shark stories', we can leave aside the 'man-eater' stories, for these have already been dealt with in Chapter 5. We will also leave aside the stories dealing with certain supposed by-products of sharks, a subject dealt with in the next chapter. The true by-products are sufficiently numerous for it not to be necessary to add imaginary ones to the list. However, I cannot resist quoting one such example, from Joseph de Maistre (*Les Soirées de Saint-Petersburg*, 7th entretien). 'One knows how many barrels of oil the head of a shark or a sperm-whale (can produce) . . . '

This is all very well in the case of the sperm-whale, from which the spermaceti is extracted for use in the manufacture of candles or ointments. But, contrary to Joseph de Maistre's opinion, it is certainly not known how many barrels of oil could be extracted from the *head* of a shark – for the simple reason that there is no oil there at all, not even a thimbleful: the oil is extracted from the *liver*. A man of letters, an essayist, a master of language, can perhaps ignore such details. Agreed, but much better to leave aside this kind of uninformed writing. Moreover, most of the inexactitudes that crop up can be quite easily checked by a perusal of the Petit Larousse dictionary for schoolboys. With regard to the Basking Shark fishery at Trevignon off the coast of Brittany in the winter of 1943–4, one read the following: 'The flesh of the *cetaceans* is in fact quite edible.' (*Le Nouvelliste*, Rennes, 25 February 1944.) 'In a few days, they (i.e. Parisians) will be able to have a piece of these formidable *cetaceans* on their plates. . . .' (*La Légia*, Liège, 20 February 1944.)

A small transgression, perhaps, but why perpetrate it when it could easily have been avoided; and in any case, what purpose did it serve? In the same vein, but more laughable, was the notice appended to a photograph of a Basking Shark in the Fish Market in Paris: 'This is a giant fish known as a *pélerin*. It is related to the sharks and the dolphins.' (*La Depêche*, Tours, 9 December 1940.) One wonders whether it would be the butcher or the fishmonger who would be employed to carve or fillet the beast.

There are many errors of interpretation. At the same time that the Basking Sharks were hitting the headlines, a journalist had the bright idea of getting some more precise information from the late Professor L. Bertin, the Director of Ichthyological Department of the Muséum National d'Histoire Naturelle in Paris. The latter, having given some details on the systematics and relationships of the Basking Shark, went on to mention that the oil from shark's livers has a remarkable feature. It contains more or less large quantities of a hydrocarbon called *squalene*. He ended by some general remarks on the possible animal origin of oil-bearing strata. This information, quite exact as it stood, was subjected to a process of journalistic metamorphosis, which produced the following result: 'Would you like shark with black butter, or would you rather have kerosene? As for the experts, they have all exclaimed "Stop! we shall take charge of the catch: it is for making lamp oil!" ' (*L'Echo de la France*, Paris, 24 February 1944.) 'But let us rejoice, however, since these animals can, it is said, provide us with lamp oil.' (*Le Patriote*, Chateaudun, 15 March 1944.)

This paragraph was, moreover, reproduced in exactly the same form by many Parisian and provincial newspapers in March 1944. There were those who were not content merely with vague statements, but wanted to add more technical precision. 'Besides, nothing would be lost, for these marine monsters, conveniently ground up and put through a press would, it is said, provide good quality lamp oil. It only remains now to catch enough of them for our lighting.' (*Petit champenois*, Chaumont, 19 March 1944.)

We can pass over the gross errors, such as the photograph of a swordfish with the title 'South Sea shark caught in Australian waters.' (*La France*, Bordeaux, 26 August 1941.) But it saddened me to find, from the pen of an otherwise excellent and well-informed author, the following lines. 'I say emphatically, in fact, that certain sharks do not have a central nervous system. This is the case of the Greenland Shark, in which each part of the body seems to have a life of its own: the head, when separated from the body, is still capable of snapping at a leg or a foot.' (*Le Journal*, 10 April 1940.)

It is useless to protest that there are no sharks which lack a central nervous system; that *Somniosus microcephalus*, the Greenland Shark, like any other shark, has a perfectly well-developed brain and spinal cord. As for the vitality shown by *Somniosus*, and taken by the author as proof of his contention, we have already seen that this is common to all sharks, the jaws of a severed head continuing to snap and the heart to beat long after its removal from the body (p. 128). In the present case, the author seems to have relied on the word of some highly misinformed observer.

There are also the 'facts-are-stranger-than-fiction' type of article in newspapers and magazines: when carefully checked, however, they throw considerable doubt on that thesis! Here is an example. 'DID YOU KNOW THAT . . . the most voracious of all fishes is the shark? The latter are viviparous and bring forth only a single offspring at one time, but from its birth the latter is as hungry as its parents, and is armed with jaws capable of cutting a human leg into two without effort.' (*Independent*, Salonique, 14 April 1939; *Echo de l'Est*, Bar-le-Duc, 16 April 1939.) It is best we pass over these astonishing details, for it is well nigh impossible to answer such nonsense in just a few words.

There are also the stories of the pearl-fishermen coming to grips with these monsters of the depths. Pliny and his 'dogs' looks tame when compared with the following article, which was published in two newspapers, with a slight interval between. (*Parlementaire*, Paris, 25 February 1940, and *Radical*, Marseilles, 4 March 1940.)

If a [pearl] diver is taken by surprise by a shark on the sea bottom, he does not make distractedly for the surface. He knows very well that the shark would very quickly attempt to bite at a limb exposed in swimming. On the contrary, he crouches, throwing out his chest in order to use the least of his reserves of air. In spite of his precarious position in an element in which he cannot breathe, he is ready to save himself with the utmost energy. He looks danger in the face, and is not afraid of the sight of his implacable enemy. When the rapacious shark prepares to seize him, turning swiftly on its side and thus exposing its belly, the native, with a lightning movement, plunges his knife into its entrails, making a wound as deep as possible. Thus mortally wounded, the shark zigzags away, and the hero of this adventure makes for the surface and the life-giving air. Such heroice scenes are not rare: to us simple mortals they appear unbelievable.

The herculean strength of these chaps is prodigious. A traveller recounted an adventure that happened recently on one of his cruises. A sailing ship had been wrecked on a coral reef in the Red Sea. Broken in half, the boat had been lost, and the shipwrecked crew prepared to swim to dry land when all at once numbers of sharks appeared. They devoured five members of the crew. Amongst the survivors was a native of exceptional size. He accomplished an extraordinary and almost superhuman feat of strength. Almost at the shore, he felt the swirl of a shark trying to seize him. Seeing that his position was hopeless, he made a supreme decision. With a sudden movement, he hugged the beast to his body. The latter, in spite of furious thrashing, could not disengage itself from the formidable grasp of the native, who swam like this towards a sandbank. He only released the dangerous beast when the latter showed no further signs of life. This almost incredible story was vouched for by the companions of this new kind of Hercules. As proof of their veracity, they showed a traveller who had come to their aid the gasping corpse of the shark lying on the sandbank (which had served as their refuge).

And there it is. The author, who is anonymous, does not give the date, nor the location (Red Sea is too vague), nor the name of the witness to this mighty feat. Strangling a monstrous man-eater, towing it while swimming to the sandbank, and then abandoning it as a gasping corpse – this is surely a unique feat!

Dates, names and places, however, cannot always be guaranteed to be authentic, and the most circumstantial stories can leave large areas of baffling uncertainty. An example of this is what could be called the 'Chenille de mer' (literally 'sea caterpillar') affair.

In 1939 (on 11 June to be precise), the *Eclaireur de l'Est* of Rheims published quite a long article entitled:

The Capture of an Enormous Chenille de Mer

It is a most curious animal that we present to our fellow-citizens, which will arouse no little curiosity in them. This animal, which is a marine dweller of the family *Squales* (sharks) has come to us, by what mysterious chance? from the coast of Florida, and it was caught off the Cordouan lighthouse. The Chenille de mer is a truly bizarre animal, as much in its general appearance as in the composition of its skin. Weighing 245 kilograms and measuring 2·60 metres in length and 1·35 metres around, at its greatest girth, this fish derives its name from the way that it progresses in the water, which curiously recalls that of caterpillars moving by undulations across a cabbage leaf.

Its mouth opens on the underside of the head, as in all sharks, its short fins lying towards the rear; as regards the tail, this is composed of only a single lobe. The skin of the animal is made up of a multitude of bony particles which, from their hardness and sheen, have the appearance of white marble. . . .

The Chenille is a great destroyer of fishes. Its stomach can cope with 50 kilos of fish, a quantity which it is able to consume many times a day. . . . A fearless animal, the Chenille attacks man not to eat him, as does the Blue Shark, but in the spirit of battle. It can bite viciously, and, with a blow of its tail, knock a person senseless and can even upset a boat.

M. Barnet and his companion, Giricq, who caught this animal, had a homeric battle with it, and it was only when they had harpooned it that they gained mastery over it. . . . We have seen marine animals, and some most curious ones, but we have never seen this creature before. One can believe that it must be of real interest, since the Centre de Pisciculture maritime de Boston [*sic*] have bought it for 14,000 francs.

In conclusion it can be said that this unique specimen is on view in Rheims, 11 rue de Tallyrand; thereafter it will be on view in London.

This sensational news item contains too many extraordinary details for us to spend time pointing them all out. However, it can be deduced that this 'phenomenal' Chenille de mer is nothing more than a Bramble Shark (*Echinorhinus brucus*), a relative of the Greenland Shark (*Somniosus*); its skin is in fact irregularly strewn with areas of large spiny protuberances having the structure of placoid scales and resembling the 'bucklers' of the Thornback Ray. In France, the common name of this shark is Bouclé, which like the English name, refers to the prickly skin. Along the coast of Vendée, Charente-Maritime and Gironde, however, it is also given the name 'Chenille', not for the manner in which it swims, but presumably for its resemblance to a hairy or spiny caterpillar. The Bramble Shark is neither exceptional nor fabulous. Its method of swimming hardly differs from that of other sharks; its range is not limited to the Florida coast – it is known to be quite common from Bidassoa to Adour, and Moreau has reported it in large numbers off Saint Jean-de-Luz, although it becomes rare beyond Gironde. The Paris Museum has five specimens. Even being charitable, one must admit that the *Eclaireur de l'Est* managed to embellish the facts in quite a remarkable manner!

One of the most curious aspects of the report is the statement that the 'Centre de Pisciculture maritime de Boston' (whatever organization this might be) solemnly bought this worthless animal for the sum of 14,000 francs (1939 value), and that the said 'Chenille', caught at Royan, was exhibited at Rheims and then in London, before being sent to the United States, where no doubt it was anxiously awaited by its happy purchasers!

All this is plainly of little intrinsic importance and would hardly merit inclusion in our dossier, were it not for another 'scoop' by the Press which revived the affair. Three years later, on 17 October 1942, the *Dépêche de Berri* of Bourges announced, in its turn, the 'Capture of an Enormous Chenille de Mer' by two fishermen at Royan, a 'phenomenal beast' which weighed no less than 245 kilos and measured 2·60 metres in length and 1·55 metres in girth. The journalist elaborated on the story for the benefit of readers who had demanded further information on the ways of these fantastic 'fishes'.

Here is what can be said about it, in full agreement with sea-going people and competent fishermen: The Chenille de mer lives and reproduces in the depths off the coasts of Florida; it does not possess lungs, but has a swim-bladder, a reservoir of air which it distends or contracts at will, and which allows it to adjust its volume in order to maintain itself at the depth which suits it. It possesses, like the shark, a dental arsenal . . . etc.

A character common to *all* sharks is precisely that they do *not* have a swim-bladder (although such is present in most bony fishes). Of less importance is the fact that the animal was to be exhibited at Vierzon, in the Place Aristide-Briand.

Thus, within a space of three years, two *Echinorhinus* are caught at Royan by two fishermen, and strangely enough they have the same weight and dimensions. It is, of course, possible, but it seems a remarkable coincidence.

But we have not finished yet. On 8 May 1943, the *Dépêche d'Eure-et-Loir* of Chartres published a headline, 'Two Fishermen off Cordouan Catch an Enormous Chenille de Mer. It Will be Exhibited in Chartres', reproducing underneath word for word the article printed by the *Eclaireur de l'Est* four years before – even to the size and weight of the animal, even to the names of the fishermen and details of this 'phenomenal Chenille'! The same *Dépêche*, on 14 May, announcing that the 'monster' would be exhibited at Nogent-le-Rotrou, rounded off the bulletin by reproducing with scrupulous fidelity, the phrases used by the previous newspaper. There was only one difference: the Chenille could not, and for good reason, be bought by America, and had been made over to the Palais Berlitz in Paris for the sum of 22,000 francs. Which, if nothing else, shows that the price of Bramble Sharks had risen appreciably since 1939. . . .

So, if one were to believe all that one reads, the same two fishermen caught, in the same place, within the space of four years, *three Echinorhinus* of exactly the same size and weight (1·55 metres girth in some reports, 1·35 in others, but this is probably just a typographical error). This is more than mere chance or coincidence – it threatens to become a habit! There is something a little miraculous in this succession of phenomenal catches of Chenille by the two fishermen.

But wait; the miracles continue. . . . Three years later, on 2 April 1946, the *Hebdo-Variétés* reproduced the original article on the Chenille de mer, adding all kinds of absurd supplementary data: the monster was about 300 years old, it feeds not for nourishment but to destroy, it was now immersed in a special liquid – a strong poison – which ensured perfect preservation, it had been bought for the sum of 44,000 francs by the Director of Olympia in London, etc. Finally, the *Patriote du Charolais* (24 August 1946) announced, after some preliminaries, that the Chenille de mer would be exhibited on 28 August at Charolles in the Place de l'Eglise; after which, Olympia of London having acquired this unique specimen for 75,000 francs. . . .

So traditions arise. The subject of spectacular and ill-informed reporting could easily fill a whole volume. To conclude, one can cite the notice given in the *Bulletin du Commerce* of Noumea (4 February 1939):

BEWARE OF SHARKS! Recently, in the neighbourhood of Artillerie, a woman who was bathing a short distance from the shore caught sight of a shark swimming between her and the land. At the screams of terror from the bather, the shark made off. The woman, benumbed by fear, fainted on the shore. She received the help of people who hastened to her cries.

This serves to show that (1) the shark had very keen hearing, (2) it must have been timid by nature to have been frightened into flight at 'hearing' the woman's cries, and (3) the person who reported this fact must have been a remarkable 'psychologist', since he appears to have deduced in a flash what was the factor that made the shark act as it did.

The Press are not the only culprits when it comes to shark stories. One can cite numerous instances of this kind of thing in works which are intended to be quite serious. Adventure stories, memoirs, accounts of voyages, these are all veritable mines of misinformed opinion on the subject of sharks. There is a great deal of wisdom in the remark made by K. Guenther (1931) apropos sharks and the bad reputation accorded them. He said that the authors of adventure stories, and especially those writing for the young, have a marked tendency to exaggerate the danger of these savage beasts; these writers stupidly imagine that a reader is only interested in an animal if the latter is either a ferocious killer or one that is itself killed.

There are also oral traditions. When showing off his shark, from Australia, at Saint Kilda, Slocum in his book *Sailing alone around the world* (p. 140) had engaged an Irishman, Tom Howard, who was said to be an expert in the matter of sharks, and had charged him with the job of replying to any questions asked by visitors. Some days later, being amongst the crowd, Slocum heard Howard holding forth on the ways of sharks in such an extravagant and fantastic vein that within the hour he parted company with so imaginative a lecturer. It is quite possible that some of these extravagant ideas made their way around the world and ended up by being quoted as 'first-hand information from an irrefutable source'.

At Le Havre a few years ago, some fishermen on the Southampton Quay were showing a Porbeagle (*Lamna nasus*) of $4\frac{1}{2}$ feet which they had caught by chance in their nets. When asked for information, they replied quite rightly that it was a kind of shark. To which a spectator replied categorically that he could not accept this, for the shark had a tail like *this*, that the shark was quite *different* in appearance, that the shark's teeth . . . etc.

177

Let us close this dossier of 'stories', merely noting that some of the modern misconceptions about sharks which appear in print in this scientific age are, in their way, no less extraordinary than those of earlier periods which we rather condescendingly term 'quaint' or 'primitive'. The examples in this chapter show how such stories can arise, become enlarged, prosper, and finally pass into the realm of accepted facts.

Chapter 9

Fisheries and the Utilization of Sharks

Our ancestors, while recognizing that sharks are edible, did not exhibit much enthusiasm for them. These 'vile beasts that eat up men' engendered, because of such a reputation, a revulsion which was in no way helped by the discouraging comments on the gastronomic qualities of shark flesh. 'Flesh hard, of poor flavour, which smells bad, difficult to digest, but once digested is greatly nourishing' (Rondelet, 1554).

The latter statement shows that robust stomachs were not to be put off because the flesh was coarse. Père Labat also found that the *Requien* has a flesh 'leathery, usually lean, cartilaginous, of a bad taste' and that one had to be very hungry to eat it. Only the part under the belly, sprinkled with salt for 24 hours and well cooked, could be eaten with oil, salt and vinegar. One could also deal with the offspring found in a fat female, leaving them to clear in a tank of water for a day or two, after which they were good to eat.

Rabelais informs us that the Gastrolâtres, sacrificing on fast-days to their god Ventripotent, included in their list of '*Entrées de Table*', besides '*caviat*' and '*boutargue*',[1] dogfish and monkfish. At the same time, however, Rabelais affirms that the flesh of dogfish 'smells bad. It is loathsome and hard to digest.'

Thus the general concensus of opinion was not, on the whole, in favour of shark flesh. In antiquity, only the common people ate shark. It was not a sought-after dish, and this outlook has changed little up to the present day amongst Europeans, but we shall return to this later on and see what can be made of it.

Regarding the liver of sharks, this was more valued. It was used in stews, or in omelettes. Rondelet considered the liver of the Blue Shark (*Prionace glauca*) to be particularly edible. 'It is above all esteemed when fried. One keeps it salted, then eats it cooked in wine or roasted; it is very good boiled

---

[1] A dish prepared from the eggs of the mullet (*Mugil*), sun-dried and salted, eaten in Provence and in certain parts of Italy and the Orient. The word may derive from the arabic *boutarkha*.

with hyssop, bay leaves and some herbs, adding to it cinnamon, nutmegs and whole cloves.'

Clearly, the sauce helped the fish down! But if sharks have not been of much use to the table or the kitchen (or even the lamp!), they have on the other hand played their part in the apothecary's trade. Ancient therapeutic formulae included those in which the by-products of sharks reputedly played a beneficial role.

The oil from the liver of some sharks (*Centrina, Prionace*) had a reputation for easing hardness of the liver in men. The gall bladder of *Centrina*, taken with honey, was good for cataract. The baked ashes of the same animal were recommended for ringworm. The ashes of the Blue Shark and the Smooth Hound (*Mustelus*) were good for teething pains in children. Adults, however, could resort to Pliny's prescription: 'Rub the teeth, once a year, with the brains of a dogfish which had been cooked and kept in olive oil'; he also deemed it useful to scarify the gums with the 'sting' of a Stingray (*Dasyatis*); or again, to use the dorsal spines of the Spur Dog (*Squalus acanthias*), 'taking care to press the point against the bad tooth'.

Sharks' brains, when dried, become extremely hard. They can then be grated and added to white wine; in England, this was considered helpful for women in labour (Labat). Powdered sharks' brains came to be esteemed for their laxative and diuretic properties. The teeth of sharks, also reduced to powder, were reputed to help stem haemorrhages and to destroy gall stones. The latter property would have been especially appealing to those who feared having to submit to the 16th-century operating techniques described by Ambroise Paré (1510–90), the Father of modern surgery.

Little by little one passes from medical and pharmaceutical practices to those which are hardly a step removed from pure magic. The goldsmiths, for example, mounted teeth from the Great White Shark (*Carcharodon*) in gold settings and these were hung round children's necks. They were referred to as 'snakes' teeth', and it was thought that, being so much larger than the child's own teeth, they would guard the child from nocturnal evils. They were also reputed, by sympathetic magic, to give the child a healthy appetite.

The teeth from fossil sharks were used until the 16th century as poison indicators. The teeth themselves were known as *glossopetrae*, that is to say, they were taken to be the petrified tongues of snakes (or birds). Legend relates how the Apostle Paul landed at Malta, an island infested with huge snakes, and turned the latter to stone. The first fossilized sharks' teeth to come to the notice of naturalists were indeed from the island of Malta, and it was perhaps not unreasonable in those days to assume that these dated from Saint Paul's visit.

The Middle Ages and the Renaissance were a time when men constantly lived in fear of being poisoned. The very existence of *praegustatores* is an indication of the scant confidence men placed in the food and wine that were set before them. Various objects were used to detect poisons. They included, in addition to the *glossopetrae* or shark's teeth, the horn of the unicorn (in reality the tusk of the Narwhal[1]), flint arrow-heads, certain hard, coloured stones, and so on. Usually set in rich gold mountings, these were part of the tableware in princely houses or wherever there was fear of 'powders' being used. Their method of use was simple: one plunged the object into the food or drink that was to be consumed – if poison was present the object either changed colour or else showed a telltale exudation at its surface. The same thing happened to knife handles made from unicorn horn, when the blade of the knife cut through poisoned meat.

The illusory nature of such ideas did not, of course, escape the notice of certain of the more enlightened spirits of the age. Ambroise Paré, talking with the chief physician to King Charles IX, one Chappelain, asked him to abandon 'this custom whereby one must needs steep of piece of unicorn horn in the cup from which the King drinks, fearing poison'. Chappelain merely replied, not without malice, that as far as he was aware, there was no virtue in the unicorn horn, but that he noticed that faith in it was so deep-rooted and confirmed in the minds of princes and the masses that he saw no way to remove it, so strong was their need of faith in it. He added that, if this superstition had no real effect, at least it did no harm except to the purse of those who bought them for much more than their weight in gold.

The *glossopetrae* had, for this purpose, less of a reputation than the unicorn horns, not because they were less effective but because the latter not only warned of the presence of poison: it actually neutralized it. The unicorn horn was used for making drinking goblets, vessels, water butts, safe since it then took on the power of an effective and all-round antidote. As an antidote, it acted both against poison which was ingested orally as well as that introduced by poisoned arrows.

If to the list of uses one adds the abrasive properties of shark skin, one has virtually completed the contribution that sharks have made in past times to the culture and welfare of man. Thus, regular and intensive fisheries for sharks do not appear to have existed, even in areas where sharks abound. In current idiom, it would seem that hitherto sharks have not 'paid'.

In the same way, the technique of catching sharks remained for a long time

---

[1] In the Narwhal (*Monodon monoceros*), there are two teeth in the upper jaw. Both are concealed in females; in the male, the right tooth is concealed but the left grows out at the front of the head, spiralling anticlockwise (very rarely both are developed).

very much as described by Père Labat and as illustrated, for example, by the painter Louis Garneray (1783–1857); and as is practised, even today, on board ship whenever there is the leisure to indulge in this pastime. When the shark has taken the bait and the hook is firmly grasped, the line is hauled in so as to raise the head of the shark out of the water. Another line, with a running noose, is slipped over the first and is carefully worked down until it encircles the caudal peduncle of the shark. Hauling on the second line, the shark is lifted into the boat tail first. Extreme caution must be exercised if the shark is lifted aboard by the mouth like a roach. For, with its tail free, it can cause great damage to the legs to anyone standing by. On the other hand, the technique of pulling the animal up by its tail completely neutralizes this dangerous part of the body, and a blow with a machete or heavy instrument can then put the shark out of action.

Louis Garneray, painter of seascapes, gave an accurate rendering of shark fishing in one of his paintings. It shows the moment when the sailors are endeavouring to catch the tail in a running noose. It is certain that Garneray himself had assisted in this operation, for prior to devoting himself to the arts (and rising to be Conservateur of the Rouen Museum), he had sailed for many years, particularly under the privateer Robert Surcouf.

The same procedure was used on the long-haul sailing ships or in general whenever a line-caught shark had to be hauled from the water, either from a wharf or from the deck of a ship. Naturally, an enormous hook is used for this type of fishing, mounted to a swivel on a strong chain – the most massive trace a fisherman could dream of.

If 'defensive behaviour' and 'fight' were simply and directly related to the size and weight of a fish, then shark fishing would be one of the finest sports in the world. But one is deceived if one thinks that the 'Tiger of the Seas' offers incomparable sport, for, on the whole, sharks do not exhibit the kind of 'fight' that one would expect from such muscular and powerful animals. There are, however, differences between the species. A Greenland Shark (*Somniosus microcephalus*) or a Nurse Shark (*Ginglymostoma*) allow themselves to be hauled up quite passively, like great big heavy sacks. A Tiger Shark (*Galeocerdo*) is more recalcitrant, and it can fight vigorously and for a considerable time. The great pelagic sharks also put up a sporting fight most of the time, especially those belonging to the family Isuridae. A large Mackerel Shark, suitably enraged and reluctant to be torn from its natural element, can undoubtedly provide a most enjoyable and exhilarating battle for any angler. It is mostly a trial of brute strength, which is not always to the liking of those sportsmen who prefer to fish with finesse; in this respect, many such fishermen prefer the Tarpon (*Megalops*) or the Swordfish

(*Xiphias*). It is agreed, however, that the sporting qualities of certain sharks are all that can be desired by a sea fisherman. Ranked beside the great sporting fishes such as the swordfish, the Sailfish (*Istiophorus*) or the tarpon, the specialists also include the Mako (*Isurus*).

To descend to a less sporting level, the harpoon is the classical weapon of shark fishing. In actual fact, its use is rather limited; it requires that the animal come alongside the ship or vice versa. This cannot often be arranged, except perhaps for Basking Sharks which tend to lounge at the surface. In many places where sharks are known to be abundant, one hardly sees them at the surface and there is nothing to indicate their presence. The technique then is to try to attract them, either with a carcass (preferably one that is beginning to decompose) or by the well-known method of lowering a container of coagulated blood, pierced with holes. In this way one can hope to draw the shark's attention to the presence of the ship. One of the advantages of harpoon fishing, and not the least appreciated of its attractions, is that it permits the harpooner to adopt suitably athletic poses, particularly if he is within range of a camera!

Finally, although this is not strictly a fishing method as such, it sometimes happens that a shark is rammed by a boat. The latter continuing on its way, the shark finds itself held against the bows of the ship by the pressure of the water; photographs have recorded this unusual sight. Gudger (1940, 1941) made a study of all reports of such occurrences. In every case the shark concerned was the Whale Shark, *Rhincodon typus*, that enormous and inoffensive beast that is sometimes found sunning itself at the surface even more unconcernedly than does the Basking Shark, *Cetorhinus maximus*. A few of these accidents have been recorded from a wide range of localities: the Red Sea (twice), the Straits of Bab-el-Mandeb, the Gulf of Aden, off Colombo (Ceylon), along the coast of West Africa, off the coast of Panama, in the Pacific, and in the neighbourhood of Touamotou. Almost always the animal was killed by the impact and as the ship slowed down, it slipped away since it was no longer held by the force of the water. On one occasion, involving the Italian steamship *Francesco Crispi* (on 14 May 1934), they were able to haul the shark aboard.

There are even two ships which have bagged a 'brace' of Whale Sharks. The Dutch passenger ship *Johan van Oldenbarnevelt*[1] collided with its first Whale Shark in November 1932, 150 miles west of Colombo. Exactly one year later, in November 1933, it collided with its second Whale Shark in the Straits of Bab-el-Mandeb near Perim Island (the true oceanographic

[1] Bought back by the Greek shipowners, it was renamed *Lakonia*; during the winter of 1963 it caught fire and sank, with the loss of 121 lives.

entrance to the Red Sea). The American liner *President Wilson* killed its
first Whale Shark on 28 January 1936, a little north of Sokotra while returning to Suez from Bombay. The second was rammed in the South Red Sea on
1 April 1937, to the north-east of Massawa during a voyage from Colombo
to Suez.

Any other shark, threatened by the on-coming bows of a ship, will escape
collision by immediately changing course. Only the Whale Shark seems to
be oblivious of what is going on around it. Whether it lies at the surface
motionless, or whether its course takes it across the bows of a ship, it seems
to have no awareness of the impending danger. Gudger (1940) recorded
that a Whale Shark spent an entire day in front of a ship, travelling so close
that only a few inches separated the two, yet the impassive animal showed
not the least concern. This explains the relative frequency of collisions with
these sharks.

For thousands of years, fishes have been subjected to a very simple kind of
classification: either they were edible, or they were not. The aim of fishermen, from earliest times until the present day, has been to catch the first,
and if by chance the second were mixed in with them, they were merely
rejected as 'not really fish'. Such a concept speaks volumes for the amount
of interest accorded to the second group. Moreover, it was only the strictly
edible parts of food fishes which were of interest, that is to say, mainly the
fillets, although occasionally the ovaries or soft roe (testes) were included.
The remainder was the refuse, the scraps which were returned to the sea.

Certain species with livers rich in oils, such as the Cod (*Gadus morhua*)
however, show that fish can provide more than just flesh. The Menhaden
(*Brevoortia tyrannus*) of the American Atlantic coasts, perhaps the most
abundant single species of fish in the world, has been fished chiefly for the oil
derived from it. As a rule, however, fishes are mainly caught for their edible
qualities and not solely for their by-products.

The flesh of sharks, however, has traditionally been considered rather
unappetizing. Possibly some basis to the unpopularity of sharks as table fish
may lie in the fact that the muscles contain a certain amount of urea. The
urea seems to be the precursor for the formation of large quantities of
ammonia during storage. To overcome the general prejudice against
dogfishes, they are now marketed in England as 'flake', in Canada and the
United States as 'grey fish' and in Germany as '*See-aal*' (i.e. Sea Eel).
Similarly, the rather unattractive Wolffish (*Anarrhichas*) is sold as 'rock
salmon', or 'rock turbot' in Scotland. What has made sharks even less
attractive has been the idea that these 'Tigers of the Sea' are inveterate

man-eaters, so that by eating a slice of shark one risked being a kind of cannibal, albeit at second remove. In actual fact, there is only a chance in a million that the shark in question has ever eaten a living man. Even those that have taken a mouthful or two from dead bodies must be extremely rare. Indeed, this is a poor pretext to pick on; other things being equal, gastronomy is not necessarily deterred by such things. For I can bring to mind numbers of marine animals that do not disdain human flesh when the opportunity presents itself, but this does not prevent them from repeatedly appearing at table and without anybody objecting. Is this mere ignorance on the part of the diner? If so, then perhaps we should drop the subject. . . . However, there is one fish which deserves mention here, the Barracuda (*Sphyraena* spp.), which is highly esteemed as a table fish in some parts of the world. The only reproach levelled at the barracuda is that perhaps, and in some circumstances, it may have been the culprit in cases of fish poisoning.

Up to the early years of the present century, sharks were mainly considered as harmful animals which were of no benefit to man simply because they did not supply him with food. Not that there was any lack of evidence of the value of selachians in other respects, other than as food. Their hide had for a long time been used in the manufacture of scabbards and leatherwork, quite apart from their use as abrasives. Neither was the liver overlooked, which is full of oil that had been used since early times. On the whole though, the exploitation of these by-products did not pass beyond the empirical and artisan stage.

The commercial exploitation of sharks dates from the period between the two world wars. Some fisheries, with the production of sharkskin as their primary object, drew attention to other by-products that could be derived from sharks. With an enthusiasm not a little excessive, sharks came to be considered as the most important element of the ichthyological fauna.

At first, this helped to change the general prejudice against shark flesh, which hitherto had been little appreciated for a number of reasons, the most valid being that the flesh was mainly dry, tough and not very tasty. Some species are, however, better than others. Coles (1919) claims that the White Shark (*Carcharodon*) is 'the most delicious meat that [he] had ever tasted'. While most sharks have flesh which is very pale in colour and poor in oil, that of the White Shark is, on the contrary, reddish like salmon and fat, soft and appetizing. There is something ironical in the fact that the most tasty of sharks is precisely the White Shark, the man-eater. Be this as it may, Coles says that on one occasion he ate almost two pounds of the White Shark for supper. Unfortunately, the White Shark is not very commonly caught, while most other sharks must indeed be classed as rather poor eating. This does not mean that the latter are inedible. There is no doubt that they would be eaten much more freely were it not for the man-eating bogy that has been attached to them. But this reputation is not immutable, for in Paris during the Occupation, the markets began to stock sharks, and at times the Porbeagle, Basking Shark and Blue Shark still appear in the Halles Centrales, although they cannot be said to have exactly stormed the citadels of gastronomy (they are all but dismissed by the *Larousse Gastronomique*).

There is one aspect of shark-eating that shows no signs of diminishing popularity, for still the best-known edible parts of a shark are undoubtedly the fins. Sharkfin soup is one of the classical dishes of Chinese cooking, and in the Far East there appears to be an unlimited market for this product. The classifying of fins destined for this dish is complex; there are many and variously valued categories, depending on the size and colour and on which particular fin is used. For the fishermen, the preparation of the fins is reduced to a minimum. He merely cuts them off close to the body, removing the mass of associated muscles, and dries them without further ado. In a short while the fins harden and can be packed and sent off. However, they are not eaten in this state, but are then subjected to quite a complicated pre-paratory process. For it is not the flesh that is eaten, but the *ceratotrichia* or elastoidine fibres[1] which, with the cartilaginous radials, serve to support the fin (Figure 49). The shark fin is then transformed into the commercial product. First the skin is removed from both sides, and then all the muscular tissue is carefully extracted in such a way as to leave only the cartilaginous skeleton and the ceratotrichia. Finally, the latter alone are kept and are pressed into discs of about 9 inches in diameter and about half an inch thick. These discs are something like matted coconut fibres to the touch, but are pale yellowish and slightly glossy. It is these felt-like discs, made up of the elastoidine fibres from the fins, that are used in the preparation of sharkfin soup.

According to McCormick, Allen & Young (1963), sharkfin is not so popular in Japan but a number of dishes are prepared from shark meat, including the famous *kamaboko*. The latter is made by crushing the flesh of sharks, adding cornstarch and other ingredients, shaping it into a round or rectangular form about the thickness of a pancake, and then steaming or roasting it. Apparently, other fishes are used to make different kinds of

[1] Or 'horny rods'. Elastoidine is a special scleroprotein which differs from collagen in certain ways such as the presence of sulphur, a compact structure not broken down into simple elements, and so on; it does not yield gelatin on boiling (Faure-Fremiet, 1936). Engeland and Bastian (1938) have recognized many amino-acids in elastoidine: glycol alanine, serine, oxyproline.

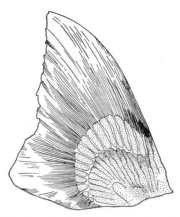

Fig. 49   Pectoral fin of shark with the skin removed to show the bars of cartilage and the elastoidine fibres.

kamaboko. The total production of *kamaboko* throughout Japan was at that time an astonishing 420,000 tons and this was reflected in the considerable rise in the Japanese shark fisheries since the end of the war.

When sharkskin is merely dried and used without any special preparation, the cutaneous (dermal) teeth in the skin are of no other use than as abrasives if drawn, so to speak, against the grain. Since the cusps of the teeth are, in the majority of cases, directed backwards, the rasp only works in one direction, i.e. from tail to head. One need only stroke the flank of a dogfish back and forth to appreciate this; the difference is immediately obvious.

For centuries, men have been aware that the hide of sharks is strong, thick and flexible and could be used for purposes other than as an abrasive. One such use was to prevent wear on oars where chafed by the rowlocks. At some point, sharkskin came to be known as *shagreen*, a word which according to McCormick, Allen & Young (1963) derives from the term *saghari* (Persian) or *sagri* (Turkish):

Saghari or *sagri* is the tough skin of the rump of a horse, which was made granular by imbedding hard seeds into the softened skin, then drying it. The seeds fell out, leaving permanent indentations in the skin. Sharkskin, with its patterns of denticles, resembled *saghari* or *sagri*, though in sharkskin the denticles were permanent fixtures.

The Persian *saghari*, with its rough, granular surface, was found to be ideal for sword hilts, for it gave swordsmen a good purchase on their weapons.

The Japanese are believed to have been the first to have used sharkskin and rayskin for this same purpose.

According to Whitley (1940), 'the French verb *chagriner* comes from the

Turkish and our word chagrin evolves from a metaphorical use of the word shagreen for friction'. He instances the play upon the word in the title of one of Balzac's short stories, Peau de Chagrin, which deals with a magical piece of skin or parchment and the fate that befalls its owner, each gratified wish shortening his life and shrinking the piece of skin. In French, *chagrin* means a tanned goat or sheepskin.

In Europe, oriental polished sharkskin-covered objects began to appear in the 17th century, and by the 18th century European craftsmen had begun to practise this art. McCormick *et al.* mention the shagreen workers' (*segrynwerkers*) guild of Holland as an indication of the development of this craft. It was in France, however, that the most famous of the shagreen craftsmen lived.

In France, the word '*galuchat*' has come to be attached to sharkskin. It should, however, be spelt with two *l*s since it commemorates Jean-Claude Galluchat who, towards the end of the reign of Louis xv, prepared shark and dogfish skins for covering sword handles, scabbards, cases, etc. Galluchat had a '*boutique de gainier*' in Paris in about 1769 on the Quai des Morfondus (now Quai de l'Horloge), and the goods bearing his name were very much in vogue. He died on 8 March 1774. His son Denis-Claude Galluchat had died before him, and none of his direct descendants succeeded to his business. During the Revolutionary period, two legal documents of the 20th Frimaire An II and the 22nd Messidor An IX of the republican calendar (10 December 1793 and 6 August 1801) specified that '*galuchat*' should be written with two *l*s and that it was due to an error that this family name had become misspelt (C.Dufeu).

But, in spite of this official correction, France has continued to use '*galuchat*' for the skin of a selachian worked in a particular manner and commemorating the name of the originator of this process. Even then, however, the word has come to be misapplied, for in certain otherwise well-informed books I have found the word *galuchat* used in reference to certain dogfishes. This is a misuse of the word. The true *galuchat* comes from the skin of a Stingray, *Dasyatis sephen*, a species first described by Per Forsskål from the Red Sea. In this species the dorsal surfaces are covered with a coat of dermal spicules which are set very close together. By grinding these spicules carefully, and by using dyes which stain dentine, enamel and skin differentially, the particular appearance of *galuchat* is produced. Green is most often used, partly because it is easier and partly because the result is so beautiful. Also, it may perhaps be a question of fashion. But it is the various shades of green produced which give the skin such a pleasing and elegant look.

The technique developed by Galluchat in the 18th century can obviously be applied to other rays, as well as to sharks, dogfishes, etc, and these were eventually used also by the craftsman of the Quai des Morfondus. But a glance at the true *galuchat* is enough to recognize the type of spicule arrangement found in *Dasyatis sephen* (commonly called the Chinese Ray since its range extends across the Indian Ocean to the East Indies). One should, by the way, beware of referring to dogfishes, or *Dasyatis sephen* for that matter, as *galuchat*, for this would be like referring to a bull or a cow as a 'hide' or a 'leather'.

The use of *galuchat* was restricted to a very narrow luxury trade and it could never be more than a rather whimsical product prone to all the exigencies and fluctuations of fashion. Much used in the 18th century, it suffered an almost total eclipse in the 19th century. After 1918 some of the more artistic decorators used it anew, but this revival was neither long-lasting nor widespread. *Galuchat* has never recovered the popularity that it had at the time of its invention.

It is, however, in some ways thanks to *galuchat* that attention was drawn to the possible use of selachian hide, and especially that of sharks, in the leather industry. The skin of sharks is made up of a very thick dermis of *very long* connective fibres interwoven into a dense and regular network, from which one would expect a leather of rather exceptional qualities. The drawback lies in the presence of the placoid scales: should these be kept, or should they be removed? And in the latter case, how?

The skin of some species can be cured with the spicules intact, a notable example being *Centrophorus granulosus* (Müller & Henle) (family Squalidae), a species with a strong spine in front of each dorsal fin and living in deep water in the Mediterranean and neighbouring parts of the Atlantic. Between the wars, excellent results were obtained from the hide of this species, which was found to be amenable not only to the manufacture of luxury leather goods, but also to shoes. The cutaneous teeth in this species take the form of tiny squares, evenly grooved, without salient points or cusps and set in regular diagonal lines. The whole forms a pleasing surface which is quite smooth and free of projections. It is exactly these qualities which allow the skin to be used directly and without the need to remove the spicules. But one still has, as with true *galuchat*, a hide for luxury use, with only limited applications. It was hardly possible to establish an industry of any size on the basis of only a single species of shark, and that a small one whose fishery could not be enlarged.

In the more typical sharks, on the other hand, the removal of the outer covering of placoid scales is absolutely necessary. For these scales, usually bearing more or less sharp cusps or crests, are precisely the feature which renders sharkskin such a useful abrasive for industrial purposes. This covering makes sharkskin inappropriate for most other uses: shoes, furniture, suitcases, fancy leather-work, etc. The effect of the denticles on clothes, coats, the hems of dresses, would be absolutely disastrous. Young, incidentally, tells an anecdote of a trick wallet made from sharkskin covered with spicules: it was easy to slip into the pocket, but very difficult to withdraw it. One can see an application for this kind of thing in combating pick-pockets. But, of course, were the wallet to be rotated by 180°, it would be equally impossible to pocket it.

There are two ways in which the placoid scales can be removed. The first consists in employing purely mechanical means, in other words merely grinding them away in one way or another. This is the technique currently used in Denmark for dealing with the hides of the Greenland Shark (*Somniosus microcephalus*). In this case, the basal plate of each spicule is left in the skin, which gives the latter a rather pleasing speckled appearance. The skin of the Greenland Shark lends itself well to this type of preparation, since the spicules are distributed unevenly, with bare patches in between. But this is a special case. The general rule in sharks is for the scale cover to be very dense, with the denticles closely juxtaposed, sometimes overlapping (imbricating). Their mechanical removal, leaving the basal plates intact, does not give very satisfactory results, since the skin then lacks suppleness and is difficult to cut. Furthermore, this type of grinding down of the skin is a delicate operation and little applicable to the skins of typical sharks.

It is therefore necessary to have recourse to chemical agents, enabling the whole denticle, basal plate and all, to be extracted. The problem is a tricky one. It is necessary to remove the dermal denticles without at the same time damaging the dermal layer of fibres or altering the superficial layer of skin whose grain imparts a definite quality to the finished product. The first steps in this direction were taken in 1919–20. Theodore Kohler, an industrial chemist, and then Allen Rogers, a leather chemist, of the United States, carried out research which was soon crowned with success, and an American concern, the Ocean Leather Corporation, took up the development of the process, and a patent was taken out for it. Since then, other enterprises have been started, but their initial ventures have not been without a certain amount of testing and experiment.

The skins of sharks have some extremely attractive properties. In mammals, the skin is made up of *extremely short* connective fibres, some fractions of an inch in length only. In sharks, on the other hand, the connective fibres are very long. Thus, in a skin prepared by the process used by

F. & J.Gerin of Grenoble, I have been able to draw out fibres of 8 to 10 inches in length, and even then it was not certain that this was the limit because there comes a time when the fibres break with further pulling and it is hardly possible to draw them out all in one piece. It has even been claimed that in sharks these fibres may run uninterrupted the entire length of the body, from head to tail, but I cannot see what the basis of this claim is, nor how indeed it could be verified. Still, the fact remains that these fibres are exceptionally long and robust. The skin of a shark can, in some ways, be compared to a piece of material, whereas in mammals the skin much more nearly resembles a piece of felt. That is why the former is superior to the latter in strength and suppleness. When the two skins are compared, the difference is quite striking, especially when seen under a microscope.

At this point, we can recall our collection of 'shark stories' mentioned in Chapter 8, for one comes across statements from time to time of this kind: 'The skin of the shark is so thick that one can slice it fourteen times in a horizontal direction.'

One knows perfectly well that this habit of talking about *the* shark has no real meaning. The animal whose skin can be cleaved in this way is the Whale Shark, *Rhincodon typus*, a rather rare species and one whose capture is usually such as to be reported in scientific journals; it does indeed have a remarkably thick skin. In most sharks and certainly in those usually caught by fisheries, the skin is of normal thickness and can be used in the normal way; there is no question of being able to cleave it into numerous layers. The one and exceptional case is the Whale Shark, but this cannot be taken as a general rule.

Many 'informative' articles have been written on the tanning of 'the stomach and intestines of sharks, which produce a leather comparable to that of lambs or sheep'. Many authors, writing briefly or at length on the utilization of sharks, have repeated this statement, some of them even specifying that this extraordinarily fine leather 'can be used for making women's gloves', while others affirm that it yields a product resembling a kind of sheepskin. Some even give details, such as 'the intestine is turned inside out, and one then obtains . . .'

It is, of course, quite impossible to turn the intestine of a shark inside out! The spiral valve completely prevents such an operation. It would be necessary to make a particularly fine dissection in order to remove the internal folds and keep for curing the outer portions. Even admitting that the latter could provide a commercial product, it certainly would not be profitable since it would involve excessive hand labour. Moreover, the insertion of the plates of the spiral valve on the lining of the intestine would give the skin a

191

rather bizarre appearance and would hardly be suitable for the manufacture of ladies' gloves. In fact, I have never come across a cured shark's intestine, and the least that can be said is that such a product is unlikely to come on to the market for some years.

Another fancied use to which the intestines of sharks are put is 'the manufacture of strings for musical instruments'. Here, the origin of this erroneous information can be tracked down. It is merely a confusion between sharks and porpoises. The digestive tract of the porpoise (like that of other large cetaceans, such as whales) has been the object of considerable research in the United States with a view to its use commercially. Allen Rogers is said to have obtained an *ersatz* cat-gut from the intestines of the porpoise, which was suitable for use in musical instruments. From a zoological point of view, a shark is a long way from a porpoise, but popular writers are not always much concerned with such niceties. After all, both are large marine animals, so why quibble over details? We have seen the same kind of mistake made in connection with 'shark oils'.

Regarding the stomachs of sharks, the situation is a little different. Allen Rogers (1922) made some attempts at tanning which showed promise, but these were not taken beyond laboratory techniques and no large-scale industrial process was evolved. There is no doubt that it was the hopes raised by the work of this American chemist which led to the later affirmation that there is, in the curing of sharks' stomachs, a means of producing a very fine type of leather. Some similar trials were made in France by F.& J. Gerin, who had succeeded so well with the tanning of sharkskins. But the results have been disappointing, the first samples splitting in a waferlike manner. This, of course, is to be expected, for the stomach lining is made up of alternate layers of muscle and connective tissue. During the curing operations, the layers necessarily become separated, since the tanning agents act only on the connective tissue and not on the muscle. Hence the disconcerting 'leafing' of the leather.

There are two layers in the stomach lining which can be cured.

(1) The deep part of the chorion, where the fibres are crowded together in a thin, compact layer, known as the *stratum compactum* or Membrane of Zeissl.

(2) The *submucosa*, a much thicker layer, but one made up of fine interlacing fibres which form a kind of mat.

The fibres in the Membrane of Zeissl are larger, stronger and more regularly orientated, but the whole layer is very thin and the curing process must be carried out very delicately. The submucosa, being thicker but having finer fibres, seems more likely to give a better leather. The two connective layers are separated by a muscular layer (*muscularis mucosae*) which, although very thin, is sufficient to divide the two layers. They are linked, however, by villosities of the chorion, and this does not fail to show in the finished product. In any case, the stomachs of mammals are already being cured, the results are quite acceptable, and there seems little advantage in turning to the stomachs of sharks.

A final observation can be made, concerning the oft repeated assertion, 'The rugosities [i.e. placoid scales] are removed by treatment with hydrochloric acid . . .' and later on we come across 'these rugosities find a use in the manufacture of abrasives: . . . Their hardness makes them a product of the first order.' Moreover, one learns that 'shagreen' (i.e. the denticles), having been removed by a chemical agent, is used in 'the manufacture of anti-slip articles, the polishing of diamonds', and that it is harder than steel.

The chemical action destined to remove the denticles has precisely the effect of decalcifying them, softening them and thus rendering them quite useless as abrasives. I have, on my work-bench, many tubes of such denticles taken from skins cured by the process of removing such denticles by chemical means. The consistency of the denticles resembles ordinary cartilage; they can be cut quite easily with a scalpel or razor blade. Of their original hardness, nothing remains. Obviously, such spicules could never be used in the way that the authors have stated.

In the years following the First World War, the curing of sharkskins seemed to promise a glowing future. Almost everywhere, factories were set up for this industry. It is true that, technically speaking, the tanning processes had been mastered, with or without the spicules. But in Europe at least, the commercialization of the product did not respond to earlier hopes, and sharkskins have almost completely disappeared from the European market. The Ocean Leather Corporation in the United States at least until 1963 produced luxury goods made from shark hides – including 'unscuffable' toe-caps for children's shoes!

Fishes spoken of as 'lean' are those in which the muscles contain little or almost no fatty matter, but which localize their lipids in the liver, as for example, does the Cod (*Gadus morhua*). Fat fishes have livers which are much less rich in fatty tissue, the latter impregnating the muscles of the fish: this is the case in the scombroid fishes (mackerel, tunas, etc) and the clupeoid fishes (herrings, sardines, anchovies).

Sharks are very lean fishes. Their flesh is especially dry, while the liver, as we have seen, is a voluminous organ almost always full of great quantities of oil, sometimes in quite incredible amounts. It is the search for this liver oil which has given importance to such sharks as the Greenland Shark (*Somniosus microcephalus*) in the Iceland fishery, and the Basking Shark (*Cetorhinus maximus*) in the fishery off the west coast of Ireland (where they are called *muldoans*). Grossly extracted, either by putrefaction or by heating, these oils have a number of different industrial and domestic uses, and have even been used to fraudulently simulate the required olive oil content in cooking oils. During the last war, a veritable gold-rush on sharks, and especially the Soupfin Shark (*Galeorhinus zyopterus*) began off the west coast of the United States and Canada. The attraction was the liver and the very high proportion of Vitamin A that it contained. At the height of the boom the livers reached a price of $14.25 per pound, and at this time shark liver oil supplied three-quarters of the Vitamin A produced in the United States.

The oils from sharks' livers were originally used in a number of different industries: for tanning, for chamois-dressing and for 'nourishing' skins, in soap-making, in metallurgy for tempering high-grade steel, and so on. In fact, there is nothing very unusual about this list, since all these are normal uses for fish oils. However, in the early part of this century, the Portuguese (Louis Castillo, 1906) claimed that the oil from the liver of the 'Tollo', a Smooth Hound of the genus *Mustelus*, has the same curative properties as cod liver oil.

One thing should be emphasized here: the expression 'shark liver oil' used in the singular, is meaningless, although it is commonly used. Just as there is no *one* shark, so there is no *one* shark liver oil. The constituents in the oils derived from the livers of sharks vary enormously, depending not only on the species involved, but also on the sex of the individual, its state of sexual maturity, the season, its feeding habits and condition, etc. Thus, it can be said that the different qualities of shark oils can, theoretically speaking, be much more numerous than the species of sharks, since within any one species the oil can vary with all the factors listed above. This simple fact gives some indication of the complexity of the subject.

The literature concerning the liver oils of sharks is already copious and this is no place to review it in any detail. These oils have, indeed, been subjected to considerable research in the last few years by numerous chemists. In general, fish oils are mainly composed of triglycerylesters (i.e. glycerides) of fatty acids, with small quantities of free fatty acids, hydrocarbons, vitamins, sterols, and so on. Fish oils differ markedly from vegetable oils in their great variety of fatty acids, particularly the highly unsaturated fatty acids. The proportion of the latter with C_{18} is higher in sharks than in other marine groups.

One of the most curious facts about shark liver oils is that certain of them, in contrast to ordinary fish oils, contain enormous quantities of unsaponifiable matter (i.e. which cannot be combined with an alkali to form a soap). The very high figures obtained by Marcelet, Tsujimoto and Chapman, all of which are in agreement with each other, show that the quantity may exceed 80 per cent in certain species, particularly in *Centrophorus* and *Scymnorhinus lichia*. Conversely, there may be only traces of unsaponifiable matter in the oils from other species.

Working on oils extracted from sharks on board the yacht of the Prince of Monaco, Henri Marcelet noted in 1914, the presence of this unsaponifiable matter and he then isolated a highly unsaturated terpenic hydrocarbon, samples of which he sent to Dr Richard, director of the Musée Océanographique in Monaco, and also to Professor Imbert of the Department of Pharmacology at Montpellier. All this took place in July of 1914. Marcelet then had to interrupt this work a few weeks later on joining the armed forces, and he did not publish the results of his discovery. As sometimes happens in scientific research, it would seem that the time was ripe for this discovery, for two years later, a Japanese chemist, Tsujimoto Mitsumaru, found this unsaturated hydrocarbon in the livers of certain Japanese dogfishes, and he gave it the name of *squalene*. Almost simultaneously, A.C.Chapman (1917–18) reported the presence of such a hydrocarbon in small sharks caught off the coast of Morocco, and he christened it *spinacene*. Tsujimoto's papers date from 1916; Chapman's work was published a few months afterwards. Priority must be accorded to the Japanese chemist, and some years later, when squalene and spinacene were found to be identical, the name squalene was officially adopted. It is remarkable that Chapman and Tsujimoto, each working independently, at opposite sides of the world and not in direct contact with each other, should have stumbled on this same discovery within a few months of each other.[1]

The figures given on the next page, taken from Marcelet (1924), give an idea of the amount of variation in the percentage of unsaponifiable matter in the oils from various species of shark.

Squalene is present in very varied amounts in the species studied. What role does this hydrocarbon play in the physiology of sharks? The question remains open. Chemists have not abandoned the problem and are still searching for an answer. It is of interest to note that sharks with a high squalene level tend to have a proportionately lower Vitamin A content in the liver oils (Tsuchiya, 1961).

[1] According to Tomotaro Tsuchiya (1961), Tsujimoto had in fact first isolated this hydrocarbon from the liver oils of the Black Shark (*Centroscyllium ritteri*) as early as 1906.

Species	% unsaponifiable matter	Observer
Lamna cornubica	1·58	Hansval & Huvart
	3·6	Tsujimoto
Cetorhinus maximus No 1	48·4	–
No 2	41·9	–
No 3	55·5	–
	41·92	–
	22·80	Marcelet
Carcharhinus glauca	8·4	Tsujimoto
Sphyrna zygaena	1·7	–
Heptranchias deani	9·8	–
Hexanchus griseus	2·58	Marcelet
Galeocerdo arcticus (= *G. cuvieri*)	11·48	Yoshiyuki Toyama
Squalus mitsukurina No 1	90·17	Tsujimoto
No 2	87·32	–
Somniosus microcephalus	16·2	–
	10·2	Lewkowitsch
	20·8, 21·8	Bull
Acanthias vulgaris	12·31	T. Lexow
Centrophorus acus	62·9	Tsujimoto
C. atromarginatus	58·3	–
C. calceus	60·61	Marcelet
(small individuals)	76·64	–
C. squamosus No 1	84·26	–
No 2	86·39	–
C. squamosus	71·87	–

The essential character of most shark oils is, however, their rich content of Vitamin A. It is precisely the presence of this vitamin in the oils which makes for the prosperity of the shark fisheries. This aspect could well form a chapter on its own, for all the other by-products derived from sharks pale to insignificance in the face of Vitamin A – to such an extent that in certain of the shark fisheries, the carcasses are simply thrown back into the sea once the livers have been removed. A more precise picture is gradually being built up of the way in which Vitamin A occurs in shark liver oils, and its relation to the species, its sex, condition, maturity and so on. But around 1950, the appearance of synthetic Vitamin A marked a decline in the production of it from natural sources, or at least from sharks.

There is another point about shark livers which should be mentioned.

This is the recent discovery (Heller *et al.*, 1963) of the presence in the livers of sharks of a 'reticulo-endothelial-system stimulating agent', which has been christened RESTIM after its initials. Research was carried out on various sharks of the Gulf of Mexico – Nurse Shark, Great Hammerhead, Lewin Hammerhead, Blacknose Shark (*C. acronotus*), Bull Shark, Tiger Shark, Brown Shark, Dusky Shark, and Lemon Shark (*Negaprion brevirostris*). The working technique is very difficult, for the liver must be removed within 15 to 20 minutes after the death of the shark. Moreover, only livers which are light yellow-brown in colour can be used, the darker ones with brown or blackish marks being rejected. J. H. Heller and his team of workers are continuing their work on RESTIM and its properties.

Finally, a word about the 'oil from sharks' jaws'. It is not rare to find, in a list of the by-products derived from sharks, mention of 'oil extracted from the jaws, used for the lubrication of accurate timepieces'. This statement is found in almost all articles on the commercial aspects of sharks, and the authors never fail to stress the properties of this marvellous oil, which does not become sticky and never congeals, even at the lowest temperatures. One only needs to know a little of the anatomy of sharks to begin to have doubts about all this. For one cannot see where in the jaw of a shark such a reserve of adipose tissue could be sited. When a jaw is boiled up (I have assured myself on this), a certain *very small* amount of oil comes to the surface, exactly as it does when one boils up any other part of a shark's body, except of course the liver. Some small traces of fatty matter are in fact always present in the tissues, however lean the fish may be. But in the case of the jaw, the principal result of boiling is the transformation of cartilage to gelatin and the liberation of the teeth, which become detached and fall off after a few minutes of boiling. (Incidentally, this is the best method for removing the teeth.)

This claim that a special oil can be derived from the jaws of sharks is, in fact, a complete falsehood. It results from a confusion regarding the origin of this oil. There is indeed a 'jaw oil', but this comes from aquatic mammals, i.e. from the Dolphin (*Delphinus delphis*) or from other delphinids (*D. longirostris* for example, studied by Tsujimoto), or from the Porpoise (*Phocaena phocaena*). On the inner face of the lower jaw in these cetaceans, there is a depression or cavity in which fatty matter is found from which is extracted an oil whose special properties have been studied by many chemists. One only obtains relatively small quantities, however, each animal providing about ½ pint. It is used, after careful preparation, for the lubrication of delicate machinery. But for the last fifteen years, the important problem of lubricating clocks and other delicate mechanisms of high precision has been resolved by using quite different oils, some synthetic and developed since the end of the Second World War. As a result, even if the 'shark jaw oil' were other than a complete myth, it would still not figure amongst the by-products of the shark industry.

During the period between the wars, the shark industry rocketed, if one can use the expression. The policy can be summed up by the phrase 'Everything about a shark is of use except the snap of its jaws' (and the lash of its tail, one might add). In this respect, it comes close to the pig, for which there is the well-known phrase of the Chicago meat-packers 'We can everything but the squeal'. Amongst the by-products from sharks, one can list: liver oil, edible flesh, skin, fish meal (sometimes incorrectly termed *guano*), fins, and so on, in addition to certain hormones such as insulin, although the extraction of the latter presents as yet almost insurmountable difficulties for profitable commercial production.

The commercial exploitation of sharks has suffered from diverse fortunes. Certain industries, especially in the early days, were concerned with the skin for tanning. But very quickly, interest switched to the production of Vitamin A, and these latter fisheries had no other object than the production of shark liver oil with the richest content of vitamins. The appearance of synthetic Vitamin A was fatal to this industry. Regarding the edible flesh and the fins, there has evidently always been a market for them, especially in the East, but the western market has remained limited, and from about 1950 onwards the shark industry as it had stood for a number of years, had almost completely disappeared. The last word has not been said, however. As mentioned earlier, squalene may yet provide a stimulus for the commercial exploitation of sharks.

In spite of fluctuations in the fortunes of the shark fisheries, the scientific interest displayed by men towards sharks has not shown any signs of diminishing. On the contrary, one could almost say that this interest has been stimulated by the decline in shark production. Already, numerous biologists have raised the dogfish 'to the dignity of a laboratory animal', as Professor Prenant once remarked, with the elegant research of Professor Wintrebert on the embryos of *Scyliorhinus* in mind. All zoology students have had to carry out the classical dissection of the dogfish. But it is enough to cast one's eye over the mass of scientific works published in the last twenty years, on the biology of sharks, to be convinced of the fact that, while commercial interest has not flourished as one would have hoped, scientific interest has grown enormously. Thanks to such installations as the large shark tanks and pens, anatomists, physiologists and biologists are now in a position to attack and resolve some of the classic shark 'problems' once thought to be insoluble. And a remarkable feature of such research is its *international* character. The scientific workers of the United States, Australia and South Africa, to name but three of the countries involved, act and work in constant liaison. Studies on marine fauna give many examples of such co-operation, as in the case of research into whales, tunas, sardines and shrimps, which include species of considerable and worldwide importance.

Sharks, beside their study from the point of view of the dangers that their behaviour presents to man, are nowadays often associated with what is termed (a little abusively) 'pure' research. But Louis Pasteur saw quite clearly the artificial nature of any line drawn between 'pure' and 'applied' science. He summed this up in the following way: 'There is no such thing as applied science; there is science, and there are the applications of science; the two are united as the fruit is to the tree that bears it.' Surely a fitting remark on which to end.

Glossary of Common and Latin Names for Sharks

Alopias spp. Thresher Sharks

Angel Fish *Squatina* spp.

Basking Shark *Cetorhinus maximus*

Black-nosed Shark *Carcharhinus acronotus*

Black Shark *Centroscyllium ritteri*

Black-tipped Reef Shark *Carcharhinus melanopterus*

Blue Pointer *Isurus* spp.

Blue Shark (USA) *Lamna* spp.

Blue Shark (Britain) *Prionace glauca*

Bonnet-nosed Shark *Sphyrna tiburo*

Bramble Shark *Echinorhinus brucus*

Broad-headed 7-gill Shark *Notorynchus maculatum*

Brown Shark *Carcharhinus milberti*

Bullhead *Heterodontis* spp.

Bull Shark *Carcharhinus leucas*

Carcharhinus acronotus Black-nosed Shark

C. falciformis Silky Shark

C. gangeticus Ganges Shark

C. leucas Cub or Bull Shark

C. limbatus Small Black-tipped Shark

C. longimanus White-tipped or White-tipped Oceanic Shark

C. maculipinnis Large Black-tipped or Spinning Shark

C. melanopterus Black-tipped Reef Shark

C. milberti Brown Shark or Sandbar Shark

C. nicaraguensis (= *C. leucas*) Nicaraguan Shark (= Bull Shark)

C. obscurus Dusky Shark

C. platyrhynchus White-tip Reef Shark

C. zambezensis (= *C. leucas*) Zambezi Shark

CARCHARHINIDAE Grey or Requiem Sharks

Carcharhinus spp. Grey Sharks, Whalers (Aust.)

Carcharodon carcharias Great White Shark, White Pointer

Carpet Sharks ORECTOLOBIDAF

Cat Sharks SCYLIORHINIDAE

Centroscyllium ritteri Black Shark

Cephaloscyllium spp. Swell Sharks

Cetorhinus maximus Basking Shark

Chlamydoselachus anguineus Frilled Shark

Comb-toothed Sharks HEXANCHIDAE

Common Hammerhead Shark *Sphyrna zygaena*

Cow Sharks HEXANCHIDAE

Cub Shark *Carcharhinus leucas*

DALATIIDAE Sleeper Sharks, Spineless Dogfishes

Dogfishes SCYLIORHINIDAE (but commonly used for a variety of small sharks)

Dusky Shark *Carcharhinus obscurus*

Echinorhinus brucus Bramble Shark

False Cat Sharks PSEUDOTRIAKIDAE

Frilled Shark *Chlamydoselachus anguineus*

Galeocerdo cuvieri Tiger Shark
Galeorhinus galeus Tope
G. zyopterus Soupfin Shark
Ganges Shark Carcharhinus gangeticus
Ginglymostoma cirratum Nurse Shark
Goblin Shark Mitsukurina sp.
Great Blue Shark Prionace glauca
Great Hammerhead Shark Sphyrna mokarran (formerly S. tudes)
Great White Shark Carcharodon carcharias
Greenland Shark Somniosus microcephalus
Grey Nurse Shark Odontaspis arenarius
Grey Sharks CARCHARHINIDAE

Hammerhead Sharks Sphyrna spp.
Heptranchias perlo Narrow-headed 7-gill Shark
Heterodontus spp. Port Jackson, Horn, Bullhead Sharks
HEXANCHIDAE Cow, Comb-toothed 6- and 7-gilled Sharks
Hexanchus griseus 6-gilled or Cow Shark
Horn Sharks Heterodontus spp.

Isurus oxyrinchus Sharp-nosed Mackerel Shark
Isurus spp. Mako or Mackerel Sharks

Lamna spp. Porbeagles (Britain), Blue Sharks (USA)
Large Black-tipped Shark Carcharhinus maculipinnis
Larger Spotted Dogfish Scyliorhinus caniculus
Lemon Shark Negaprion brevirostris
Lesser Spotted Dogfish Scyliorhinus stellaris

Mackerel Sharks Isurus spp.
Mako Sharks Isurus spp.
Midwater Shark Squaliolus laticaudus
Monkfish Squatina spp.
Mustelus canis Smooth Hound
Mustelus spp. Smooth Dogfishes

Narrow-headed 7-gill Shark Heptranchias perlo
Negaprion brevirostris Lemon Shark
Nicaraguan Shark Carcharhinus nicaraguensis
Notorhynchus maculatum Broad-headed 7-gill Shark
Nurse Shark Ginglymostoma cirratum
Nurse Sharks ORECTOLOBIDAE

Odontaspis arenarius Grey Nurse Shark
O. taurus Sand Shark
Odontaspis spp. Ragged-toothed or Sand Sharks
ORECTOLOBIDAE Carpet, Nurse and Zebra Sharks, Wobbegongs
Orectolobus spp. Wobbegongs

Piked Dogfish Squalus acanthias
Porbeagles Lamna spp.
Port Jackson Sharks Heterodontus spp.
Prionace glauca Great Blue Shark, Blue Shark (Britain)
PRISTIOPHORIDAE Saw Sharks
PSEUDOTRIAKIDAE False Cat Sharks

Ragged-toothed Sharks Odontaspis spp.
Requiem Sharks CARCHARHINIDAE
Rhincodon typus Whale Shark

Sand Shark Odontaspis taurus
Saw Sharks PRISTIOPHORIDAE
SCAPANORHYNCHIDAE Goblin Sharks
Scoliodon sp. Sharp-nosed Sharks
SCYLIORHINIDAE Spotted Dog-fishes, Cat Sharks and Swell Sharks
Scyliorhinus caniculus Larger Spotted Dogfish
S. stellaris Lesser Spotted Dogfish
Sharp-nosed Mackerel Shark Isurus oxyrinchus
Sharp-nosed Sharks Scoliodon sp.
Shovel-nosed Shark Sphyrna tiburo

Silky Shark *Carcharhinus falciformis*
Six-gilled Shark *Hexanchus griseus*
Sleeper Shark *Somniosus microcephalus*
Sleeper Sharks DALATIIDAE
Small Black-tipped Shark *Carcharhinus limbatus*
Smooth Dogfish *Mustelus* spp.
Smooth Dogfishes TRIAKIDAE
Smooth Hound *Mustelus canis*
Somniosus microcephalus Sleeper or Greenland Shark
Soupfin Shark *Galeorhinus zyopterus*
Sphyrna tiburo Bonnet- or Shovel-nosed Shark
S. mokarran Great Hammerhead Shark
S. zygaena Common Hammerhead Shark
Spineless Dogfishes DALATIIDAE
Spinning Shark *Carcharhinus maculipinnis*
Spiny Dogfishes SQUALIDAE
Spotted Dogfishes *Scyliorhinus* spp.
Spur Dog *Squalus acanthias*
SQUALIDAE Spiny Dogfishes
Squaliolus laticaudus Midwater Shark

Squalus acanthias Spur Dog or Piked Dogfish
Squatina spp. Monkfish, Angel Fish
Stegostoma fasciatum Zebra Shark
Swell Sharks *Cephaloscyllium* spp.

Thresher Sharks *Alopias* spp.
Tiger Shark *Galeocerdo cuvieri*
Tope *Galeorhinus galeus*
TRIAKIDAE Smooth Hounds, Smooth Dogfishes

Whale Shark *Rhincodon typus*
Whalers (Aust.) *Carcharhinus* spp.
White Pointer *Carcharodon carcharias*
White-tip Oceanic Shark *Carcharhinus longimanus*
White-tip Reef Shark *Carcharhinus platyrhynchus*
White-tipped Shark *Carcharhinus longimanus*
Wobbegongs *Orectolobus* spp.

Zambezi Shark *Carcharhinus zambezensis* (= *C. leucas*)
Zebra Shark *Stegostoma fasciatum*

Bibliography

ALDROVANDI, U. (1613) *De Piscibus libri V et de Cetis liber unus.* J.C. Uterverius, Bononiae, 732 pp.

ALEEV, YU.G. (1963) Functional basis of the exterior structure of fish. *Izdat. Akad. Nauk SSSR, Moscow* (in Russian, with English summary).

ALEXANDER, R.McN. (1965) The lift produced by the heterocercal tails of Selachii. *J. experim. Biol.*, **43**: 131–8.

—— (1967) *Functional design in fishes.* Hutchinson University Library, London, 160 pp.

AMANS, P.C. (1906) Du rôle des formes animales dans les progrès de la navigation aerienne et aquatique. *Bull. Sci. France Belg.*, ser. 5, **9**: 207–28.

APPLEGATE, S.P. (1967) A survey of shark hard parts. Chapter 2 in Gilbert, Mathewson & Rall, *Sharks, Skates and Rays (loc. cit.).*

ARISTOTLE. *Historia Animalium.* The works of Aristotle translated into English under the editorship of J.A.Smith . . . W.D.Ross, 1910. See especially, Vol. 4 by d'Arcy Wentworth Thompson.

AUBREY, J.D.d' (1961) Shark survey off the east coast of South Africa. *Bull. S. Afric. Assn. mar. biol. Res.*, **2**: 12–18.

—— (1964) Preliminary guide to the sharks found off the east coast of South Africa. *Rept. oceanogr. Res. Inst. Durban*, No 8: 95 pp.

BACKUS, R.H. (1963) Hearing in Elasmobranchs. Chapter 7 in Gilbert, *Sharks and Survival (loc. cit.).*

BARETS, A. and SZABO, T. (1962) Appareil synaptique des cellules sensorielles de l'ampoule de Lorenzini chez la Torpille, *Torpedo marmoratus. J. Microsc.*, **1** (1): 47–54.

BARNARD, K.H. (1925) A monograph of the marine fishes of South Africa. *Ann. S. Afric. Mus. Cape Town*, **21**: 1–418.

BELON, P. (1551) *L'histoire naturelle des étranges poissons marins avec la vraie peinture et description du Daulphin, & de plusiers autres de son espèce.* R. Chaudière, Paris, 2 pts., ff. 55.

—— (1555) *La nature et la diversité des poissons avec leurs pourtraicts, représentés au plus près du nature.* C.Estienne, Paris, 448 pp.

BERNARD, F. (1952) La digestion chez les poissons. *Trav. Lab. hydrobiol. Pisc. Grenoble*, **44**: 61–95.

BERTAUT, S. (1837) Mœurs des Négriers. *La France Maritime*, edited by Amédée Gréhan, vol. 2, Pilout, Paris, 117–20 and 128–9.

BERTIN, L. (1958a) Organes de la respiration aquatique. Pp. 1303–41 in P.-P. Grassé (1958) *Traité de Zoologie*, **13** (2).

—— (1958b) Appareil digestif. Pp. 1248–1302 in P.-P.Grassé (see above).

BIBLIOGRAPHY

BERTIN, L. and ARAMBOURG, C. (1958) Systématique des poissons. Pp. 1967–83 in P.-P.Grassé (see above).

BIGELOW, H.B. and SCHROEDER, W.C. (1948) The fishes of the Western North Atlantic. *Sears Foundation for Marine Research, New Haven*, No 1, Part 1, Lancelets, Cyclostomes and Sharks, 576 pp.

—— (1961) *Carcharhinus nicaraguensis*, a synonym of the Bull Shark, *C. leucas. Copeia*: 359.

BLACK, V.S. (1957) Excretion and osmoregulation. Chapter 4 in Brown, M. (editor) *The physiology of fishes*, Academic Press, New York, 447 pp.

BOESEMAN, M. (1964) Notes on the fishes of Western New Guinea, III. The freshwater shark of Jamoer Lake. *Zool. Meded. Leiden*, **40** (3): 9–22.

BOLAU, H. (1881) Ueber die Paarung und Fortpflanzung der Scyllium-Arten. *Zeitschr. Wiss. Zool.*, **35**: 321–5.

BONE, Q. (1966) The function of the two types of myotomal muscle fibre in elasmobranch fishes. *J. mar. biol. Assoc. U.K.*, **46**: 321–50.

BONNELL, B. (1961) Structure and action of the sucker of *Echeneis. Nature*, **191**: 403.

BOUIN, P. (1932) *Elements d'Histologie*. F.Alcan, Paris, 2 vols.

BOYLAN, J.W. (1967) Gill permeability in *Squalus acanthias*. Chapter 12 in Gilbert, Mathewson & Rall, *Sharks, Skates and Rays (loc. cit.)*.

BRASSEY, LADY ANNE (1885) *In the Trades, the Tropics and the Roaring Forties*. New York, pp. 168–9.

BREDER, C.M. (1926) The locomotion of fishes. *Zoologica*, **4** (5): 159–297.

BUDDENBROCK, W. VON (1952) *Vergleichende Physiologie*, Band 1: *Sinnes-physiologie*. Basle, 504 pp.

BUDKER, P. (1937) Sur les changements de coloration d'un Ange de Mer (*Rhina squatina* (L.)) et son comportment en aquarium. *Bull. Stat. Biol. Arcachon*, **33**: 229–34.

—— (1938) Les cryptes sensorielles et les denticules cutanés des Plagiostomes. *Ann. Inst. oceanogr.*, **18** (3): 207–88.

—— (1948) Un tam-tam et un pied humain trouvés dans l'estomac de deux Requins Tigres. *La Nature*, Sept. 1948: 263.

—— (1949) Note préliminaire sur le placenta et le cordon ombilical de trois sélaciens vivipares de la Côte Occidentale d'Afrique. *Comptes-rendus 13th Int. Congr. Zool.*, Paris 1948: 337–8.

—— (1953) Sur le cordon ombelical des squales vivipares. *Bull. Mus. Hist. Nat. Paris*, ser. 2, **25** (6): 541–5.

BURGER, J.W. (1967) Problems in the electrolyte economy of the Spiny Dogfish, *Squalus acanthias*. Chapter 10 in Gilbert, Mathewson & Rall, *Sharks, Skates and Rays (loc. cit.)*.

BURGER, J.W. and HESS, W.N. (1960) Function of the rectal gland in the Spiny Dogfish. *Science*, **131**: 670–1.

CADENAT, J. (1962) Notes ichtyologique ouest-africaine, 38. Documents pour servir à la recherche des mécanismes de déplacement et de remplacement de dents chez les Requins. *Bull. Inst. franc. Afr. noire.*, **24** (A): 551–605.

CAHN, P.H. (1967) *Lateral line detectors*. Indiana Univ. Press, 496 pp.

CASTILLO, L. (1906) *El tollo aprovechamiento industrial*. Cervantes ed., Santiago, Chile, 7 pp.

204

CHAPMAN, A.C. (1917) Spinacene: a new hydrocarbon from certain fish liver oils. *J. Chem. Soc.*, 3: 56.

— (1918) Spinacene and some of its derivatives. *J. Chem. Soc.*, 113: 459.

— (1918) Dogfish liver oil. *Analist*, 43: 156–8.

CLARK, E. (1962) The maintenance of sharks in captivity (capture, feeding, enclosures, behavior). *1st Congr. Internat. Aquariolog. Monaco*, vol. A: 7–13; vol. D: 1–10.

— (1963) The maintenance of sharks in captivity, with a report on their instrumental conditioning. Chapter 4 in Gilbert, *Sharks and Survival* (*loc. cit.*).

CLARK, E. and SCHMIDT, K. VON (1965) Sharks of the central Gulf Coast of Florida. *Bull. Mar. Sci. Miami*, 15 (1): 13–83.

COLE, F.J. (1944) *A history of comparative anatomy from Aristotle to the eighteenth century*. Macmillan, 524 pp.

COLES, R.J. (1915) Notes on the sharks and rays of Cape Lookout, N.C. *Proc. Biol. Soc. Washington*, 28: 89–94.

— (1919) The large sharks of Cape Look-out, North Carolina. The White Shark or Maneater, Tiger Shark and Hammerhead. *Copeia*: 34–43.

COPPLESON, V.M. (1962) *Shark attack*. Angus and Robertson, Sydney, 266 pp.

— (1963) Patterns of shark attack for the world. Chapter 14 in Gilbert, *Sharks and Survival* (*loc. cit.*).

CORDIER, R. (1939) Les composants fonctionnels des nerfs craniens chez les vertébrès. *Actualites Scientifiques et Industrielles: Histophysiologie*, 8, Herman, Paris, 57 pp.

COUSTEAU, J.-Y. (1953) *The silent world*. Hamish Hamilton, 148 pp.

CUÉNOT, L. (1932) *La genèse des espéces animales*. Alcan, Paris.

DANIEL, J.F. (1934) *The elasmobranch fishes*. Univ. of California Press, Berkeley, 332 pp.

DAUZAT, A. (1938) *Dictionnaire Etymologique*. Larousse, Paris.

DAVIES, D.H. (1963) Shark attack and its relationship to temperature, beach patronage and the seasonal abundance of dangerous sharks. *Rept. oceanogr. Res. Inst. Durban*, No 6: 1–43.

— (1964) *About sharks and shark attack*. Shuter & Shooter, Pietermaritzburg, 236 pp.

DAVIES, D.H. and CAMPBELL, G.D. (1962) The aetiology, clinical pathology and treatment of shark attack (based on observations in Natal, South Africa). *J. roy. mar. Med. Serv.*, 48 (3): 1–27.

— (1963) First aid treatment of shark attack victims in South Africa. Chapter 20 in Gilbert, *Sharks and Survival* (*loc. cit.*).

DEMPSTER, R.P. and HERALD, E.S. (1961) Notes on the Hornshark, *Heterodontus francisci*, with observations on mating activities. *Occ. Paps. Calif. Acad. Sci.*, No 33: 1–7.

DENTON, E.J. and NICOL, J.A.C. (1964) The chorioidal tapeta of some cartilaginous fishes (Chondrichthyes). *J. mar. biol. Assoc. U.K.*, 44: 219–58.

DESOLA, C.R. (1932) Fishing with the fisherman fish in West Indian waters. *Bull. N.Y. Zool. Soc.*, 35 (3): 74–92.

DESYLVA, D.P. (1963) Systematics and life history of the Great Barracuda *Sphyraena barracuda* (Walbaum). *Stud. trop. oceanogr. Miami*, No 1: 1–179.

BIBLIOGRAPHY

DIJKGRAAF, S. (1934) Untersuchungen über die Funktion der Seitenorgane an Fischen. *Z. vergl. Physiol.*, **20**: 162–284.

— (1963) The functioning and significance of the lateral line organs. *Biol. Rev.*, **38**: 51–105.

— (1964) Electroreception and the ampullae of Lorenzini in Elasmobranchs. *Nature*, **201**: 523.

— (1967) Biological significance of the lateral line organs. Chapter 7 in Cahn, *Lateral line detectors (loc. cit.)*.

DOTTERWEICH, H. (1932) Bau und Funktion der Lorenzini'schen Ampullen. *Zool. Jahrb.*, **50**: 347–418.

DuTERTRE, J.B. (1667–71) *Histoire General des Antilles*, 2. *Histoire Naturelle*. Th. Jolly, Paris.

EKMAN, V.W. (1906) On dead water, in *The Norwegian North-Polar Expeditions: Scientific results* (1893–6). Edit. Fridtjof Nansen, Vol. 5, 152 pp.

ENGELAND, R. and BASTIAN, A. (1938) Contribution à la connaissance de l'élastoidine. *C. R. Acad. Sci.*, Paris, **207**: 945–7.

ENGLEHARDT, R. (1913) Monographie der Selachier der münchener Staatssammlung (mit besonderer Berücksichtigung der Hai fauna Japans), 1. Tiergeographie der Selachier. *Abh. bayer. Akad. Wiss.* (suppl.), **4** (3): 1–110.

FAURE-FREMIET, E. (1936) La structure des fibres d'élastoidine. *Arch. Anat. Microsc.*, **32**: 249–70.

FIELD, I.A. (1906) Inutilized fishes and their relation to the fishing industries. *Bureau of Fisheries, Rept. Comm. Fish. Washington*: 7–50.

FONTAINE, M. (1953) La fonction hypophyso-thyroidienne des poissons dans ses rapports avec leur morphologie et leur comportement. *J. Cons. Int. Explor. Mer* (I.C.E.S.), **19** (1): 23–38.

FORSTER, R.P. (1967) Osmoregulatory role of the kidney in cartilaginous fishes (Chondrichthyes). Chapter 11 in Gilbert, Mathewson & Rall, *Sharks, Skates and Rays (loc. cit.)*.

FORTIS, ABBÉ A. (1778) *Travels in Dalmatia*, London, pp. 260–3.

FOWLER, H.W. (1936) Marine fishes of West Africa. *Bull. Amer. Mus. nat. Hist.* **70** (1 and 2): 1–1493.

FRISCH, K.VON (1941a) Die Bedeutung des Geruchsinnes im Leben der Fische. *Naturwissensch.*, 29th year: 321–33.

— (1941b) Über einen Schreckstoff der Fischhaut und seine biologische Bedeutung. *Z. vergl. Physiol.*, **29**: 46–145.

GANS, C. and PARSONS, T.S. (1964) *A photographic atlas of shark anatomy: the gross morphology of Squalus acanthias*. Academic Press, London & New York.

GARMAN, S. (1913) The Plagiostoma (Sharks, Skates and Rays). *Mem. Mus. comp. Zool. Harvard*, **36**: 528 plus atlas.

GARRICK, J.A.F. (1967) A broad view of *Carcharhinus* species, their systematics and distribution. Chapter 5 in Gilbert, Mathewson & Rall, *Sharks, Skates and Rays (loc. cit.)*.

GARRICK, J.A.F. and SCHULTZ, L.P. (1963) A guide to the kinds of potentially dangerous sharks. Chapter 1 in Gilbert, *Sharks and Survival (loc. cit.)*.

GEOFFROY SAINT-HILLAIRE, E. (1807) Observations sur l'affection mutuelle de quelques animaux, et particulièrement sur les services rendus au requin par le pilote. *Ann. Mus. Hist. nat. Paris*, **9**: 469–76.

GESNER, K. (1558) *Historia animalium*. Tiguri, 5 vols, 1551–87.

GILBERT, P.W. (1962) The behaviour of sharks. *Scientific American*, **207**: 60–68.

—— (1963a) *Sharks and Survival*, edited by P.W.Gilbert. D.C.Heath, Boston, 578 pp.

—— (1963b) The AIBS Shark Research Panel. Chapter 22 in Gilbert, *Sharks and Survival* (*loc. cit.*).

—— (1963c) The visual apparatus of sharks. Chapter 9 in Gilbert, *Sharks and Survival* (*loc. cit.*).

GILBERT, P.W., MATHEWSON, R.F. and RALL, D.P. (1967) *Sharks, Skates and Rays*, edited by Gilbert, Mathewson and Rall, John Hopkins Press, Maryland, 624 pp.

GILBERT, P.W. and SPRINGER, S. (1963) Testing shark repellants. Chapter 19 in Gilbert, *Sharks and Survival* (*loc. cit.*).

GILL, T. (1911) The Glanis of Aristotle. *Science*, **33**: 730–8.

GRASSÉ, P.-P. (1957) Les sens chemique. In *Traité de Zoologie*, edited P.-P. Grassé, vol. **13** (2): 925–39. Masson, Paris.

—— (1958) Agnathes, Poissons. *Traité de Zoologie*, as above.

GRUBER, S.H. (1967) A behavioral measurement of dark adaptation in the lemon shark *Negaprion brevirostris*. Chapter 32 in Gilbert, Mathewson & Rall, *Sharks, Skates and Rays* (*loc. cit.*).

GRUBER, S.H., HAMASAKI, D.I. and BRIDGES, C.D.B. (1963) Cones in the retina of the lemon shark (*Negaprion brevirostris*). *Vision Res.*, **3**: 397–9.

GUDGER, E.W. (1907) A note on the Hammerhead Shark (*Sphyrna zygaena*) and its food. *Science*, **25**: 1005.

—— (1918) The myth of the shipholder: studies in *Echeneis* and *Remora*. *Ann. Mag. nat. Hist.*, (9) **2**: 271–306.

—— (1919) The use of the sucking fish for catching fishes and turtles. *Amer. Naturalist*, **53**: 289–311; 446–67; 515–25.

—— (1922) An odd place of refuge; the habit of the shark sucker, *Echeneis* or *Remora*, of taking shelter in the gill chamber or mouth cavity of its host. *Nat. Hist.*, **22**: 243–9.

—— (1940) Whale sharks rammed by ocean vessels. *New England Naturalist*, No 7: 1–10.

—— (1941) The Whale Shark unafraid. The greatest of the sharks, *Rhineodon typus*, fears not shark, man nor ship. *Amer. Naturalist*, **75**: 550–68.

—— (1946) Oral breathing valves in fishes. *J. Morph.*, **79** (2): 263–8.

—— (1952) The Butterfly Ray, *Pteroplatea maclura*, and its intra-uterine-fin-tailed embryo. *J. Elisha Mitchell Sci. Soc.*, **68** (2): 195–8.

GUENTHER, K. (1931) *A naturalist in Brazil: the flora and fauna and the people of Brazil*. Trans. by B.Miall, London.

HALSTEAD, B.W. (1959) *Dangerous marine animals*. Cornell Maritime Press, 146 pp.

—— (1963) First-aid treatment of shark bites: general comments. Chapter 20 in Gilbert, *Sharks and Survival* (*loc. cit.*).

HARDMAN, E.F. (1884) Sea-fish in fresh-water rivers. *Nature*, **29**: 452–3.

HARRIS, J.E. (1936) The role of the fins in the equilibrium of the swimming fish, I. Wind tunnel tests on a model of *Mustelus canis* (Mitchill). *J. Exper. Biol.*, **13**: 476–93.

—— (1938) The role of the fins in the equilibrium of the swimming fish, 2. The role of the pelvic fins. *J. Exper. Biol.*, **15**, 32–47.

HASSE, C. (1879) *Das natürliche System der Elasmobranchier auf Grundlage des Baues und der Entwicklung ihre Wirbelsaule. Eine morphologische und paläontologische Studie.* Gust. Gischer, Jena.

HELLER, J.M., PASTERNAK, V.Z., RANSOM, J.P. and HELLER, M.S. (1963) A new reticuloendothelial system stimulating agent (Restim) from shark livers. *Nature*, **199**: 904–5.

HERRICK, C. (1903) On the morphological and physiological classification of the cutaneous sense organs of fishes. *Amer. Naturalist*, **37**: 313–18.

HESSE, R. (1910) *Tierbau und Tierleben in ihren Zusammenhang betrachtet*, by Hesse R. & Doflein, R.F., Berlin.

HOFER, B. (1908) Studien über die Hautsinnesorgane der Fische, I. Die Funktion der Seitenorgane bei den Fischen. *Ber. K. bayer. biol. VersStn. München*, **1**: 115.

HOLDER, C.F. (1905) The remoras. *Scientific American*, **33**: 162–3.

HOUSSAY, F. (1912) *Forme, puissance et stabilité des poissons.* A.Herman, Paris, 372 pp.

HUBBS, C.L., IWAI, T. and MATSUBARA, K. (1967) External and internal characters, horizontal and vertical distribution, luminescence, and food of the dwarf pelagic shark, *Euprotomicrus bispinatus*. *Bull. Scripps Inst. oceanogr.*, **10**: 1–64.

HUGHES, G.M and BALENTJIN, C.M. (1965) The muscular basis of the respiratory pumps in the dogfish (*Scyliorhinus canicula*). *J. Exper. Biol.*, **43**: 363–83.

HUMBOLDT, A.VON and BONPLAND, A. (1814) *Voyage aux régions équinoxiales du Nouveau Continent. Relation historique*, vol. I. F.Schoell, Paris, 546 pp.

JARVIK, E. (1960) *Théories de l'évolution des vertébrés* (preface and translation by J.P.Lehman). Monographies scientifiques, Paris, 104 pp.

—— (1964) Specialization in early vertebrates. *Ann. Soc. roy. Zool. Belg.*, **94** (1): 12–95.

KALMIJN, A.J. (1966) Electro-perception in sharks and rays. *Nature*, **212**: 1232–3.

KELLER, O. (1909–13) *Die Antique Tierwelt.* Engelmann, Leipzig.

KLAUSWITZ, W. (1962) Wie schimmen Haifische? *Natur und Museum*, **92** (6): 219–26.

—— (1965) Die Bewegungsweise der Geigenrochen aus funktioneller und stammesgeschichtlicher Sicht. *Natur und Museum*, **95** (3): 97–108.

KOEFOED, E. (1957) Notes on the Greenland Shark *Acanthorhinus carcharias* (Gunn.), 2. A uterine foetus and the uterus from a Greenland Shark. *Rept. Norweg. Fish. mar. Invest.*, **11** (10): 8–12.

KRAMER, E.V. (1960) Zur Form und Funktion des Lokomotionsapparates der Fische. *Z. Wiss. Zoo.*, **163**: 1–36.

LABAT, PÈRE J.-B. (1728) *Nouvelle relation de l'Afrique occidentale contenant une description exacte du Sénégal et des païs situés entre le Cap-Blanc et la Rivière de Serrelionne . . .* (compiled from the notes of A.Brue, etc.) 5 vols, Paris.

LACEPÈDE, COMTE DE (1798) *Histoire naturelle des poissons*, 1. Plassan, Paris, 532 pp.

LANDELLE, G. DE LA (1842) *Galerie Maritime*. Pt. 3, *L'Equipage: Les Caliers*, in *La France Maritime*, edited Amédée Gréhan, vol. 4, Pilout, Paris, 330–2 pp.

LANG, T.G. (1966) Hydrodynamic analysis of cetacean performance. Chapter 19 in Norris, K.S., *Whales, Dolphins and Porpoises*, University of California Press, 789 pp.

LE MAIRE, J.J. (1696) *A Voyage of Sieur Le Maire to the Canary Islands, Cape Verde, Senegal and Gamb under Monsieur Dancourt* ... (English translation). London.

LEVY-BRUHL, L. (1938) *L'expérience mystique chez les primitifs*. N.R.F., Paris.

LIMBAUGH, C. (1963) Field notes on sharks. Chapter 2 in Gilbert, *Sharks and Survival (loc. cit.)*.

LINEAWEAVER, T.H. and BACKUS, R.H. (1970) *The natural history of sharks*. André Deutsch, 256 pp.

LLANO, G.A. (1963) Open-ocean shark attacks. Chapter 13 in Gilbert, *Sharks and Survival (loc. cit.)*.

LÜTKEN, C. (1880) Smaa Bidrag til Selachiernes Naturhistorie. *Vidensk. Foren. Kbh.*, **56**: 45–68.

McCORMICK, H., ALLEN, T. and YOUNG, W.E. (1963) *Shadows in the Sea*. Sidgwick & Jackson, London, 415 pp.

MAGNAN, A. (1929) Les caractéristiques géométriques et physiques des poissons, avec contributions à l'étude de leur équilibre statique et dynamique. *Ann. Sci. Nat. (Zool.)*, **12**, 5–133.

—— (1930) *Idem*, **13**: 335–489.

MAGNAN, A. and SAINTE-LAGÜE, A. (1928) Sur l'équilibre statique des poissons. *C. R. Acad. Sci. Paris*, **187**: 388–90.

MAGNUSON, J.J. (1970) Hydrostatic equilibrium of *Euthynnus affinis*, a pelagic teleost without a gas bladder. *Copeia*: 56–85.

MARCELET, H. (1924) *Les huiles d'animaux marins*. Librairie Polytechnique, Ch. Beranger, Paris.

MARTYR, P. (1511) *De Orbe Novo*. Translated by F.A.MacNutt, 1912. Putnam, New York, 2 vols.

MATTHEWS, L.HARRISON (1962) The shark that hibernates. *New Scient.*, **13**: 756–9.

METTEN, H. (1939) Studies on the reproduction of the Dog-Fish. *Phil. Trans. Roy. Soc. London*, ser. B, **230**, 217–38.

MOREAU, E. (1881) *Histoire naturelle des poissons de la France*. Paris, 3 vols.

MOSS, S.A. (1967) Tooth replacement in the Lemon Shark, *Negaprion brevirostris*. Chapter 22 in Gilbert, Mathewson & Rall, *Sharks, Skates and Rays (loc. cit.)*.

MOULE, T. (1842) *The heraldry of fish*. John van Voorst, London, 250 pp.

MÜLLER, J. and HENLE, F.G. (1838–41) *Systematische Beschreibung der Plagiostomen*. Berlin, 200 pp.

MURPHY, R.C. (1947) *Logbook for Grace*. Macmillan, New York.

MURPHY, R.C. and NICOLS, J.T. (1916) The shark situation in the waters about New York. *Brooklyn Mus. Quart.*, **3** (4): 145–60.

MURRAY, R.W. (1962) The response of the ampullae of Lorenzini of elasmobranchs to electrical stimulation. *J. Exper. Biol.*, **39**: 119–28.

MURRY R. W. (1967) The function of the ampullae of Lorenzini of Elasmobranchs. Chapter 18 in Cahn, *Lateral line detectors* (*loc. cit.*).

NAGEL, W.A. (1894) Vergleichende physiologische und anatomische Untersuchungen über den Geruchsund Geschmackssian und ihre Organe. *Bibl. Zool.* Stuttgart, **7**: 1–207.

NEEDHAM, J. (1950) *Biochemistry and morphogenesis.* Cambridge, 788 pp.

NELSON, D.R. (1969) The silent savages. *Oceans Magazine*, **1** (4): 8–22.

NICOL, J.A.C. (1961) The tapetum of *Scyliorhinus canicula. J. mar. biol. Assn. U.K.*, **41**: 271–7.

NORMAN, J.R. and FRASER F.C. (1948) *Giant fishes, whales and dolphins.* Putnam, London, 361 pp.

ORR, R.T. (1959) Sharks as enemies of sea otters. *J. Mammal.*, **40**: 617.

PARKER, G.H. (1912) The relations of smell, taste, and the common chemical sense in vertebrates. *J. Acad. nat. Sci. Philad.*, **15**: 221–34.

PARKER, G.H and PORTER, H. (1934) The control of the dermal melanophores in elasmobranchs. *Biol. Bull. Wood's Hole*, **66**: 30–7.

PARSONS, J.J. (1962) *The green turtle and man.* Univ. of Florida Press, 126 pp.

PETIT, G. (1930) L'industrie des pêches à Madagascar. Sté. ed. *Géogr. Mar. et Col.*, Paris, 8th edn.

PIVETEAU, J. (1934) L'histoire du tissu osseux. *La terre et la vie*, **4** (9): 515–22.

PLINY SECUNDUS. *The Natural History of Pliny.* Translated with . . . notes and illustrations, 1855–7, by J.Bostock and H.T.Riley. London, 6 vols.

POSTEL, E. (1958) Sur la présence de *Carcharodon carcharias* (L., 1758) dans les eaux tunisiennes. *Bull. Mus. Nat. d'Hist. nat.*, Paris, (2) **30**: 342–4.

PURVES, P.E. (1963) Locomotion in whales. *Nature*, **197**: 334–7.

RABAUD, E. (1942) *Transformisme et adaptations.* Flammarion, Paris.

RANDALL, J.E. (1963) Dangerous sharks of the western Atlantic. Chapter 11 in Gilbert, *Sharks and Survival* (*loc. cit.*).

RANZI, S. (1929) Ricerche di embriologia sperimentale nei cichlostomi. *Atti. Acc. Lincei*, **10**: 111–15.

—— (1932) Le basi fisiomorphologiche dello sceluppo embrionale dei selaci, Pt. 1. *Publ. Staz. Zool. Napoli*, **12**: 109–290; Pt. 2 & 3. *Ibid.*, **13**: 331–437.

RICHET, C. (1945) Notes médicales sur le camp de Buchenwald. *Bull. Acad. Méd.*, **129**: 377–88.

ROCHON-DUVIGNEAUD, A. (1943) *Les yeux et la vision des vertébrés.* Masson, Paris, 720 pp.

ROGERS, A. (1922) *Practical tanning.* New York.

RONDELET, G. (1554) *Libri de piscibus marinis.* Lugduni, fol.

ROSEN, M.W. (1959) Waterflow about a swimming fish. *Tech. Publ. U.S. Naval Test Station, China Lake, Calif.*: NOTS TP 2298: 1–94.

SAND, A. (1938) The function of the ampullae of Lorenzini, with some observations of the effect of temperature on sensory rhythms. *Proc. roy. Soc. London*, **125** B: 524–53.

SAUVAGE, H.E. (1888) Sur le foetus de l'aiguillat commun. *Bull. Soc. zool. France*, **13**: 219–20.

SAVE-SODERBERG, G. (1934) Some points of view concerning the evolution of the vertebrates and the classification of this group. *Ark. Zool.*, **26** A (17): 1–20.

SCHAEFFER, B. (1967) Comments on elasmobranch evolution. Chapter 1 in Gilbert, Mathewson & Rall, *Sharks, Skates and Rays (loc. cit.)*.

SCHWARTZ, F.J. (1959) Two eight-foot cub sharks, *Carcharhinus leucas* (Müller and Henle), captured in Chesapeake Bay, Maryland. *Copeia*, 1959, No 3: 251–2.

SHELDON, R.E. (1911) The sense of smell in selachians. *J. exper. Zool.*, **10**: 51–62.

SLOANE, SIR HANS (1707–25) *A voyage to the islands Madera, Barbados, Neives, S. Christophers, and Jamaica, with the natural history . . . of the last of those islands.* London, 2 vols.

SLOCUM, J. (1948) *Sailing alone around the world, and voyage of the Liberadade . . .* with an introduction by Arthur Ransome. Rupert Hart-Davis, London, 384 pp.

SMITH, H.W. (1936) The retention and physiological role of urea in the elasmobranchii. *Biol. Rev.*, **11**: 49–82.

SMITH, H.W. and SMITH, C. (1931) The absorption and excretion of water and salts by the elasmobranch fishes. I. Freshwater elasmobranchs. *Amer. J. Physiol.*, **98**: 279–95.

— (1948) Oviphagous embryos of the Sand Shark, *Carcharias taurus*. *Copeia*: 153–7.

SPRINGER, S. (1954) Laboratory experiments with shark repellants. *Proc. Gulf. Caribb. Fish. Inst.*, 7th Annual Session.

— (1957) Some observations on the behaviour of schools of fishes in the Gulf of Mexico and adjacent waters. *Ecology*, **38**: 166–71.

— (1960) Natural history of the Sandbar Shark, *Eulamia milberti*. *Fish. Bull. Fish Wildl. Serv.*, **61** (178): 1–42.

— (1963) Field observations on large sharks of the Florida–Caribbean region. Chapter 3 in Gilbert, *Sharks and Survival (loc. cit.)*.

— 1967. Social organization of shark populations. Chapter 9 in Gilbert, Mathewson & Rall, *Sharks, Skates and Rays (loc. cit.)*.

SPRINGER, S. and GILBERT, P.W. (1963) Anti-shark measures. Chapter 18 in Gilbert, *Sharks and Survival (loc. cit.)*.

SPRINGER, V.G. (1964) A revision of the carcharinid shark genera, *Scoliodon, Loxodon* and *Rhizoprionodon. Proc. U.S. natl. Mus.*, **115** (3493): 556–63.

SPRINGER V.G. and GARRICK, J.A.F. (1964) A survey of vertebral numbers in sharks. *Proc. U.S. natl. Mus.*, **116** (3496): 73–96.

STEAD, D.G. (1906) *Fishes in Australia*, 1. Sydney, 278 pp.

STENO, N. (1673) Ova viviparorum spectantes observationes factae . . . In Thomas Bartholini, *Acta medica et philosophica Hafniensia*, 2. P.Haubald, Hafniae, 219–32.

SVENSSON, G.S.O. (1933) Freshwater fishes from the Gambia river (British West Africa) – Results of the Swedish Expedition, 1931. *K. Svensk. Vetensk, Akad. Handl.*, (3) **12**: 1–102.

TESTER, A.L. (1963a) The role of olfaction in shark predation. *Pac. Sci.*, **17** (2): 145–70.

— (1963b) Olfaction, gustation and the common chemical sense in sharks. Chapter 8 in Gilbert, *Sharks and Survival (loc. cit.)*.

TESTER, A.L. and NELSON, G.J. (1967) Free neuromasts (pit organs) in sharks. Chapter 34 in Gilbert, Mathewson & Rall, *Sharks, Skates and Rays (loc. cit.)*.

TEWINKEL, L.E. (1963) Note on the smooth dogfish, *Mustelus canis*, during the first three months of gestation. *J. Exper. Zool.*, **152** (2): 123–38.

BIBLIOGRAPHY

THORSON, T.B., COWAN, C.M. and WATSON, D.E. (1966a) Sharks and sawfish in the Lake Izabel–Rio Dulce system, Guatemala. *Copeia*: 620–2.

—— (1966b) The status of the freshwater shark of Lake Nicaragua. *Copeia*: 385–402.

TORTONESE, E. (1950) Studi sui Plagiostomi, 3. La viviparita un fondamentale carattere biologico degli squali. *Arch. Zool. Ital.*, **35**: 101–55.

TOWNSEND, G.H. (1915) The power of the Shark-sucker's disc. *Bull. N.Y. Zool. Soc.*, **18**: 1281–3.

TSUCHIYA, T. (1961) Biochemistry of fish oils. Chapter 7 in Bergstrom. G., *Fish as food*, Academic Press, 725 pp.

TSUJIMOTO, M. (1906) On the liver oil of the Kurokazame (*Centroscyllium ritteri* Jord. & Fowler). *J. Soc. Chem. Ind. Japan*, **9**: 953–8.

—— (1916a) A highly unsaturated hydrocarbon in shark liver oil. *J. Industr. Engin. Chemistry*, **8** (10): 889.

—— (1916b) On an unsaturated hydrocarbon in shark liver oil. *J. Soc. Chem. Ind. Japan*, **19**: 277–80.

—— (1920) Squalene. A highly unsaturated hydrocarbon in shark liver oil. *J. Ind. Engin. Chemistry*, **12** (1): 63–73.

TUVE, R.L. (1963) Development of the U.S. Navy 'Shark Chaser' chemical shark repellant. Chapter 17 in Gilbert, *Sharks and Survival (loc. cit.)*.

VAN BENEDEN, P.J. (1870) Les Echeneis et les Naucrates dans leurs rapports avec les poissons qu'ils hantent. *Bull. Acad. roy. Sci. Bruxelles*, (2) **30**: 181–5.

VERRIER, M.L. (1928) Recherches sur les yeux et la vision des poissons. *Bull. Biol. France Belg.*, Suppl. **11**: 222 pp.

VILTER, V. (1941) Polarisation dorso-ventrale de la livrée pigmentaire, sa physiologie et ses origines. *Bull. Mus. Marseilles*, **1**: 157–87 and 259–71.

WAHLERT, G.VON (1965) The role of ecological factors in the origin of higher levels of organisation. *Syst. Zool.*, **14** (4): 288–300.

WARING, H. (1938) Chromatic behaviour of elasmobranchs. *Proc. roy. Soc. London*, **125** B: 264–82.

WHITE, G.E. (1936) The classification and phylogeny of the elasmobranch fishes. *Amer. Mus. Novit.*, No 837: 1–16.

WHITLEY, G.P. (1940) *The fishes of Australia*, Pt. 1. The sharks, rays, devil-fish and other primitive fishes of Australia and New Zealand. Sydney, 280 pp.

—— (1963) Shark attacks in Australia. Chapter 10 in Gilbert, *Sharks and Survival (loc. cit.)*.

WU, TAO-TSU (1961) Swimming of a waving plate. *J. Fluid. Mech.*, **10** (3): 321–44.

ZANGERL, R. (1966) A new shark of the family Edestidae, *Ornithoprion hertwigi*, from the Pennsylvanian Mecca and Logar Quarry shales of Indiana. *Fieldiana Geol.*, **16** (1): 1–43.

Index